A Human Rights-Based Approach to Justice in Social Work Practice

A HUMAN RIGHTS-BASED APPROACH TO JUSTICE IN SOCIAL WORK PRACTICE

Shirley Gatenio Gabel

OXFORD
UNIVERSITY PRESS

Oxford University Press is a department of the University of Oxford. It furthers
the University's objective of excellence in research, scholarship, and education
by publishing worldwide. Oxford is a registered trade mark of Oxford University
Press in the UK and certain other countries.

Published in the United States of America by Oxford University Press
198 Madison Avenue, New York, NY 10016, United States of America.

© Oxford University Press 2024

Library of Congress Cataloging-in-Publication Data
Names: Gabel, Shirley Gatenio, author.
Title: A human rights-based approach to justice in
social work practice / Shirley Gatenio Gabel.
Description: New York, NY : Oxford University Press, [2024] |
Includes bibliographical references and index.
Identifiers: LCCN 2023017312 (print) | LCCN 2023017313 (ebook) |
ISBN 9780197570647 (paperback) | ISBN 9780197570661 (epub) |
ISBN 9780197570678 (online)
Subjects: LCSH: Social service—Practice. | Human rights. | Social justice.
Classification: LCC HV10.5 .G33 2024 (print) | LCC HV10.5 (ebook) |
DDC 361.3/2—dc23/eng/20230626
LC record available at https://lccn.loc.gov/2023017312
LC ebook record available at https://lccn.loc.gov/2023017313

DOI: 10.1093/oso/9780197570647.001.0001

Printed by Marquis Book Printing, Canada

To my partner in life, Ken, who always reminds me of what I can do.

CONTENTS

PREFACE

At the founding of the social work profession, social workers were human rights defenders who sought justice for the people they worked with by advocating for societal reforms and helping people manage everyday challenges in their lives. Social work pioneers fought against social exclusion and discriminatory practices that voided the human rights of the people with whom they worked (Gatenio Gabel et al., 2022). Over time, clinical approaches to social work practice in the United States became more dominant, and the bulk of advocacy was left to those working in communities or at policy levels. This resulted in casting a false division within social work into two dominant forms of practice—micro and macro. Micro-practitioners focused on professionalizing social work by creating theories and interventions to guide social work practice, and justice was no longer the driving force in this newly created body of knowledge informing social work practice. The role of social workers as human rights defenders faded as the place of justice in social work receded. Social work practice moved away from instigating change toward maintaining the existing social infrastructure.

The focus on human rights and justice distinguished social workers from other helping professionals. As social workers, not only did we want to right the injustice that was done to those we worked with directly but we also understood that it was the obligation of our profession to change the system that created the injustice. It didn't matter whether we were working one on one in therapeutic settings, organizing groups in communities, or advocating elected officials to enact legislation for the benefit of those we served—we all had the same professional obligation to fight for a just society that recognized and accorded all humans their rights.

Over time, we neglected this holistic approach in social work and focused instead on developing professional standards, and specialties and subspecialities. True, we gained a better understanding of our skill sets, integrated evidence-based methods into standard practices, and carved our professional niche in interprofessional approaches. Still, in the process, we quieted our unique voice among the helping professions to stand up to injustice, to shake up unjust systems and practices, and to remind others that we can always do better.

The professional organizations representing social work noted the uneven path social work was taking and have tried to rebalance social work practice. The centrality of human rights in promoting social, economic, and environmental justice in social work is recognized by the International Association for Schools of Social Work, the International Federation of Social Workers, and the U.S. Council on Social Work Education.

According to the Global Standards of the International Association of Schools of Social Work & International Federation of Social Workers (2020, p. 19):

> Social, Economic, and Environmental Justice are fundamental pillars underpinning social work theory, policy and practice. All schools *must*:
>
> a. Prepare students to be able to apply human rights principles (as articulated in the International Bill of Rights and core international human rights treaties) to frame their understanding of how current social issues affect social, economic and environmental justice.
> b. Ensure that their students understand the importance of social, economic, political, and environmental justice and develop relevant intervention knowledge and skills.
> c. Contribute to collective efforts within and beyond school structures in order to achieve social, economic and environmental justice.

In its Global Definition of the Social Work Profession, the International Federation of Social Workers (2014) states, "Principles of social justice, human rights, collective responsibility and respect for diversities are central to social work."

> Social workers understand that every person regardless of position in society has fundamental human rights. Social workers are knowledgeable about the global intersecting and ongoing injustices throughout history that result in oppression and racism, including social work's role and response. Social workers critically evaluate the distribution of power and privilege in society in order to promote social, racial, economic, and environmental justice by reducing inequities and insuring dignity and respect for all. Social workers advocate for and engage in strategies to eliminate oppressive structural barriers to ensure that social resources rights, and responsibilities are distributed

equitably and that civil, political, economic, social, and cultural human rights are protected.

Social workers:

a. advocate for human rights at the individual, family, group, organizational, and community system levels; and
b. engage in practices that advance human rights to promote social, racial, economic, and environmental justice.

(Council on Social Work Education, *2022, Competency 2*)

Human rights and justice are at the core of social work, recognized at global and national levels. Nevertheless, our educational and training materials in social work, for the most part, do not integrate human rights perspectives on justice (Chen et al., 2015; Swigonski, 2011; Gatenio Gabel & Mapp, 2020; Gatenio Gabel et al., 2022).

A human rights approach brings justice as the focal point to all forms of social work practice: micro, macro, community, policy, and international (Androff & McPherson, 2014). Introducing this perspective to students as they begin their training as social work professionals is essential. Learning about a human rights-based approach to justice and how to apply it to social work practice early on in one's professional education and training guides students' perspectives and understanding of social issues throughout their training and as their practice skills advance. In a rights-based approach to achieving justice in social work practice, our imposed divisions as clinicians, community workers, or policy practitioners do not exist (Androff & McPherson, 2014; Gatenio Gabel et al., 2022). All social workers must understand the implications of policies on communities, groups, and individuals. All social workers must comprehend how communities can support and harm individuals and groups. All social workers must appreciate that advocacy is essential to their work, regardless of whether it is in a job description and whether they are working with individuals, groups, communities, organizations, or policies.

When social workers understand human rights and apply this perspective to further justice, they can pass this knowledge on to the people and communities with whom they work. A human rights-based approach is empowering. Human rights belong to all human beings. Human rights are not earned, merited, or awarded to the favored—we are all entitled to our human rights by virtue of being human. This perspective can be transformative, especially for those denied their rights, oppressed by others with power, or unaware of their rights. Applying a human rights-based approach in social work practice moves us toward achieving justice.

This book introduces readers to human rights, human rights principles and instruments, human rights dilemmas, and the application of human rights in social work practice. Through U.S.-based and international examples, the book helps learners think critically about the potential of social work practice from a human rights-based approach.

Our purpose as social workers is to bring dignity and respect to the lives of all people. A human rights-based approach is built on this concept.

The book is premised on the belief that the realization of human rights will bring justice to all. Although there are many different interpretations of justice, human rights are realized when governments, businesses, and people respect one another's human rights. Justice is achieved when human rights are realized without discrimination, prejudice, and favor.

The book has three main sections. The first section introduces learners to human rights—its history, evolving interpretations, the main instruments and their application today, key human rights mechanisms at the United Nations, and some of the controversies regarding human rights such as the dominance of Western philosophy, universalism and cultural relativism, and exceptionalism (as in the case of the United States). Brief biographies of social work pioneers are offered as examples of how social workers intertwined human rights and social work practice from the earliest decades of the profession.

Before we can move on to learning about justice, we must understand the ways in which our current systems and structures oppress some and privilege others. Oppression, privilege, and power are unpacked in the book's second section. The section also introduces us to the intersectionality of our identities and our positionality within society—how the different identities we each have may privilege and oppress us simultaneously and why some persons suffer more significant inequities than others in our society. We learn about how we may view others and how others may perceive us based on our positionality.

The third section explores the concept of justice and its many interpretations. We learn that we may all be fighting for justice, but our goals can vary greatly. We then explore social, economic, and environmental justice individually by understanding how each concept has evolved and is defined and why each is important to social work practice.

The final section integrates the concepts of human rights, oppression and privilege, intersectionality, and justice into social work practice. Case examples are used to demonstrate the application of these concepts.

The book will train new social workers to become human rights defenders of justice in all types of practice methods and levels and for all people.

REFERENCES

Androff, D., & McPherson, J. (2014). Can human rights-based social work practice bridge the micro/macro divide? In K. Libal, L. Healy, R. Thomas, & M. Berthold (Eds.), *Advancing human rights in social work education* (pp. 23–40). Council on Social Work Education. https://doi.org/10.4324/9781315885483

Chen, H. Y., Tung, Y. T., & Tang, I. C. (2015). Teaching about human rights in a social work undergraduate curriculum: The Taiwan experience. *British Journal of Social Work, 45*(8), 2335–2350. https://doi.org/10.1093/bjsw/bcu068

Council on Social Work Education. (2022). *Educational policy and accreditation standards for baccalaureate and master's social work programs 2022.* https://www.cswe.org/getmedia/94471c42-13b8-493b-9041-b30f48533d64/2022-EPAS.pdf

Gatenio Gabel, S., & Mapp, S. C. (2020). Teaching human rights and social justice in social work education. *Journal of Social Work Education, 56*(3), 428–441. https://doi.org/10.1080/10437797.2019.1656581

Gatenio Gabel, S., Mapp, S., Androff, D., & McPherson, J. (2022). Looking back to move us forward: Social workers deliver justice as human rights professionals. *Advances in Social Work, 22*(2). https://journals.iupui.edu/index.php/advancesinsocialwork/article/view/24971

International Association of Schools of Social Work & International Federation of Social Workers. (2020). *Global standards for social work education and training.* https://www.iassw-aiets.org/global-standards-for-social-work-education-and-training/

International Federation of Social Workers. (2014). *Definition of social work.* https://www.ifsw.org/what-is-social-work/global-definition-of-social-work/

Swigonski, M. (2011). Claiming rights, righting wrongs: Educating students for human rights. *Journal of Baccalaureate Social Work, 16*(2), 1–16. https://doi.org/10.18084/basw.16.2.dp1ht167100h1819

ACKNOWLEDGMENTS

The spirit of my grandparents, David and Raschel, my aunts, Beatrice and Stella, and the many great-aunts, great-uncles, and cousins I never met but who were murdered in the death camps during the Holocaust are the force behind my interest in human rights and justice. I have traveled to the city and region where they once lived, hoping to gain more insight into their lives. I have often contemplated what it must have been like for them to be pulled from school and lose their livelihoods, homes, families, and ulti-mately their lives, not because of their actions but simply because of who they were. Thinking about them has opened my eyes to the symptoms that lead to genocide, racism, and other forms of oppression that exist today and drive my work to uphold human rights and justice. By pursuing this work, I honor the memories of my family and all those whose lives are taken or diminished because of how they are labeled in society.

Throughout my journey to deepen my understanding of human rights and justice in contemporary societies, I have been fortunate to work with Susan Mapp, who came to this topic from a different path. We have created together, written together, and spent many hours researching and conversing on these and related topics. Together with our colleagues, we founded the *Journal of Human Rights and Social Work* to provide a platform for voices from around the world to share their experiences and research on human rights and social work. I've drawn inspiration and energy from past and current members of the journal's board, our authors, and reviewers. I continue to grow from working with my new co-editor, Cathryne Schmitz.

Discussions with my colleagues throughout the United States, Europe, Africa, the Middle East, and Asia reinforced my observation that students should know early on how these key concepts in social work—human rights, oppression, privilege, intersectionality, and social, economic, and environmental justice—are interrelated and interdependent. This served as the motivation for writing this textbook.

I have learned so much about different perspectives and the challenges of opening oneself to a new framework from exposing students to the topics. Input from students, administrators, and full-time and part-time faculty at Fordham's Graduate School of Social Service helped me better understand what was needed to address the gap in social work literature that pulled these critical concepts together for social work students.

Thank you, too, to my editors at Oxford University Press, Dana Bliss, Alyssa Palazzo, and Mary Funchion, for guiding me to complete the book.

The world we live in today is far from perfect. We all have the option to make it better. I hope this book will inspire students to take up the charge to give respect and dignity to the lives of others and, in doing so, create a better world than the one they found.

CHAPTER 1

Ethics, Morals, Human Rights, and Justice in Social Work Practice

Most of us chose social work because of our interest in improving how we treat one another in our society and helping individuals reach their potential. In short, we want to change situations for the better. Change is a critical part of social work. Change is a process that social workers help the individuals, communities, or systems we work with go through so that we can evolve into a better place. But what is "better"? We will likely have different opinions on what form change for the better should take. Yet we are all social workers; shouldn't we have the same vision or strive for the same goals?

Without question, social workers have lots of opinions. We may be affiliated with different political parties or religions or rely on different philosophies to understand our world. We value diversity in social work— diversity in culture, thought, and ways of living. Diversity helps us all learn from one another.

As new social workers, you want to learn about the appropriate and professional way to handle situations. No rule book could exist for every situation we might encounter. Still, we have a professional code of ethics to provide guidelines on responding to the social situations we are likely to encounter. These guidelines encapsulate a vision of who we are as a profession and how, as social workers, we see the world.

A Human Rights-Based Approach to Justice in Social Work Practice. Shirley Gatenio Gabel, Oxford University Press.
© Oxford University Press 2024. DOI: 10.1093/oso/9780197570647.003.0001

Each of us belongs to groups, and each of those groups has expectations regarding our choices, behaviors, and perspectives on issues. We may not always be conscious of the expectations because they may be unspoken, but the expectations guide our actions and way of thinking. These expectations inform our values, and these values help us prioritize what's important and our decision-making. When we are faced with a conflict, we depend on our values to help us see our way through the conflict. Social work values are embedded in the profession's national and international codes of ethics (International Association of Schools of Social Work, 2018; International Federation of Social Workers & International Association of Schools of Social Work, 2018; National Association of Social Workers, 2021).

The core values of social work are the foundation of social work practice and inform our purpose and perspective on social issues. Six core values and ethical standards guide U.S. social workers. The first is service to others, then social justice, followed by the dignity and worth of each person. The other values are the importance of human relationships, integrity, and competence as professional workers. There is no hierarchy among these values. They are all equally crucial, though some may weigh in more prominently than others as you work through a conflict.

Values reflect our ideals, but ethics relate more directly to our behaviors. Ethics are closely related to morals. Morals reflect our belief system. For many of us, the foundation of our morals is religion. Morals tend to inform what is acceptable or unacceptable, virtuous or non-virtuous actions or ways of seeing situations. Morals help us evaluate a situation or actions and tend to be personal. We typically don't have professional morals, but we have professional ethics.

Ethical standards guide professional decision-making and actions. Professional ethics are usually codified in a formal system or set of rules. We are more likely to use professional standards to consider whether a social worker has acted ethically than to judge their morality. When we say a social worker acts unprofessionally, we often refer to whether they have served ethically in their professional roles.

In the United States, the National Association of Social Workers (NASW) is the member organization of our profession. NASW performs several essential roles, including establishing a code of ethics for social work. The NASW Code of Ethics, last updated in 2021, serves as a guide for all social workers on professional conduct and identifies the core values of social work (National Association of Social Workers, 2021). The Code of Ethics summarizes ethical principles and standards to guide professional social work practice, identifies relevant factors to consider when obligations conflict or uncertainties arise, and discusses professional and public accountability. The Code of Ethics also helps socialize new social work professionals, like yourselves, and articulates the standards that the profession can use to assess whether professional conduct is ethical. New to the 2021 version is the importance of professional self-care in social work.

The ethical principles and standards in the NASW Code of Ethics lead us through conflict situations. Typically, conflict comes about when standards direct us to pursue different paths. For example, let's say I am working in a program funded by a government grant at a social service agency. All is well until one day, the type of assistance that the grant directs me to offer the individuals I am working with is very different than the kind of help the service users are telling they need. I have a conflict. The Code of Ethics can provide guidance.

The ethical standards articulated within the NASW Code of Ethics describe our responsibilities in practice settings, as professionals, and to clients, colleagues, the profession, and broader society. Self-determination and autonomy, as well as informed consent, are critical parts of these standards. Fundamental to social work practice and a human rights-based approach (you'll hear more about this soon) is that we respect the individuals and communities we are working with to make their own decisions. We may not always agree with the decisions made, but the standards guide us to prioritize self-determination and empower individuals as professionals. Our role is to help the people and communities we work with understand the potential consequences of their actions. Related to this is informed consent. We are obligated to inform the populations we are working with of the likely course of action and help them set expectations accordingly. Social work ethical standards also stress the importance of privacy and confidentiality. When we work with individuals, families, or groups, we are obliged to keep any confidential information private unless situations are disclosed that may harm the people we are working with or others. As professionals, we are required to report these.

Another ethical standard is non-discrimination. Regardless of our own beliefs, we must treat the people and communities we work with equally and with respect for all. We must continually check ourselves on this, which is why another ethical standard is that we commit to ongoing supervision so that as we practice, we also reflect on what we are learning and enlist the help of supervisors to help see us through situations where we may be unaware of our own biases affecting our practice.

In addition to the NASW Code of Ethics, a code of ethics exists for social work professionals globally. The Global Social Work Statement of Ethical

Principles can be found on the website of the International Association of Schools of Social Work (2018) and the website of the International Federation of Social Workers (2018). When we compare the Global Statement of Ethical Principles with our national code of ethics, it's interesting to see what is emphasized and included in each. In doing this comparative exercise, students have remarked how much broader the international ethical principles seem to be and the greater emphasis on human rights. The Global Social Work Statement of Ethical Principles is based on international human rights conventions. It is broader because people from around the world developed it, and the intention was for each country to be able to make the guidelines more specific to their culture and tailored to their sense of what is best practice for a social worker. Absolute positions are avoided in favor of allowing for culture-specific interpretations, thereby respecting different cultures and ways of thinking. The reference to human rights in the Global Statement of Ethical Principles reflects the global view of the alignment of social work values with international human rights instruments.

Ethical behavior is the bedrock of social work practice, wherever one chooses to practice. The ability and the commitment to act ethically are essential components of the quality service we offer as social workers. When applying a rights-based approach to justice in social work practice, respecting one's human rights is core to achieving justice.

INTEGRATING A RIGHTS-BASED APPROACH TO JUSTICE IN SOCIAL WORK PRACTICE

Social work grew out of humanitarian and democratic ideals. Social work values are based on equal respect, worth, and dignity for all people. Since the founding of the social work profession over a century ago, social work practice has focused on meeting human needs and developing human potential. Human rights and justice are the motivation and justification for social work action. In solidarity with those who have been marginalized, oppressed, and excluded, the profession strives to promote social inclusion and equity and to celebrate diversity.

Yet, social workers often work for or with governments (or organizations) that do not have the best interests of all people in their policies and practices. Social workers can find that they are torn between their duties to their employer and the best interests of the people they serve. There are too many examples in history when social workers sided with serving the interests of their employers or government at the expense of individuals and communities. For instance, during World War II, authoritarian regimes used social workers to gather information from individuals that was later used to imprison or justify murdering these individuals (Gatenio Gabel, 2016). We can look to practices today, albeit with less drastic consequences for the most part, to see how this practice continues in the United States and around the world.

Human rights provide a normative framework for our ethical standards. Jim Ife has remarked that human rights present a road map for ethical social work practice (Ife, 2012). It is an aspirational framework. As such, human rights provide us direction toward normative standards and behaviors. By striving for these standards as social workers, we facilitate the realization of social, economic, and environmental justice on behalf of people, their communities, and society at large.

Using a human rights framework allows different cultures to decide what ethical standards mean for them and to adjust these standards as their own cultures evolve. Cultures are constantly changing and evolving, and this should be reflected in ethical standards. The international human rights treaties coming from the United Nations respect individual cultures and see culture as central to one's identity as an individual. However, there are some circumstances when local cultural practices are viewed as oppressive and in violation of human rights by international standards. For example, many cultures continue to deny women's rights and punish, alienate, and exclude persons with specific diseases such as albinism or HIV/AIDS, or sexual preferences or identities beyond heterosexual, binary options. As champions of justice, social workers often navigate rough waters while trying to obtain services and benefits needed by the people they are working with from sources that hold punitive attitudes toward the populations.

The Global Ethical Principles of the International Association of Schools of Social Work and the International Federation of Social Workers provide guidelines on the role of culture in social work practice. They instruct that culture should not be used to justify committing human rights violations or maintaining traditional values. In many African cultures, the chastity and loyalty of a wife are essential, and a cultural ritual called female genital mutilation (or cutting) is performed on young women or girls to ensure their purity. This ritual varies greatly from one culture to another, but the typical result is that sexual intercourse is often an uncomfortable or painful experience for women. This voluntary practice asserts male superiority over women, reducing any temptations for women to stray from their husbands by largely eliminating sexual desire and pleasure from women.

On the other hand, a girl or woman who refuses to participate in the ritual is likely to diminish her marriage prospects. Because her economic well-being is dependent on marriage, her future economic well-being is also compromised. Mothers will risk their daughters' health and emotional well-being to ensure their social and economic futures.

The conflict we would face as social workers is whose culture to respect. Do we prioritize local culture that shapes the social and economic infrastructure? Should we evaluate local culture against international human rights standards? How would we want others to judge how we were raised or how we raise our own children?

As powerful as our human rights instruments can be, they will not eliminate the ethical conflicts that we are likely to face as professionals. Like our cultures and sense of justice, our ethical standards need to change to adjust to the evolving perspectives. Rights-based standards encourage us to consider different points of view and give respect and dignity to each, and instruct us how to consider the factors that affect the lives of those we seek to help.

As social workers, we have the responsibility to investigate whether human rights are being violated or upheld and work toward practicing in a way that facilitates the realization of human rights for all. This book will introduce the human rights framework and how it can be used to achieve social, economic, and environmental justice.

The book will explain the basics of the modern human rights framework, its evolution and instruments, the unique position of the United States related to human rights, and how one can advocate for human rights as a practicing social worker. It then turns to concepts of diversity, oppression/privilege, and intersectionality and demonstrates how they are linked to our concepts of justice. The book will unpack social, economic, and environmental justice relating to social work and human rights and then demonstrate how social workers can integrate these concepts of justice into practice using the human rights approach at micro, mezzo, and macro levels of practice.

Section 1 introduces readers to human rights as they stand in international law. It will explain the history, culture, and principles of human rights. The Universal Declaration of Human Rights will be discussed, as will other core international covenants and conventions, including their implementation and monitoring. It will discuss the responsibilities inherent in a human rights-based approach. A chapter in this section discusses which, where, and how human rights can be found in the United States by walking readers through the Bill of Rights, courts, and state/local laws. Exercises are provided in each section to help students review the concepts discussed and test their understanding of these concepts. The section concludes with a chapter describing the rights-based approach to social work practice. It explains how social workers can practice from a rights-based approach in diverse settings and using different skills in direct and community-based social work practice, policy, and research. The differences between charity-, needs-, and rights-based approaches are explained.

Section 2 explores the relationship between diversity, oppression, and privilege, focusing on the United States. Differences in a society often lead to preferences that become privilege and power. To maintain the distribution of power and resources, societies often oppress those who may pose a challenge to existing privilege and power. This section will relate this to the populations social workers typically work with and will then introduce the concept of intersectionality to demonstrate that privilege and oppression is relative and that most of us embody elements of both. Students first learn about intersectionality and then engage in an interactive exercise to understand the sources of their own power and privilege. Students will use this to understand whose human rights are often upheld and whose are not.

Building on the previous two sections, Section 3 explains how one's conceptualization of human rights and privilege/oppression affects one's sense of social, economic, and environmental justice specified in our educational standards. Social justice has been synonymous with social work for decades, but most social workers are less familiar with economic and environmental justice. This section begins with a chapter discussing different definitions and types of justice. The section discusses how justice is tied to time and place and is continually evolving, and offers a rights-based definition of justice.

Three chapters follow. The chapter on social justice discusses the importance of social justice and social work throughout the profession's history, different theories of informing social justice, and the significance of seeking racial justice. Examples of social justice and their relevance to social work practice are presented. The next chapter discusses how for decades economic justice was part of social justice in social work and why we have differentiated social and economic justice. Opposing views of economic justice are presented and readers are asked to reflect about their own definition of economic justice and how it may affect their practice as social workers. Following this is a chapter on environmental justice and social work practice. Addressing social inequities and human suffering in our communities is part of larger efforts to restore ecological balance and sustainability. Neither can be achieved without clean air and water and healthy and balanced ecosystems.

Section 4 of the book applies human rights and the right-based approach in practice, whether the social worker is working with individuals, families, groups, communities, or organizations. It will describe specific ways of helping and demonstrates how human rights and justice can be integrated into social work practice, policy, and research.

Human rights are much more than a list of standards. They make up a framework for understanding ways we can interact with one another, wherever we may live and practice, that can lend dignity and respect to each and every one of us. In doing so, we believe justice will be achieved.

SECTION 1
Human Rights

CHAPTER 2
Human Dignity and Respect for All

Dignity is "the state or quality of being worthy of honor or respect."
Oxford Languages, n.d.

[T]he inherent dignity and of the equal and inalienable rights of all members of the human family is the foundation of freedom, justice and peace in the world.
Preamble, International Covenant on Civil and Political Rights, 1966;
Preamble, International Covenant on Economic,
Social and Cultural Rights, 1966

At the heart of human rights is human dignity. Human dignity connotes that all human beings possess equal and inherent value and should be accorded respect regardless of gender, sexuality, age, race or ethnicity, health, religion, socioeconomic status, political affiliations, or any other socially constructed classification.

Discussions of human dignity can be traced back to Roman times. However, the work of the German philosopher Immanuel Kant in the late 18th century anchored and profoundly influenced our thinking on human dignity (Sensen, 2011). According to Kant, human beings are unique in that they have freedom (autonomy), reasoning, and the ability to follow moral law to do good. Acting to do good (being moral) becomes a means and an end that distinguishes humankind. In Kant's view, acting morally or respecting others gives all humans intrinsic dignity, and by acting with dignity, we enhance our own dignity and the dignity of others.

At some point in our lives, we have all found ourselves in situations with those whose perspectives on an issue differed from ours. For example, Janine was excited to start her social work program and enthusiastically participated in her social policy class on the first day. It was an election year, and Janine soon realized that almost everyone in the class was supporting a different candidate than the one she favored. Janine was not shy about expressing her opinion, but the eye-rolling and facial gestures of the other students made it clear that no one was listening to her reasons for supporting her candidate. When class was over, Janine was left alone in the classroom as the other students scrambled to go to lunch together with the new friends they had made in class. Janine felt that she had been disrespected and that her perspective was unheard.

Like most social work students, Janine was interested in social work because she wanted to help others improve their lives. Her life experiences led her to favor a particular candidate. She is bright, involved in her community, and committed to helping others. When she expressed her opinion, Janine felt shunned or marginalized by the other students.

Imagine how this scenario would have played out differently if the other students had listened to Janine's reasoning when she spoke, perhaps even challenging her rationale by asking her questions. Janine surely would have felt respected, and this would have given her dignity. And if Janine had responded respectfully to the students' questions, she would have enhanced the dignity of the others. Perhaps both sides would have learned something and found common ground to speak with one another. Respecting one another's views does not mean we agree; rather, it is about a willingness to hear one another.

TIME FOR REFLECTION AND DISCUSSION

Write down two qualities you admire about yourself—for instance, you may be compassionate or a good listener. Write down how you typically react when you recognize these qualities in someone else (e.g., in a work situation or social gathering). Now, note what it feels like when someone recognizes these qualities in you.

How do you feel when colleagues, friends, or family do not recognize these qualities? Picture yourself, for example, in a meeting where your ideas are not recognized or are dismissed.

Now think of the opposite. Place yourself in a meeting where your ideas were supported, appreciated, or heard. How did that feel?

When we hear others, acknowledge their perspectives, and support others, we give dignity. We are more likely to treat others with dignity and respect when we treated are treated with dignity. Every time we do this for someone, it enhances the likelihood of others being treated with dignity and respect, including ourselves.

Some philosophers and scholars believe that human dignity gives us human rights and makes human rights *inalienable*, meaning no one can take them away from anyone (Beyleveld & Brownsword, 1998; Dicke, 2002). Human rights enable us to fully develop those uniquely human traits of reason, morality, and autonomy that give us dignity.

In social work, we learn to respect all persons and treat all with dignity. To do this, we must seek to uphold the human rights of all persons.

According to international law, the relationship between human dignity and human rights is the one between a foundational principle of equal respect for every human being and the concrete norms that are needed to flesh out that principle in social life. Human dignity is the foundation of human rights; rights *derive* from human dignity. Human dignity is . . . the ultimate source of all rights. The notion of human dignity attempts to respond to the question "why do human beings have rights?" And the answer is that they are entitled to rights precisely because they possess intrinsic worth. (Andorno, 2014, p. 49; emphasis original)

The idea of human rights goes back to biblical times and has evolved since then. Today when we speak of human rights, we generally refer to the human rights articulated by the United Nations (UN) in the Universal Declaration of Human Rights (UDHR; United Nations General Assembly, 1948).

The UN was created in 1945 at the end of World War II. Worldwide, nations were in ruin, and the world had to figure out how to put itself back together. For two months, representatives of 50 countries gathered at the UN Conference on International Organization in San Francisco to draft and then sign the UN Charter, which created a new international, intergovernmental body, the UN, whose primary purpose is to prevent another world war and other wars. Maintaining peace and security was the foremost goal for the world leaders. To do this, they realized that it must begin with mutual dignity and respect for all people. The Preamble of the UN Charter (United Nations, 1945) states:

We the peoples of the United Nations [are] determined . . . to reaffirm faith in fundamental human rights, in the dignity and worth of the human person, in the equal rights of men and women and nations large and small.

Recognizing that views of human rights differed around the world and within countries, the UN leaders decided to create a document that would articulate the UN's vision of human rights and guide the implementation of human rights worldwide. The UN worked on this document in various newly founded UN bodies, eventually creating a Commission on Human Rights to draft the final document. The Committee was composed of eight members from diverse political, cultural, and religious backgrounds. Eleanor Roosevelt, the widow of American president Franklin D. Roosevelt, chaired the UDHR drafting committee. The other members were René Cassin of France, Rapporteur Charles Malik of Lebanon, Vice-Chairman Peng Chung Chang of China, John Humphrey of Canada, Alexandre Bogomolov of the USSR, Charles Dukes from the United Kingdom, and William Hodgson of Australia.

Countries around the world agreed to emphasize the notion of human dignity to prevent "barbarous acts which have outraged the conscience of mankind" from ever happening again (United Nations General Assembly, 1948, Preamble). At the very beginning, the Declaration puts forward that "all human beings are born free and equal in dignity and rights" (United Nations General Assembly, 1948, Article 1).

The human rights declared in the UDHR have been expanded upon in subsequent treaties and declarations and are discussed further in the next chapter. Human rights appear in numerous national constitutions and as the bases for domestic legal frameworks. Curiously, as much as human rights have increased in international and domestic laws and goals, resistance to fully embracing human rights has also grown. Regilme (2019) argues that the integration of human rights has been undermined by reactions to 9/11, the U.S.-led war on terror, the rise of neoliberalism and populism both within and beyond states that have been champions of human rights, and the Global North and South tensions around approaches to human rights. Regilme feels we should respond by shifting the focus to human dignity:

The notion of dignity avoids the unnecessary political tensions between states and key actors of the North and South. It guarantees equal normative value for both socioeconomic rights often dismissed by the Global North and political and civil rights that many regimes in the Global South perceive as less important. By invoking dignity, actors from the North and the South are placed on equal political footing. The debate then becomes post-ideological as the terms of conversation shift toward actual policies and governance structures. (Regilme, 2019, p. 287)

THE UDHR IS NOT PERFECT

The UDHR and the major conventions and treaties that followed have been criticized for embracing Western or Global North perspectives of human dignity and human rights, to the exclusion of other views. For example, the conception of human dignity and its relation to human rights embraced by the individualist cultures of Europe, North America, and elsewhere is not widely accepted by people in communitarian cultures of Asia and Islam (Mattson & Clark, 2011). Communitarian cultures tend to emphasize people's duties and obligations rather than their rights (Suh, 2000). In communitarian cultures, dignity comes from fulfilling one's obligations or duties, which are often seen as collective rather than relating to the individual. Individuals derive dignity from being acknowledged for what they have done for others. These differences in how dignity is understood affect one's concept of human rights as well.

TIME FOR REFLECTION AND DISCUSSION

What do you think? Is a focus on human dignity more appealing to you? Do you think it would be a way to open dialogues among neighbors, family members, and colleagues who have very different points of view from yours? Would it allow for broader interpretations of human rights (e.g., individualism vs. communitarian views)?

As social workers, regardless of our political, philosophical and religious leanings, our professional values guide us to fight for respect and dignity for all.

CHAPTER 3
Evolving Concepts of Human Rights

As we learned in our previous chapter, the values that drive social work practice align with human rights and justice. Social workers are committed to helping others navigate the complicated world we have constructed as humans, internally and externally. As social workers, our experiences with our families, communities, and the larger society inform how we feel about ourselves and our lives. By prioritizing human rights in social work practice, we allow individuals to change the way society has treated them, feel differently about themselves and their lives, and expect they are a part of creating and implementing public policies that respect the dignity of all members of the society.

Social workers most often work on local issues pertaining to those who live in communities in the United States, whether this work is with individuals, groups, or communities or at the policy level. However, as the boundaries of our world expand, so do the boundaries of social work. Increasingly, issues confronted on a local level in countries in the West or Global North are the same issues faced by people struggling across the world. However, they take a different form depending on the cultural context.

What Are Human Rights?

Let's begin by unpacking what we mean by human rights. The term may be familiar, but many of us may not have given thought to what it means, even though we may have often referred to our "right" to act in a certain way or our expectation that the government act in a particular way.

A Human Rights-Based Approach to Justice in Social Work Practice. Shirley Gatenio Gabel, Oxford University Press.
© Oxford University Press 2024. DOI: 10.1093/oso/9780197570647.003.0003

Human rights are not earned, nor are they awarded. They are ours simply because we are human beings. As human beings, we all have the same rights. Because all humans have the same rights, we promote everyone's rights when we promote "our" rights.

Origins of Human Rights

Human rights have a long history. Like most ideas, identifying the specific moment an idea was conceived is difficult, if not impossible, because new ways of seeing things build from previous perspectives. Human rights emerged from the claims of people suffering and seeking justice. Throughout history, human rights reflect the cultures, morals, and religious beliefs of a period and the challenges to culture, religion, and morality at the time.

Scholars have traced the notion of human rights to religious and philosophical concepts of compassion, charity, justice, individual worth, and respect for all life found in Hinduism, Judaism, Buddhism, Confucianism, Christianity, and Islam (Marks, 2016). Some scholars claim that the origins of human rights can be ascribed to the ancient codes of Hammurabi in Babylon (about 1772 BCE) (Lauren, 2013). The Code of Hammurabi includes some of the earliest examples of civil rights, such as the right to freedom of speech, the presumption of innocence, the right to present evidence, and the right to a fair trial by judges (Lauren, 2013). The Charter of Cyrus the Great in Persia (about 535 BCE) is another commonly cited source of early human rights (Figure 3.1). Cyrus the Great was viewed as a liberator, not a conqueror, because upon entering ancient Babylon, he freed the enslaved people, declared that all people had a right to choose their religion and where they wanted to live and that there should be equity among all humans (Lauren, 2013). Some scholars look to the edicts of Asoka in India (about 250 BCE) for the roots of human rights and in the rules and traditions of pre-colonial Africa and pre-Columbian America (Marks, 2016). The Edicts of Asoka address respect for all life, equal protection under the law regardless of political belief or caste, the administration of justice, social and environmental protection, the prohibition of slavery, and the banning of torture (Lauren, 2013).

The natural law theories from ancient Greece and Rome, such as the writings of Plato, Aristotle, and Cicero, are also thought to be the roots of human rights (Lauren, 2013). The Christian theology of the Middle Ages, especially the English Magna Carta of 1215, is a crucial contributor to the

Figure 3.1. The Cyrus Cylinder was discovered in Babylon, Mesopotamia, in March 1879 and is currently located in the British Museum, London.

conceptual development of human rights. The Magna Carta introduced the "rule of law" concept and delineated rights and liberties such as protection against arbitrary prosecution and incarceration. These concepts were developed further during the Enlightenment and the declarations that launched the French and American revolutions. Before this, it was commonly believed that justice was divine and that monarchs had divine authority to deliver justice from their perspective.

The success of the American Revolution in overthrowing a monarch and creating a new government with legal protections for freedoms and other rights encouraged the French to challenge the privilege and power in France. The ideas of the Enlightenment and the U.S. Declaration of Independence had a profound effect on galvanizing other countries and peoples in the world struggling against abuse and oppression. They also heavily influenced France's Declaration of the Rights of Man and Citizen (Lauren, 2013), which states that all "are born and remain free and equal in rights . . . These rights are liberty, property, security, and resistance to oppression" (Élysée, n.d.). It sets out the "natural and inalienable" rights: freedom, ownership, security, and resistance to oppression; it recognizes equality before the law and the justice system and affirms the separation of powers.

Rights related to personal liberty and protecting individuals from being abused by powerful rulers are considered political and civil rights. These are sometimes referred to as negative rights (things that governments and others cannot do) or the first generation of rights.

The second generation of human rights peaked after World War II. Also known as positive rights, they generally refer to the actions that governments should take to protect and promote the well-being of their citizenry. Generally, they relate to economic, social, and cultural rights such as education, food, housing, national security, healthcare, social security (social welfare benefits and services), information, and employment.

According to Sutto (2019), positive rights evolved from concerns raised by the League of Nations at the end of the First World War regarding the treatment of marginalized populations and the creation of the International Labor Organization (ILO) in 1919 to oversee treaties protecting workers' rights, including their health and safety. The founders of the ILO recognized how the exploitation of workers in the industrializing nations hindered the securing of peace (ILO, n.d.).

Coming out of World War II, public opinion heavily leaned toward the need to promote human dignity, even during wartime (Sutto, 2019). The world was horrified by the unprecedented cruelties perpetrated during World War II, including the extermination by Nazi Germany of over 11 million people, including Jews, Sinti and Romani, non-heterosexuals, and persons with disabilities, as well as the savage rape, torture, and mass murder of Chinese civilians and prisoners of war by Japanese forces (Dower, 1999). The international trials held in Nuremberg and Tokyo after World War II introduced the concepts of "crimes against peace" and "crimes against humanity" and fueled the embrace of modern human rights across the world.

Figure 3.2 shows how these rights evolved.

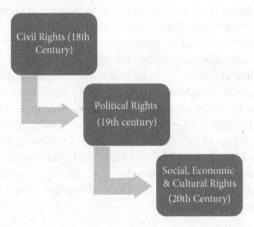

Figure 3.2. The evolution of modern human rights.

PRINCIPLES OF HUMAN RIGHTS

Definitions of human rights change over time and according to culture. The United Nations has identified the following as the basic principles of human rights (Officer of the High Commissioner of Human Rights, n.d.):

Universality: As humans, we are all entitled to the same human rights.

Equality and non-discrimination: Regardless of race, color, ethnicity, gender, age, language, sexual orientation, religion, political or other opinions, national, social, or geographical origin, (dis)ability, property, birth, or another status, all human beings are equal and should be treated with dignity.

Indivisible and interdependent: All rights are dependent on the realization of other rights, and the realization of any human right furthers other rights.

Inalienable: No one and no entity can grant or deny our human rights, except in specific situations and according to due process. For example, a person found guilty of a crime by a court of law may have the right to liberty restricted.

Rights and obligations: Every right comes with the responsibility to respect, protect, and fulfill the right. Governments bear most of the duties, but individuals also have the responsibility to respect and uphold the rights of others.

More recently, two additional concepts have been added to the list of basic human rights principles:

Participation and inclusion is now commonly included as a human rights principle because the right to participate in and access information relating to the decision-making processes that affect one's life and well-being is considered a critical ingredient in securing human rights. Rights-based approaches require a high degree of participation by communities, civil society, minorities, women, young people, Indigenous peoples, and other identified groups.

Accountability refers to the obligation that States and other duty-bearers have to comply with the legal norms and standards enshrined in international human rights instruments. Should they fail to do so, aggrieved rights-holders are entitled to redress proceedings before a competent court or other adjudicator in accordance with the rules and procedures provided by law. Individuals, the media, civil society, and the international community play important roles in holding governments accountable for their obligation to uphold human rights.

Throughout this text, we refer to the member organizations of the U-nited Nations as States (note the capital "S"). This is not to be confused with the 50 states that are part of the United States (small "s"). A State is a sovereign, political entity with legal responsibility for the security and welfare needs of its people.

Sometimes other terms, such as *nation* or *country*, are used inter-changeably with State. Unlike a State, however, a nation refers to a pop-ulation that shares cultural, spiritual, or other bonds and unity. A nation does not necessarily reference a geographical area. A country, on the other hand, is a territory with defined borders. State and country can sometimes be used synonymously, but a country may also include more than one state (e.g., the United States).

Human rights are normative standards that address how individuals and groups should treat one another and how governments and non-government actors should treat people. These norms are incorporated into national and international legal systems to protect individuals and groups against actions that interfere with fundamental freedoms and human dignity.

Human rights are commonly thought to be the rights of individuals re-garding government. Examples of this would be the freedom from slavery, torture, and discrimination or the right to express one's opinions, vote, or move freely. However, human rights standards also apply to non-State actors (such as corporations, international financial institutions, ter-rorist groups, and individuals). Non-State actors who commit human rights abuses such as violence against individuals, discrimination, and withholding information detrimental to the well-being of individuals are subject to punishments prescribed by domestic and international laws. Governments have the responsibility to monitor that non-State actors comply with human rights laws and respond accordingly if they do not.

Human rights standards have international authority from two prin-cipal sources (D'Amato, 2010):

Treaty law includes human rights law as set out in many interna-tional agreements that have been developed, signed, and ratified by States. Two examples of this are the International Covenant on Civil and Political Rights (1966) and the International Covenant on Economic, Social and Cultural Rights (1966). International treaties are legally binding on the States that are "party" to them. In turn, States incorporate the treaties into their national and local constitutions and laws. Later, we will explore the interna-tional human rights treaties and how human rights are incorpo-rated into the U.S. Constitution and laws in the United States.

Customary law refers to States' general and consistent practice followed by a sense of legal obligation. Customary law refers to international obligations arising from established practices. Customary law reflects the common practice and may or may not be documented in international declarations, recommendations, bodies of principles, and codes of conduct. These are not legally binding on States but have the moral force and provide practical guidance to States.

IS SOCIAL WORK A HUMAN RIGHTS PROFESSION?

When the profession was founded, social workers sought to transform people's lives through wide-ranging social and economic reforms as well as work with individuals and communities. Social workers treated people and communities in need with respect and dignity, breaking from past practices regarding the treatment of the poor. Worldwide, social workers have a long history of working to achieve human rights, even though the profession was founded long before the Universal Declaration of Human Rights (UDHR) was written. According to an International Federation of Social Workers policy paper, social work "has, from its conception, been a human rights profession, having as its basic tenet the intrinsic value of every human being and as one of its main aims the promotion of equitable social structures, which can offer people security and development while upholding their dignity" (quoted in Healy, 2008, pp. 735–736).

At the profession's inception, advocating for equitable treatment regardless of one's place of origin, income, gender, ability, or race was at the core of social work practice. Keep in mind that during the early 20th century, social workers' concepts of human rights may have been different from our understanding today. Social work was founded over 50 years before the UDHR was written. The biographies of our social work pioneers indicate that they wanted to right the social and economic inequities they saw in society and considered human rights as a path to justice and integral to social work practice. These pioneers were heavily engaged in reforming society by creating social infrastructure and grounding the practice of human rights principles: human dignity, nondiscrimination, participation, transparency, and accountability (Healy, 2008; Androff, 2016; Gatenio Gabel, 2016; Mapp et al., 2019).

Calls for the professionalization and legitimization of social work triumphed over social action as social work matured as a profession. Social work tilted toward direct practice methods; in doing so, the micro/macro divide widened while the prominence of human rights in the profession diminished (Haynes, 1998; Gatenio Gabel et al., 2022). Consequently, the profession focused on professionalization by developing scientific rigor in the field, and advocacy for human rights receded from center stage and was increasingly designated to macro-practitioners (Abramovitz, 1998; Haynes & Mickelson, 1992).

In the past few decades, however, calls to reintegrate human rights and advocacy into the profession's core have grown louder, helping to make social work practice whole again.

SOCIAL WORK PIONEERS' CONCEPTS OF HUMAN RIGHTS

Many of the leaders and individuals who first identified as social workers in the United States were White and from privileged class backgrounds. They did not necessarily reflect the values, goals, and cultures of the populations they sought to help. Early social workers focused on improving the lives of low-income, White migrants and European immigrants. We are beginning to learn more about how social work pioneers viewed cultural pluralism across racial and ethnic lines. For example, many of our well-respected early agencies excluded African Americans (Carlton-LaNey & Hodges, 2004). Instead, assistance to the Black community developed separately as mutual aid organizations, later evolving into orphanages, settlement houses, and other social services (Schiele & Jackson, 2020; Brantley et al., 2021). Many of the early social work agencies were sectarian and did not cross religious, racial/ethnic, and even country-of-origin lines (Friedlander, 1963; Coughlin, 1965). This paralleled immigration laws of the time that required immigrants to have sponsors or guarantors, who were often immigrants who had migrated to the United States or organizations founded by immigrants who had arrived a generation or so earlier to help their compatriots (Friedlander, 1963; Coughlin, 1965).

The brief biographies that follow will highlight how some of these pioneers understood human rights and social work practice.

JANE ADDAMS (1860–1935)

Jane Addams (Figure 3.3), who founded Hull House and was awarded a Nobel Peace Prize in 1931, is heralded as an early advocate who fought for social and racial equality and cultural pluralism (Steen, 2006; Deegan, 2010). The main focus of her efforts was securing economic and social rights of immigrants and their families, largely from Europe. She also worked to protect Blacks (who at that time were often victims of

Figure 3.3. Jane Addams, 1926.
George Grantham Bain Collection, Library of Congress Prints and Photographs Division.

lynching and mob violence) and to fight discrimination against Blacks in hiring and employment practices. She worked passionately with Black women's clubs to effect change and was a founding member of the National Association for the Advancement of Colored People. As a fierce antiwar advocate, she took a strong stand upholding the civil rights of those who were jailed because of their objections to war. Unlike many other feminists of the period, Addams did not fully embrace Marxism, or capitalism, or any feminism based on anger (Deegan, 2010). She fought for the ability of all women (not just middle- and upper-class women) to stay at home to nurture their children (Deegan, 2010). For Addams, justifying discrimination against one group was the same as justifying discrimination against any group, and she connected oppression by religion, age, disability, origin, class, employment practices, and gender in her advocacy for justice (Deegan, 2010).

JANIE PORTER BARRETT (1865–1948)

Janie Porter Barrett (Figure 3.4) was the daughter of a formerly enslaved person and was raised in the home of a wealthy White family, the Skinners, who employed her mother and educated Barrett along with their children. Barrett trained to become a teacher, and in her early work in education, she realized the importance of community in helping people live better lives. Living in Georgia, Barrett was aware of segregation and the institutions that excluded African Americans. She viewed access to social and educational support and participation as human rights and was devoted to building the institutions African Americans needed. After she married, Barrett would invite African American girls and young women to her home to teach home management and involve them in community activities. Over time this became a clubhouse and then the Locust Street Settlement, the first settlement house for Blacks in the United States. It was modeled after Hull House in Chicago. Barrett and

Figure 3.4. Janie Porter Barrett.
New York Public Library, Schomburg Center for Research in Black Culture, Jean Blackwell Hutson Research and Reference Division.

Addams were colleagues who visited one another.

Barrett founded the Virginia State Federation of Colored Women's Clubs. Through her Federation networks, she raised funds for a residential, industrial school for young African American girls who had been incarcerated (the Virginia Industrial School for Wayward Colored Girls). Barrett became the superintendent of the innovative Virginia Industrial School for Colored Girls from 1915 until her retirement in 1940. She used her influential position to advocate voting and participation in government for Blacks years before the civil rights movement. For more information about Barrett, see https://socialwelfare.library.vcu.edu/set tlement-houses/barrett-janie-porter-1865-1948-african-american-soc ial-welfare-activist/.

LILLIAN WALD (1867–1940)

Helping those in need has long been integral to Jewish life. Because Jews were most often segregated from the rest of the community, Jewish communal life was organized around the place of worship, including activities related to helping those in need. These traditions were brought to colonial America. For centuries, Jewish communities established in the United States cared for needy Jews and assisted Jewish immigrants in developing their livelihoods and families in the new world. Many social work pioneers in the late 1800s and early 1900s worked endlessly to create the social infrastructure to support their brethren.

Lillian Wald (Figure 3.5) went beyond this. She was born in 1876 in Ohio and raised in Rochester, New York. Her German ancestors may have been rabbis, but Wald was raised in a liberal Jewish atmosphere. She passionately dedicated herself to the causes of all immigrants, working women, and children. She started her career as a nurse working at the New York Juvenile Asylum but eventually left institutional nursing to become a doctor. Shortly after she began taking courses at the Women's Medical College in New York, she accepted an invitation to organize classes on home nursing for immigrant families on the Lower East Side. Her work exposed her to the deplorable conditions that families lived in and the need for social and economic reforms.

She left medical school to try to change the social and economic conditions she witnessed immigrants living in on the Lower East Side. In 1893, at the age of 25, she founded the Henry Street Settlement. She moved into the neighborhood to live and work among the poor and offer healthcare to all area residents in their homes on a sliding-fee scale. While healthcare was her priority, Wald recognized how social and economic factors contributed to the plight of the immigrants.

Figure 3.5. Lillian Wald.
Library of Congress Prints and Photographs Division, Harris & Ewing photograph collection.

Working with members of the neighborhood, the Henry Street social workers organized girls' and boys' clubs and classes in arts and crafts, English, homemaking, and drama; they held social events and union meetings. Henry Street provided vocational guidance and training, and Wald established a scholarship to allow talented boys and girls to remain in school until age 16. She spearheaded campaigns for building playgrounds and parks, improving housing, and eliminating tuberculosis, which was called the "tailors' disease" because of its preponderance among Jewish immigrants, many of whom were garment workers.

Wald spoke out against assimilation programs that forced immigrants to shed their native cultures. A New York commission to investigate immigrants' living and working conditions was established at her bidding in 1908. She spearheaded the successful campaign to create a national Children's Bureau within the Department of Labor. Wald was a staunch pacifist who vigorously opposed American involvement in World War I.

Wald was an early leader of the National Child Labor Committee, lobbied for federal child labor laws, and promoted childhood education. Concerned about the treatment of Blacks, she insisted that all Henry

Street classes be racially integrated. In 1909, she became a founding member of the National Association for the Advancement of Colored People and hosted the organization's first major public conference at the Henry Street Settlement.

Wald established herself as a courageous national leader in campaigns for social reform, public health, and anti-militarism, and as an international crusader for human rights.

ANTONIA PANTOJA (1922–2002)

Although Puerto Rico became a U.S. territory in 1898, it wasn't until after Puerto Ricans were granted U.S. citizenship under the 1917 Jones Act that Puerto Rican migration to the continental United States increased rapidly. As job opportunities decreased in Puerto Rico, many islanders migrated to New York, California, and beyond, searching for bright futures. El Barrio or Spanish Harlem in New York City became home to many new migrants from Puerto Rico. Thinking their American citizenship would provide full rights and access to economic opportunities in cities such as New York, these early migrants soon discovered that the complexities of navigating race, identity, and culture in their new home were more than expected. Many returned to Puerto Rico after a few years.

Antonia Pantoja (Figure 3.6) arrived in New York in 1944 and was among the first Puerto Rican social workers in New York. Although she had an education degree from the University of Puerto Rico, she worked as a wartime welder and helped unionize the workers at a shop in New York City. A few years later, she obtained a master's degree in social work from Columbia University and received a Ph.D. from Union Graduate School in Cincinnati, Ohio.

Pantoja established several groundbreaking institutions in New York and Puerto Rico. Witnessing the exclusion, prejudice, poverty, and racism Puerto Ricans experienced in New York, she fought for their civil rights and educational opportunities. She is best known for establishing ASPIRA in 1961, an important organization that promoted education and advancement for Puerto Rican youth in New York City by providing clubs within schools, career and college counseling, advocacy for bilingual education, and other services.

Pantoja's lifelong mission was to empower community members to speak for themselves. She saw how family lives fell apart due to poor housing, a high dropout rate from school, substance abuse, and violence, leaving Puerto Ricans voiceless. She built institutions to cultivate a "Nuyorican" identity.

Figure 3.6. Antonia Pantoja.
Antonia Pantoja Papers. Archives of the Puerto Rican Diaspora, Center for Puerto Rican Studies, Hunter College, CUNY.

In 1957 she founded the Hispanic American Youth Association, which later became the National Puerto Rican Forum, focusing on education and self-sufficiency. In 1970, she created the Puerto Rican Research and Resource Center, which led to the founding of Boricua College in the early 1970s, which continues to attract Puerto Rican, Latinx, and other underrepresented communities to higher education.

Recognizing that language barriers diminished access to opportunities, she shepherded ASPIRA's lawsuit against the New York City Board of Education, seeking to provide English for Speakers of Other Languages (ESOL) classes in New York City schools. The resulting legislation was a landmark in the bilingual education movement. She co-founded the Graduate School of Community Development in San Diego. In 1996, President Bill Clinton recognized her efforts and dedication by awarding her the Presidential Medal of Freedom; she was the first Latina to receive this honor.

ADA DEER (1935–)

For centuries, the U.S. government enacted policies that were detrimental to the well-being and culture of American Indians in the United States. Native Americans suffered systematic poverty, discrimination, and police brutality; treaty rights were violated, unemployment rates were high, and Native American education and cultural identity were suppressed as part of the plan to assimilate Native Americans into mainstream culture. Repetitive efforts were made to circumvent the preservation of Indigenous cultures. By the end of the 1950s and into the 1960s, Native Americans grew more aware and organized against the 1956 Indian Relocation Act and the subsequent Indian Relocation Act. The first of these acts encouraged thousands of Native Americans to move from reservations to cities to work by providing vocational training. The latter act offered reimbursement for relocation expenses and some job training for those moving to urban areas at a time when the federal government was reducing subsidies to Native Americans living on reservations. Those who moved to cities and accepted government assistance forfeited their land rights to the U.S. government as part of the effort to end the federal government's recognition of the sovereignty of tribes (this was part of the ongoing Indian termination policy). In reaction, the American Indian Movement (AIM) was born. During the early years leading up to the AIM, Ada Deer (Figure 3.7) came of age as a social worker, advocating for the rights of American Indians and fighting against federal policies that were detrimental to their rights.

Ada Deer was born in Keshena, Wisconsin, in 1935. In 1957 she was the first Menominee to receive an undergraduate degree from the University of Wisconsin (UW)-Madison. Four years later, she was the first Native American to receive a Master of Social Work degree from Columbia University. Deer helped organize a grassroots organization to restore federal recognition of the Menominee tribe following the federal termination policy. The group named Determination of Right and Unity for Menominee Shareholders (DRUMS) successfully fought the government policy; this success led to the Menominee Restoration Act of 1972, which officially redesignated the Menominee as a federally recognized tribe. Because of her work, Deer became the first woman to chair the Menominee Tribe in Wisconsin, which she did from 1974 to 1976.

Deer ran for Secretary of State of Wisconsin in 1978 and again in 1982. She served as vice-chair of the Mondale/Ferraro presidential campaign in 1984. In 1992, she became the first Native American woman in Wisconsin elected to Congress. The following year, Deer was appointed the head of the Bureau of Indian Affairs, the first Native American woman to hold that position. While in office, Deer helped set federal policy for more than 550 federally recognized tribes, approved tribal/

Figure 3.7. Ada Deer.
Photo by Bob Nichols. Courtesy of USDA.

state gaming compacts, extended recognition to 12 tribes, and settled a
century-long border dispute with the Crow Tribe that restored tribal
lands and provided compensation for lost coal reserves and revenue.

Deer developed groundbreaking classes in the 1970s at the UW-
Madison School of Social Work on Native American issues and multiculturalism and created the first program to provide social work training on
reservations. She also co-founded the Indian Community School in Mil-
waukee, organized leadership workshops for American Indian women,
and helped to implement American Indian participation in the Peace
Corps. In January 2000, Deer became director of the American Indian
Studies Program at UW-Madison.

The pinnacle of Deer's political career was when then-president Clinton appointed her as the Assistant Secretary for Indian Affairs in the
U.S. Department of Interior. Deer was the first woman to occupy that
post, which she held from 1993 to 1997. She used the position to establish policies for more than 550 federally recognized tribes, including
transferring greater power to tribal governments.

TIME FOR REFLECTION AND DISCUSSION

- Identify the human rights that each social work pioneer fought for.
- How does the fight for human rights bind each of the social work pioneers?
- How have the social work pioneers created a foundation of human rights in social work?

CHAPTER 4
Modern Human Rights

The 1948 Universal Declaration of Human Rights (UDHR) is the birthing document of modern human rights. The UDHR is based upon the United Nations (UN) Charter of 1945 and was inspired by U.S. President Franklin D. Roosevelt's *four freedoms* (freedom of speech, freedom of worship, freedom from want, and freedom from fear) in his 1941 State of the Union address (Marks, 2016). The UN's goals rest upon the realization of human rights worldwide. Only through exercising mutual respect can the UN's goal to avert war and conflict be achieved. Eleanor Roosevelt, the widow of President Roosevelt, served as chair of the Commission on Human Rights and shepherded the writing of the UDHR through many disputes over wording, ideological differences over the role of the State, and tensions among the member countries, all of whom were healing from World War II (Arnison, 2009; Johnson & Symonides, 1998; United Nations, n.d.). The UDHR is a unified statement of political, civil, social, economic, and cultural rights; however, as a declaration, it lacks the force of law. The decision to make it a declaration rather than a treaty was made purposefully to avoid the political travails that might occur. A treaty/convention must be signed and ratified by UN member States to become legally binding.

The UDHR introduces the concept that a government's treatment of its own citizens is a matter of legitimate international concern and not simply a domestic issue. Regardless of where they live, individuals are entitled to certain rights and freedoms despite whatever government may be in force. Withholding these rights and liberties from individuals and groups is abusive from the perspective set by the UDHR. While all freedoms and rights may be

A Human Rights-Based Approach to Justice in Social Work Practice. Shirley Gatenio Gabel, Oxford University Press.
© Oxford University Press 2024. DOI: 10.1093/oso/9780197570647.003.0004

subject to certain legal limitations, the UDHR empowers other nations to be critical of one another's policies and practices to uphold human rights.

The Preamble of the UDHR eloquently declares that the recognition of the inherent dignity and the equal and inalienable rights of all members of the human family is the foundation of freedom, justice, and peace in the world. It restates the civil and political rights that many countries, including the United States, had previously embraced in their national constitutions and laws and introduces what is sometimes called the second generation of rights, or positive rights—economic, social, and cultural rights.

Although the UDHR is a declaration, not a treaty or convention, it has acquired the status of customary international law. Table 4.1 lists the articles of the UDHR.

Table 4.1. THE UDHR ARTICLES

Article 1: Right to equality	Article 16: Right to marriage and family
Article 2: Freedom from discrimination	Article 17: Right to own property
Article 3: Right to life, liberty, personal security	Article 18: Freedom of belief and religion
Article 4: Freedom from slavery	Article 19: Freedom of opinion and information
Article 5: Freedom from torture and degrading treatment	Article 20: Right of peaceful assembly and association
Article 6: Right to recognition as a person before the law	Article 21: Right to participate in government and free elections
Article 7: Right to equality before the law	Article 22: Right to social security
Article 8: Right to remedy by a competent tribunal	Article 23: Right to work and to join trade unions
Article 9: Freedom from arbitrary arrest and exile	Article 24: Right to rest and leisure
Article 10: Right to fair public hearing	Article 25: Right to adequate living standard
Article 11: Right to be considered innocent until proven guilty	Article 26: Right to education
Article 12: Freedom from interference with privacy, family, home, and correspondence	Article 27: Right to participate in the cultural life of a community
Article 13: Right to move freely in and out of a country	Article 28: Right to a social order that articulates this document
Article 14: Right to asylum in other countries from persecution	Article 29: Community duties essential to free and full development
Article 15: Right to a nationality and the freedom to change it	Article 30: Nothing in this declaration justifies any person, group, or country taking away the rights to which we are all entitled

---

The full text for the UDHR is available at https://www.un.org/en/about-us/universal-declaration-of-human-rights and in the Appendix.

Types of Rights

One way to understand the types of human rights is to differentiate civil and political rights from social, economic, environmental, and cultural rights (Figure 4.1).

Civil rights are legal protections of individuals or groups from certain forms of oppression. The most common civil rights are (1) the right not to be discriminated against based on race, ethnicity, religion, and gender; (2) the right to personal security, including protections for persons accused or suspected of crimes; (3) the right to vote and to participate in democratic political processes; and (4) freedom of expression, association, and religion.

Political rights refer to an individual's ability to participate in civil and political life without fear of discrimination, repression, or persecution. It is tied closely to citizenship status. Examples of political rights include participating freely in political rallies and protests, voting in an election, joining a political party, and running for office.

Social rights relate to those rights needed for us to participate fully in our society. They include rights related to income and social security and access to housing, food, water, healthcare, and education. Social rights overlap with civil rights. For example, discrimination can interfere with one's right to healthcare or education.

Economic rights assume that all individuals need a minimal level of material security for human dignity. These rights include the right to work and the right to an adequate standard of living. Economic rights are highly interrelated with civil and social rights because the right to work or an adequate standard of living can be obstructed by discrimination (a civil right)

Human Rights Are:

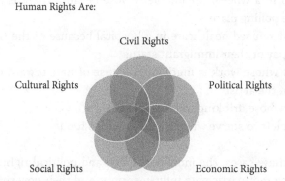

Civil Rights

Cultural Rights

Political Rights

Social Rights

Economic Rights

Figure 4.1. What are human rights?

or the lack of public benefits such as pensions or income assistance (a social right).

Environmental rights refer to the fact that a safe, clean, healthy, and sustainable environment is integral to the full enjoyment of a wide range of human rights, including the rights to life, health, food, water, and sanitation. All of us depend on a healthy environment to fulfill our life goals and live in dignity. On July 28, 2022, the United Nations General Assembly (UNGA) adopted a resolution declaring that everyone on the planet has a right to a healthy environment.

Cultural rights affect our ability to express our cultural traditions and practices freely and fully. They include the right to practice one's religion and cultural rituals, to speak a certain language, and to dress and eat foods specific to one's culture. Cultural rights are closely tied to other rights, such as the right to non-discrimination and equal protection of the law.

The UDHR makes clear the indivisibility and interdependence of human rights. Regardless of the right, all rights are linked to one another. The interrelatedness of all human rights means that promoting one right augments other rights. Conversely, violating one right hinders and may threaten the enjoyment of other rights. A civil right facilitates the realization of an economic right, and a social right enhances a political right. In the quest to realize human rights, our focus should not be limited to a particular group of rights while ignoring others, and therefore human rights are indivisible.

In some countries, such as the United States, greater attention is given to civil and political rights. However, social, economic, environmental, and cultural rights are critical human rights needed to realize civil and political rights. The following are examples of individuals denied their economic, environmental, social, and cultural rights:

- A woman paid less than her male colleague for the same work
- A person in a wheelchair unable to vote because there is no ramp to enter the polling place
- An infant refused healthcare in a hospital because of the family's inability to pay or their immigrant status
- An artist whose work is mutilated because of hate toward the cultural origins of the artist
- A family whose drinking water is unsafe
- A person left to starve when there is surplus food.

In each of these cases, the individual's civil and political rights suffer because they cannot participate fully in society, and their governments have not done enough to protect and help fulfill their rights.

TIME TO EXERCISE

- Select a social issue that is important to you.
- Choose one political, one civil, one social, one economic, one environmental, and one cultural right (consult the UDHR as needed).
- How do the six rights you selected relate to the social issue you chose?
- How would a fuller realization of the civil right you selected affect the economic right selected?

Rights and Responsibilities

As humans, we all have the same rights, and we all have the responsibility to respect other people's rights. The right to free speech, for example, does not include the right to incite hatred and violence.

Some of us live in places that honor rights more than other places. Our rights don't change if we live under an oppressive regime or an open democracy. However, realizing our rights may be different because of the laws and policies that a government or culture has implemented. Laws are legal rights and may be restricted to certain persons, but all individuals have the same human rights. The government grants legal rights through statute. This means governments can also repeal legal rights, unlike human rights, which are inalienable and universal. At the same time, laws can be used to enforce and promote rights.

Human rights entail both rights and obligations. When States ratify human rights treaties or conventions, they assume the responsibility and duties under international law to respect, protect, and fulfill human rights (Figure 4.2):

- The obligation to respect means that States must refrain from interfering with or curtailing the enjoyment of human rights.
- The obligation to protect requires States to protect individuals and groups from those who seek to undermine human rights.
- The obligation to fulfill means that States must take actions to facilitate the enjoyment of human rights.

Let's use the example of the right to work. The State must ensure that all individuals who want to work can work, regardless of race, ethnicity, culture, gender, sexual orientation, or age. There might be corporations or individuals who wish to restrict who can work. The State has an

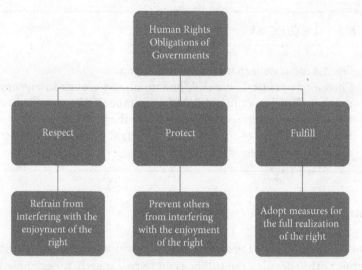

Figure 4.2. Human rights obligations of governments.
OHCHR, Factsheet 33, Frequently Asked Questions on Economic, Social and Cultural Rights.

obligation to protect or make sure that discrimination does not occur. To respect and fulfill the right to work, a State may need to establish monitoring and reporting procedures around hiring, retainment, and promotion procedures.

The primary responsibilities and obligations regarding the enjoyment of human rights are with a State. A State **cannot** forgo these responsibilities by delegating human rights obligations to non-State entities or international organizations. Non-State entities also have responsibilities to comply with human rights and abstain from violating human rights. Non-State entities take on various forms: corporations; businesses; non-governmental organizations (NGOs), both national and international; community groups; human rights defenders; religious groups; terrorists; paramilitary groups; multinational enterprises; and, finally, individuals. Some non-State groups promote human rights while others condone or even commit crimes or other violations affecting the lives and human rights of individuals. When non-State entities violate human rights, it is the responsibility of the State to address this.

The responsibility of the individual to uphold the human rights of other individuals is the subject of legal debate. Generally, when one individual commits human rights violations against another individual(s), human rights law obliges the State to regulate such conduct through its obligation to take steps to prevent human rights violations. For example, violence against women may be committed by one individual against another, but it is a State's responsibility to reasonably protect women from violence. In this way, a State may be responsible for the human rights violation because it failed to enforce laws or practices to protect women from violence.

THINKING ABOUT RIGHTS AND RESPONSIBILITIES

Parents are generally viewed as responsible for caring for, nurturing, and protecting their children. Yet, millions of children are abused and neglected every day around the world. Many parents would argue that it is their right to raise their children according to their culture and beliefs about childrearing, which may result in child marriage; child soldiers; forced labor; physical, sexual, and psychological abuse; female genital mutilation; or general neglect in terms of protection and nurturance.

The UN Convention on the Rights of the Child is the human rights treaty that establishes ethical principles and international standards of behavior toward children. It has been ratified by all but one of the 193 member States who are part of the UN. The Convention on the Rights of the Child affirms that every child has the inherent right to life, freedom of thought, conscience, and religion; requires the protection of children at home, in the workplace, and during an armed conflict from all forms of violence, injury, abuse, neglect, maltreatment, or exploitation; and calls on countries to recognize the right of every child to a standard of living adequate for physical, mental, spiritual, moral, and social development.

- What human rights are exploited when adults physically harm children or sell them as brides or laborers according to certain cultural childrearing practices?
- Who should be held responsible: parents, those guarding traditional practices, government? Are we responding appropriately when we criticize such practices?
- Who has a responsibility to rectify the situation?

Immediate and Progressive Rights

No State in our world has achieved the full realization of all human rights. As decreed in international laws, human rights reflect normative standards and are subject to interpretation. As our understanding of the complexities and intricacies of living human rights grows, so too does our interpretation of human rights and obligations. Without question, some countries score much higher in promoting and realizing human rights than other countries, but no State has achieved perfection.

There are human rights that States can realize immediately, but other rights require time and resources to implement. Civil, political, economic, social, and cultural rights all create some obligations of immediate application. Generally speaking, civil and political rights, such as those set out in the International Covenant on Civil and Political Rights (ICCPR), are interpreted as imposing obligations of "immediate effect." Governments have an immediate and ongoing duty to respect and protect the right of non-discrimination and the right to equality, for example, by refraining from discrimination in any programs and decisions and enacting legislative protection to prohibit discrimination by private actors (Porter, 2015). It is possible that to implement a legal doctrine, States may need to develop programs and other actions may require additional resources that a State commits to over time.

By contrast, many of the rights set out in the International Covenant on Economic, Social, and Cultural Rights (ICESCR) are subject to a "progressive realization" (Article 2(1)). Progressive realization obligates States to take measures toward fully realizing economic, social, and cultural rights to the maximum of their available resources. It recognizes that States may require time to garner the needed resources to realize rights fully. For example, to provide education for all, a State may need to build schools over time.

All human rights treaties impose an immediate obligation to take appropriate steps toward the full realization of all rights; lack of resources does not justify inaction or indefinite postponement of measures to implement these rights (Porter, 2015). States must demonstrate that they are making every effort to improve the enjoyment of economic, social, and cultural rights, even when resources are scarce. At the same time, the International Covenant on Economic, Social, and Cultural Rights calls for the immediate protection of the right to form and join trade unions and to strike, the right to equal pay for work of equal value without distinction of any kind, the right to free compulsory education for all, the rights for parents to choose schools for their children, and the right to respect the freedom indispensable for scientific research and creative activity (Porter, 2015). Irrespective of resources, all States should ensure that all have access to benefits and services such as food, shelter, clothing, education, and healthcare needed to survive.

Universalism Versus Cultural Relativism

The UDHR and the ensuing treaties were a bold effort to unite countries to work together rather than against one another. Declaring a set of normative human rights standards toward which all countries would work was intended to strengthen the bonds between people and countries, reinforce the dignity we bestow on one another, and, in doing so, avert conflict, marginalization, and violence.

At one extreme, cultural relativism would hold that culture is the sole source of morality or rulemaking (Donnelly, 1984). Universalism, at the other extreme, would hold that culture is irrelevant because we would judge all cultural practices against an international standard (Donnelly, 1984). Universalism has been referred to as a form of moral imperialism.

Think about that—one set of standards for all the different cultures, countries, and people in the world. Critics, such as the American Anthropological Association, argue that the UDHR espouses Western thinking of what the world should be, not necessarily reflecting the views of people from the Southern Hemisphere and those from Eastern countries. Because the UDHR emphasizes the rights of individuals rather than communal rights, the UDHR is thought by some to reflect European, Judeo-Christian (typically labeled Western) values. The danger of claiming that human rights are universal is that it may initially facilitate benign avoidance of diverse perspectives that eventually grow and undermine the cultural differences in different parts of the world. Others have further asserted that it is a deliberate effort to impose Western views on others, much like colonialism (Foday-Musa, 2010).

In response to these criticisms, the proponents of universalism say that the UDHR was written by representatives from all over the world, including Chile, China, Egypt, India, Pakistan, and Lebanon. While the majority of representatives writing the UDHR were from Western countries (37 member States held predominantly Judeo-Christian values; 11 Islamic; six Marxist; and four identified as being associated with Buddhist-Confucian traditions), two-thirds of the endorsing votes came from non-Western countries (48 in favor, none against, and eight abstentions). The emphasis on the rights of individuals was intended to transcend cultures, particularly for persons living under repressive regimes or colonialism. Almost all nations have accepted global human rights standards and incorporated elements in their domestic political institutions. They acknowledge that actual or threatened violations of these standards are reasonable grounds for external intervention (Rengger, 2011).

Most would agree that we should be somewhere between extreme universalism and cultural relativism; the issue is where, and who gets to decide. International human rights instruments are an essential tool to change situations that violate human rights, often by exerting external pressures on violators. At the same time, no one wants a world where we all eat the same food, speak the same language, practice the same rituals, and wear the same clothes. For example, the right to carry out certain cultural traditions such as marriage for young females, shunning those who have a disease or are believed to be diseased, or not educating girls and restricting their roles to mothers, homemakers, and caregivers may reflect cultural differences in practices. But others may see these practices as reinforcing the subordination of females, exclusion, and gender inequities. Who decides culture? And how?

As social workers, we often work with people who are part of cultures that are different from our own or from the dominant culture of a community or country. Social workers often have the role of explaining that failing to adhere to expectations of the dominant culture such as sending one's child to school, refraining from physically disciplining a child or wife, or allowing women to move about freely in public may result in punitive actions against an individual and family. If we lived in communities devoid of these standards, how would we feel as social workers when a parent/spouse abused members of their family, denied their children an education, or confined female members of the family to the home?

Why Wasn't the UDHR Ratified?

Tensions among nations were high prior to World War II and in its aftermath. The two superpowers emerging from World War II were the United States and the Union of Soviet Socialist Republics (also known as the Soviet Union or USSR). Relations between the two nations were strained before and at the initiation of World War II. Yet, in 1941, the United States and the Soviet Union allied to secure the defeat of Nazi Germany. Both nations realized that they needed one another's efforts to score a military victory over the Axis forces. However, the relationship between the two countries was a tense one. The United States viewed Joseph Stalin's rule of the Soviet Union as tyrannical and considered his ambitions to assert world dominance as a threat to democracy (Arnison, 2009). The Soviets resented the United States' late entry into WW II (by the end of the war, there were 20 to 30 million deaths of Soviet civilians and military) and the United States' resistance to accepting the Soviet Union as part of the international community (Johnson & Symonides, 1998).

At the end of the war, the ideological rivalry between the United States and the Soviet Union played out geopolitically, starting in Europe and quickly spreading to other world areas (Johnson & Symonides, 1998). The grievances the two nations had against one another ripened into a period of mutual distrust and enmity after World War II, known as the Cold War. The United States was suspicious of Soviet expansion, and the Soviets were wary of warlike American rhetoric and its arms buildup. By 1948 the Soviet Union politically dominated the countries of Eastern Europe that it had liberated, raising concern that this would bleed into western European countries. The Soviet Union viewed the United States' aid to western Europe under the Marshall Plan in 1947–48 as bringing western Europe under American influence (Arnison, 2009). Tensions grew, and the Cold War lasted for just over 40 years.

The mutual suspicion of these two emerging, domineering powers led to the division of rights originally unified in the UDHR into two treaties to establish the legal foundation for human rights: ICCPR and ICESCR (Johnson & Symonides, 1998). The two covenants are interconnected, and the rights contained in one covenant are necessary to fulfill the rights contained in the other. It took from 1948 until 1962 for the UN member countries to prepare the two covenants that, together with the UDHR, became the International Bill of Rights (Johnson & Symonides, 1998). The two Covenants opened for signature in 1966 and achieved enough signatures to first enter into force 10 years later, in 1976.

Major International Human Rights Treaties

Human rights became international law only after World War II, under the auspices of the UN. The UDHR of 1948 first defined human rights law in a non-binding General Assembly resolution at the international level. Since then, a series of treaties have followed. Each member State of the UN must ratify the treaty (as required by law in its State) and then integrate the treaty into its national constitutions and laws.

The main treaties of international human rights law (and the date each was adopted by the UN) are:

- International Covenant on Civil and Political Rights (1966)
- International Covenant on Economic, Social and Cultural Rights (1966)
- Convention on the Elimination of All Forms of Racial Discrimination (1965)
- Convention on the Elimination of All Forms of Discrimination against Women (1979)
- Convention against Torture and Other Cruel, Inhuman or Degrading Treatment or Punishment (1984)
- Convention on the Rights of the Child (1989)

- International Convention on the Protection of the Rights of All Migrant Workers and Members of their Families (1999)
- International Convention for the Protection of All Persons from Enforced Disappearance (2006)
- Convention on the Rights of Persons with Disabilities (2006).

In addition, international human rights law is also affected by the following regional instruments:

- European Convention on Human Rights (1950)
- American Convention on Human Rights (1969)
- African Charter on Human and Peoples' Rights (1981).

These treaties are supervised by human rights bodies, such as the Human Rights Committee for the International Covenant on Civil and Political Rights and the European Court for Human Rights for the European Convention on Human Rights.

CHAPTER 5

American Exceptionalism to International Human Rights Laws

The term "American exceptionalism" refers to the fact that the United States has exempted itself from most international human rights mechanisms while calling out other countries that have fallen short of realizing the human rights of their citizens. Paradoxically, the United States has been a driving force in promoting global human rights but at the same time has wavered in committing to international laws and conventions that protect and further human rights. Many people in the United States believe that human rights are sufficiently upheld in the U.S. Constitution and the states' constitutions. However, the absence of U.S. consent to most international human rights instruments weakens the legal standards that Americans have worked diligently to create and promulgate both in the United States and throughout the world.

U.S. EXCEPTIONALISM IN HUMAN RIGHTS TREATIES

There is a process by which UN member States assume the obligations of international human rights treaties or Conventions. The first step is for a State to sign an international human rights treaty, indicating its intention to consider ratifying the treaty. A signatory State is not bound to the treaty; however, in the period between signing and ratification of a treaty or Convention, States are expected to refrain from acts that would defeat the object and purpose of the treaty. Generally, a Head of State or Minister of Foreign Affairs signs a treaty.

A Human Rights-Based Approach to Justice in Social Work Practice. Shirley Gatenio Gabel, Oxford University Press.
© Oxford University Press 2024. DOI: 10.1093/oso/9780197570647.003.0005

The next step is ratification. Ratification binds a State to the terms of the treaty under international law. By choosing to ratify a treaty, a State is obliged to ensure that its domestic legislation complies with the treaty's provisions. The obligation includes regular reporting to and consenting to investigations by United Nations (UN) human rights bodies. Each State is required to incorporate the articles of Conventions that have been ratified into its domestic laws to guarantee specific and fundamental human rights. This process can differ according to each State's legal system. In the United States, two-thirds of the U.S. Senate must vote in favor of a treaty for ratification to occur.

As shown in Table 5.1, of the nine major human rights treaties, the United States has signed seven of them and ratified only three: the International Covenant on Civil and Political Rights (ICCPR), the Convention against Torture and other Cruel, Inhuman or Degrading Treatment or Punishment

Table 5.1. STATUS OF UN HUMAN RIGHTS TREATIES IN THE UNITED STATES, 2018

	UN Adoption	U.S. Signature	U.S. Ratification
International Convention on the Elimination of All Forms of Racial Discrimination	1965	1969	1994
International Covenant on Economic, Social and Cultural Rights	1966	1977	Not ratified
International Covenant on Civil and Political Rights	1966	1977	1992
Convention on the Elimination of All Forms of Discrimination against Women	1979	1980	Not ratified
Convention against Torture and Other Cruel, Inhuman or Degrading Treatment or Punishment	1984	1988	1994
Convention on the Rights of the Child	1989	1995	Not ratified
Convention on the Protection of the Rights of All Migrant Workers and Members of Their Families	1990	Not signed	Not ratified
Convention on the Rights of Persons with Disabilities	2006	2009	Not ratified
Convention for the Protection of All Persons from Enforced Disappearance	2006	Not signed	Not ratified

(CAT), and the International Convention for the Elimination of Racial Discrimination (CERD). The United States has also ratified the Convention on the Prevention and Punishment of the Crime of Genocide (Genocide Convention), an important treaty but not considered one of the nine key conventions.

Despite the leadership of the United States in espousing civil and political rights, it did not ratify the ICCPR until 1992—28 years after it was first adopted by the UN. The United States has also ratified optional protocols, including protocols on the sexual exploitation of children and on child soldiers, but it is the only country not to have ratified the Convention on the Rights of the Child. Notable as well is the fact that the United States did not ratify the third leg of the International Bill of Human Rights—the International Covenant on Economic, Social and Cultural Rights (ICESCR).

Almost three decades after the fall of the Berlin Wall and end of the Cold War, and almost 30 years after the reaffirmation and rejoining of human rights principles through the Vienna Declaration and Programme of Action of 1993, the United States shows no interest in ratifying the ICESCR and has made little movement toward ratifying the other major human rights instruments. To date, 168 States have ratified the ICESCR (United Nations, n.d.). The last Convention to be considered by the United States was the Convention of the Rights of Persons with Disabilities in 2012. This Convention was modeled on the Americans with Disabilities Act, which had the support of many prominent Republicans, such as the late Senate Majority Leader Bob Dole and major veterans groups and disabilities rights organizations. Despite this, its ratification was defeated due to fears that it would override U.S. domestic law (Steinhauer, 2012).

Even when the United States has ratified human rights treaties, it has done so with significant limitations. The UN allows countries to ratify treaties with reservations, meaning countries can make an exception to a treaty (i.e., provisions that the government does not accept). The United States uses reservations extensively in the treaties it has ratified. A reservation exempts a State from a particular provision of a treaty and is considered legitimate so long as the reservation is not incompatible with the treaty's purpose. The United States led the ratification of the ICCPR across UN member States. The United States also entered five reservations, five understandings, four declarations, and one proviso in ratifying the ICCPR (Carpenter, 2000). Kahn suggests this reflects the deep-seated American belief that the country's founding values are the universal embodiment of human rights—and so it need not learn from others or be subject to international scrutiny (Kahn, 2000).

Reservations to the Convention against Torture that the United States ratified in 1994 read:

> That the United States considers itself bound by the obligation under Article 16 to prevent "cruel, inhuman or degrading treatment or punishment," only insofar as the term "cruel, inhuman or degrading treatment or punishment" means the cruel, unusual and inhumane treatment and punishment prohibited by the Fifth, Eighth and/or Fourth Amendments to the Constitution of the United States. (Senate Committee on Foreign Relations, supra note 11, at 24, reprinted in 31 ILM at 660)

> Nothing in the Covenant requires or authorizes legislation, or other action, by the United States of America prohibited by the Constitution of the United States as interpreted by the United States. (Senate Committee on Foreign Relations, supra note 11, at 24, reprinted in 31 ILM at 660)

This form of exceptionalism is also known as the "Helms Proviso"—a legal clause attached to the human rights treaties (CAT, ICCPR, and CERD) that the United States has ratified (Arnison, 2009). Senator Jesse Helms offered this reservation during the U.S. ratification of the ICCPR in March 1992. This proviso means that U.S. international legal obligations to human rights are limited to those *already existing* under U.S. law. The effect then is that no additional human rights protections according to international standards are gained. The reservations to the ICCPR expressly prohibit the use of the U.S. ratification of the ICCPR to bring suit against the United States that is beyond existing law in the United States. Carpenter (2000) calls ratification of the ICCPR "toothless" for this reason.

The United States is far from alone in its use of reservations in ratifying multilateral treaties. Countries regularly employ reservations and declarations when a treaty is ratified (declarations in this process refer to a country's stated interpretation of, or position on, a treaty and are not legally binding, whereas reservations are; United Nations Treaty Collection, n.d.). Reservations and declarations facilitate the negotiation and ratification of treaties. They allow States to accept a convention without binding themselves to provisions that might conflict with certain aspects of their domestic legislation (Hill, 2016).

The common use of reservations and declarations raises the question of whether reservations undermine the universality of human rights (Hill, 2016; Ziemele & Liede, 2013) and whether there should be limits to the types of reservations allowed. Should international law override local culture and traditions as reflected in law? If the purpose of international human rights law is to eliminate practices that negate human respect and dignity, then should we allow traditional cultural practices that reinforce discrimination and class and intentionally disadvantage specific populations? For example, despite the importance of gender equality across all human rights instruments, how should the international community react to national laws that purposively position women as vulnerable, with fewer rights and fewer economic, social, and civil opportunities in society due to religious or other beliefs? What about laws that allow children, women, and marginalized groups to be beaten and abused? How do we balance the right to practice a group's traditional practices with international standards for human rights?

The types of reservations entered by countries vary and depend on the human rights instrument. Several countries assert that religious laws are of a higher order than a multilateral UN treaty, and others, such as the United States, protect the country's dominion. The Convention on the Elimination of All Forms of Discrimination against Women (CEDAW) is the international human rights convention with the most reservations by countries. The most frequent reservations to CEDAW include objections to Article 2 (integration of CEDAW into the State party's constitution, statutes, and policies), Article 9 (equality in the right to transmit nationality to one's children), and Article 16 (marriage equality) (Hill, 2016; United Nations Treaty Collection, n.d.).

TIME TO EXERCISE

Take the following quiz to test your understanding of human rights instruments and bodies.

1. What is the significant difference between the Universal Declaration on Human Rights (UDHR) and the subsequent human rights covenants, conventions, and treaties?
2. Who was the chair of the first UN Commission on Human Rights?
3. What did the UN Commission on Human Rights accomplish?
4. Why were the two covenants (ICCPR and ICESCR) created that divided rights originally unified in the UDHR?
5. Has the United States ratified the ICCPR and the ICESCR?
6. How many of the main international human rights conventions, covenants, or treaties has the United States ratified?
7. Which is the only country that has not ratified the Convention on the Rights of the Child?
8. What is a reservation to a treaty?
9. Why does the United States use reservations when it ratifies a human rights treaty?

10. What is the concern about countries using reservations when ratifying human rights treaties?

Answers:

1. The UDHR is not legally binding, and the others are.
2. Eleanor Roosevelt.
3. It created the UDHR.
4. They were divided due to ideological differences reflected in the Cold War.
5. It has ratified the ICCPR but not the ICESCR.
6. Three.
7. The United States.
8. A reservation to a treaty is a unilateral statement, however phrased or named, made by a State when signing, ratifying, accepting, approving, or acceding to a treaty, whereby it purports to exclude or to modify the legal effect of specific provisions of the treaty in their application to that State.
9. It believes that the United States should not be subject to laws beyond its existing laws.
10. The common use of reservations may undermine the universality of human rights.

THE U.S. CONSTITUTION AND THE UDHR

Although the United States has ratified only three of the major human rights treaties and has done so with significant reservations, the United States sees itself as a leader in protecting human rights. Can these two conflicting contentions coexist? The United States believes that its Constitution embodies all the rights presented in the UDHR. Is this true?

To answer this question, we begin by analyzing the rights guaranteed in the U.S. Constitution. The U.S. Constitution provides the framework for governance in the United States by separating the powers of government into three branches: the legislative branch, which makes the laws; the executive branch, which executes the laws; and the judicial branch, which interprets the laws. It sets up a system of checks and balances that ensures no one branch has too much power and divides power between the states and the federal government. The Constitution describes the scope of government power and the systems for electing representatives and for amending the Constitution. The focus of the Constitution is on government functions and governing processes.

As social workers, whether we are practicing at macro, mezzo, or micro levels, we need to understand the context of our practice. Our Constitution and federal, state, and local laws reflect the values and priorities of our communities. We should be familiar with the laws that directly and indirectly affect the populations we serve and understand how the laws protect, limit, and promote opportunities for the individuals we are working with.

The Constitution was signed in 1787 and went into effect on June 21, 1788. The first 10 amendments to the Constitution make up the Bill of Rights, which the states ratified in 1791 (Hershkoff & Loffredo, 2011). The 10 amendments were written because several states desired greater constitutional protection for individual liberties, and thus the amendments focus on the limitations of government power on individual liberties (ConstitutionFacts.com, n.d.). For example, the First Amendment protects an individual's ability to speak and worship freely as a right and prohibits Congress from making laws establishing religion or abridging freedom of speech. The Fourth Amendment safeguards citizens' right to be free from unreasonable government intrusion in their homes by requiring a warrant.

The U.S. Constitution and the Bill of Rights provide broad human rights protections equivalent to rights found in the UDHR, especially those related to political and civil liberties. Table 5.2 compares the Constitution and Bill of Rights to the UDHR.

Table 5.2. COMPARISON OF RIGHTS IN THE U.S. CONSTITUTION AND BILL OF RIGHTS TO THE UDHR

Type of Right	UDHR	U.S. Constitution
Non-discrimination	Article 2	Fourteenth Amendment
Life, liberty, security	Article 3	Fourteenth Amendment
Slavery	Article 4	Thirteenth Amendment
Cruel and unusual punishment	Article 5	Eighth Amendment
Equal protection	Article 6	Fourteenth Amendment
Equal protection	Article 7	Fourteenth Amendment
Arbitrary arrest	Article 9	Fifth Amendment
Fair trial	Article 10	Sixth Amendment
Privacy	Article 12	Fourth Amendment
Property	Article 17	Fifth Amendment
Religion	Article 18	First Amendment
Speech	Article 19	First Amendment
Freedom of association	Article 20	First Amendment
Vote	Article 21	Fifteenth, Nineteenth, Twenty-Third, Twenty-Fourth, & Twenty-Sixth Amendments

In addition, the U.S. Supreme Court has identified fundamental rights in the United States that are not explicitly stated in the Constitution, such as the presumption of innocence in a criminal trial and freedom of movement, which are included in the UDHR. U.S. courts protect people whose constitutional rights have been violated, and the U.S. Congress may also pass laws that protect constitutional rights and provide remedies for victims of human rights violations. For example, the Supreme Court ruling in *Obergefell v. Hodges* (2015) is a landmark civil rights case establishing that the fundamental right to marry is guaranteed to same-sex couples by both the Due Process Clause and the Equal Protection Clause of the Fourteenth Amendment to the U.S. Constitution. The Fourteenth Amendment is frequently used to address many aspects of citizenship and the rights of citizens that were not articulated explicitly in the U.S. Constitution. The phrase in the amendment "equal protection of the laws" figures prominently in a wide variety of landmark cases, including *Brown v. Board of Education* (racial discrimination), *Roe v. Wade* (reproductive rights), *Bush v. Gore* (election recounts), *Reed v. Reed* (gender discrimination), and *University of California v. Bakke* (racial quotas in education).

In addition to rights established by the judiciary, many federal laws have been enacted to protect human rights in the United States. For example, laws have been enacted banning child labor, limiting work hours, and facilitating access to voting. Often, federal laws are preceded by state laws on an issue, but sometimes states will expand on federal laws after enactment to clarify their interpretation of the federal law. The comprehensive legislation embodied in the U.S. Civil Rights Act of 1964 prohibits discrimination based on race, gender, and national origin in the workplace. It served as a model for subsequent anti-discrimination laws. The U.S. Civil Rights Act of 1991 created recourse for victims of such discrimination in employment situations by allowing punitive damages. Another example is the Americans with Disabilities Act of 1990, which prohibits discrimination against those with disabilities and requires institutions to provide accessibility to persons with disabilities.

Almost every U.S. state constitution explicitly addresses social and economic rights such as education, income assistance, and housing support. Some state courts have tried to enforce these provisions in the face of legislative indifference or recalcitrance (Hershkoff & Loffredo, 2011). New York State, for example, is one of about 15 states whose constitution provides a right to healthcare and mental health care.

Sometimes state statutes may address issues such as access to food and assistance as meeting a need for some defined group of people, but they do not recognize it as a right to which all people are entitled. Because many economic, social, and cultural issues are not viewed as rights enjoyed by all, public policies in the United States can exclude people from eligibility as long as they do not discriminate on prohibited grounds such as race, religion, or gender (Hershkoff & Loffredo, 2011). Curiously and despite common assumption, the U.S. Constitution does not mention a right to education, nor has the U.S. Supreme Court recognized one. All states, however, are mandated in their constitutions to offer education to the children in their states, but typically states do not offer the same education to all children. Even though education is not specifically mentioned as a right or a power of the federal government, the federal government through the Equal Protection Clause of the Fourteenth Amendment has in some cases interpreted that all children have an equal right to an appropriate education (Underwood, 2018).

Constitutional scholars such as Sunstein have argued that the federal Constitution need not be seen as excluding social and economic rights because "the meaning of the Constitution changes over time" (as quoted in Soohoo & Goldberg, 2010, p. 1006). The Constitution was written about 250 years ago and reflects the views and conflicts of the period. Our views on topics have changed over the years, and some issues were likely not on the radar of the authors of the Constitution. For example, the prohibition against gender discrimination is an interpretation of the Constitution— the Constitution does not expressly state it as such. Likewise, the rights to life and personal security have led to the adoption of domestic violence laws in the 20th century.

Soohoo and Goldberg (2010) point out that the United States protects other rights beyond the Constitution in order to protect rights found in the Bill of Rights. For example, to preserve the political and civil rights that are part of the Bill of Rights, governments may need to commit to expending funds for education, healthcare, and social assistance because without supporting these social and economic rights, our political and civil rights cannot be realized (Soohoo & Goldberg, 2010). After all, not knowing how to read and write, use computers, or do math may limit a person's ability to participate fully in our society, such as voting, or jeopardize their safety. Underwood (2018) reminds us that people cannot meaningfully exercise their First Amendment rights to free speech and association unless they have sufficient education to understand issues and gather information independently.

TIME TO EXERCISE

1. Find a copy of your state's constitution (most are available online). Does it include a right to education, healthcare, mental health care, social assistance, and social services?
2. How might having a state constitutional right to social assistance affect the types of help offered individuals in periods when politically we move further to the right or left? What effects might this have on social work practice with marginalized individuals and families?

Social workers must understand international and domestic constitutions and laws that protect and further people's rights. Some laws were put into place to promote equal access to benefits and opportunities, and social workers should ensure that the populations with whom they work are aware of these laws and benefit from them. Other laws may prevent the advancement or fair treatment of populations, and social workers need to advocate to change them.

EXCEPTIONALISM, HUMAN RIGHTS, AND THE UNITED STATES

U.S. exceptionalism in terms of international human rights treaties has a number of implications. As was demonstrated above, despite U.S. reservations to international human rights treaties and a poor record of ratifying these instruments, civil and political rights are well protected in the U.S. Constitution. However, protection of social, economic, and cultural rights is mixed in the United States because it tends to vary by state as well as according to courts' interpretation. The rights of those living in the United States are less than those articulated in the major UN human rights instruments because social, economic, and cultural rights are largely absent from the U.S. Constitution, and the laws or state constitutions where they do appear are often subject to interpretation and reinterpretation depending on the political climate.

Political climates prioritize issues, and the realization of human rights may benefit or recede as a result. Although the country once expanded and deepened its social protection programs through such efforts as the War on Poverty and the New Deal, at other times leadership has slashed social welfare programs, especially those that assist low-income households—the individuals and communities most social workers serve. During periods that prioritize business interests, a free market economy, and minimal governmental intervention, social service expenditures are typically cut. When we minimize government's role, the protection of human rights tends to diminish as a governmental responsibility. Given the vagaries of the free market, rights are not only not ensured but often are violated in pursuit of profit. Without international standards to fall back on, those who lack resources slip further away and lack redress. Protection of human rights can be swayed by political proclivities, given (1) the lack of ratification of international human rights standards, (2) the extensive use of reservations to assert U.S. sovereignty in the three covenants it has signed, (3) the politically charged will of the courts, including the Supreme Court, and (4) the ambiguity in many state constitutions around social and economic rights.

Although the United States was a leader in developing the UDHR and sees itself as a leader in human rights, it does not guarantee those rights to its citizens. Few conventions and covenants have been ratified; indeed, the United States is the only nation not to have ratified the Convention on the Rights of the Child. Human rights abuses are numerous in the United States, as exemplified in the report of the UN Special Rapporteur on Poverty (Alston, 2018).

Social workers must advocate for access to human rights for all and must incorporate a rights-based approach in their work. Social workers need to identify human rights violations that they see around them and be the force that ushers in a fuller realization of human rights.

TIME FOR REFLECTION AND DISCUSSION: WHAT'S YOUR OPINION?

- Should the United States continue to exempt itself from ratifying international human rights treaties?
- What are some of the consequences of this?
- How do you feel knowing that other countries have committed to upholding human rights to which the United States refuses to commit?
- In what ways might it be important for populations you will work with to understand the unique situation in the United States regarding human rights? And for them to understand the importance of state constitutions and laws?

SECTION 2

Diversity, Privilege, Oppression, and Intersectionality

CHAPTER 6
Diversity, Privilege, and Oppression

DIVERSITY

No two of us are exactly alike, yet any two of us are likely to have more in common than not.
When you meet someone new, do you focus on what you have in common or your differences?

Your answer to the question posed above may depend on whether you want
to become closer to the new acquaintance or keep your distance. According
to Johnson (2006), we organize our world in ways that encourage us to
use sameness and difference as means of including or excluding, rewarding
or punishing, elevating or oppressing, valuing or devaluing, crediting or
discrediting, ignoring or harassing. For much of our human history, those
who had power—whether it was a monarch, lord, elected officials, village
elders, or family members—sought ways to hold on to and to diminish
threats against their power. Those who did not hold power and were a
threat to the powerholders were dehumanized, blamed, or ignored to the
benefit of those in power (Mullaly, 2009). Eventually, this leads to marginalization and oppression of others.

Should we be focused on the similarities among us, then, rather than
our differences? Singh (1996) argues that a focus on sameness alone leads
us to be blind to or to deny differences. Denying differences means that we
repudiate differences regarding power, access to resources, opportunities,
and oppression within a society, and in rejecting these differences we facilitate the ability of those with power to maintain their privileged positions
in society.

Differences do exist among us, and deciding how a society will view those
differences and respond to them is a social construct. Social constructs are

A Human Rights-Based Approach to Justice in Social Work Practice. Shirley Gatenio Gabel, Oxford University Press.
© Oxford University Press 2024. DOI: 10.1093/oso/9780197570647.003.0006

created by humans and reflect concepts that exist because humans agree that it exists. For example, "love" is a social construct. We cannot directly see it, measure it, or confirm its existence, but we agree that it exists and have attributed emotion, standards, expectations, and even need to it. Most of the differences we ascribe to individuals are also social constructs, such as stereotypes of goodness/evil, desirability, worthiness, and societal roles. These social constructs become identities both regarding how others see us and how we identify ourselves. In turn, these identities can unite or divide us. Examples of social constructs humans have created over time to unite or divide us include, but certainly are not limited to, age, class, caste, tribe, race, ethnicity, nationality, disability and ability, gender, gender identity and expression, political affiliation, religion and spirituality, sex, sexual orientation, and marital status.

How we see these identities will depend on our larger view of society. For example, several scholars have noted that for decades, social work, particularly in North America and other Anglo democracies, has subscribed to a liberal view or liberal ideology (Mullaly, 2009; Dominelli, 2002; Leonard, 2001). The liberal view seeks to provide equal opportunities in response to the inequality in society to equalize outcomes. It implies that if given the same chance and if the same effort is exerted, equal outcomes will be achieved. Social, political, and economic differences are minimized. This recognition of inequality seems superficial. It ignores the structural inequalities that exist in society and implies that the individual alone is responsible for achievement.

In the liberal view, the views of the dominant group become the norm and other groups are expected to abide by the standards and rules established by the dominant group. Failure to succeed when given equal opportunities is likely to be attributed to the individual rather than to the social constructs embedded in a society. We'll get into more detail about this when we discuss race later in this chapter.

So, then, how should we look at similarities and differences among us? Sloan et al. (2018) urge social workers to adapt a critical multicultural perspective that begins with evaluating one's own beliefs, values, and perspectives and how these may or may not contribute to biases or discrimination against people from other identity groups. Through ongoing self-reflection, self-awareness of one's own identities develops further and one's awareness of the effects of systemic social structures grows. Later in this chapter, we'll go through an exercise demonstrating how to develop this kind of awareness about yourself and others.

Recognizing diversity is about acknowledging the differences among us but not using them as the basis of discrimination, marginalization or oppression. The Council on Social Work Education (CSWE, 2022) defines diversity as:

> The presence of differences that may include age, caste, class, color, culture, disability and ability, ethnicity, gender, gender identity and expression, generational status, immigration status, legal status, marital status, political ideology, race, nationality, religion and spirituality, sex, sexual orientation, and tribal sovereign status.

TIME FOR REFLECTION AND DISCUSSION

- When did you first become aware of race/ethnicity/tribes/castes, and how?
- What messages about race/ethnicity/tribes/castes did you receive from your family and community as a child?

PRIVILEGE

Appreciating diversity requires learning about inequity, discrimination, oppression, and privilege. Differences in power, treatment, access to resources, and opportunities affect life pathways and affect how people live together.

Privileges are benefits that accrue to certain members of society. Often, a privileged group may not be aware of the benefits bestowed upon them. For example, males may believe that the authority and position many societies bestow upon them is due to their abilities/skills. Males may not realize that females with the same abilities/skills are less likely to rise to positions of authority and influence because society sees the role and abilities of women differently. In turn, our social institutions reinforce these differences. Women are typically expected to maintain the household (cooking, cleaning, shopping, etc.); sustain socializing; and nurture and care for their parents, partners, and children (and childcare arrangements) as well as producing and competing in the workplace. Each household and partnership manages work and family responsibilities differently.

Most cisgender males are unlikely to experience sexual harassment at work. If they were to seek public office, it is unlikely that their relationship and time spent with their children would be scrutinized. They are unlikely to be accused of dressing provocatively at work. They are more likely to be considered the "person in charge" when there are mixed genders at work.

It is unlikely that their poor driving skills will be attributed to gender, and they are unlikely to be accused of letting their emotions interfere with their ability to make professional decisions.

Privileges come to people in different ways. For example, White parents typically do not have to talk with their children about how to avoid police violence, Christians generally do not need to take time off from work for religious holidays, and married couples with children typically don't have to explain to their employers why they can't spend all their time working. Privilege is given generally without cost to people; it is free and unearned and is commonly based on appearance—such as race, gender, ethnicity, or the appearance of wealth, class, or ability. Persons who have privilege often do not even notice it. When they achieve success, it is commonly attributed to their skills, talents, and acumen and the lack of these in others.

When social work was first established and for the decades that followed, social workers often had the responsibility of going into the homes of families who applied for government benefits to determine the cleanliness of the homes, signs of alcohol consumption and undisclosed males who might be living in the home. In other words, the poor had to prove their worthiness to receive assistance from the government. A few years ago, this topic as it relates to substance abuse resurfaced on social media, and State legislatures jumped on the bandwagon. Fifteen States passed legislation requiring drug testing or screening for public assistance applicants or recipients (Alabama, Arkansas, Arizona, Florida, Georgia, Kansas, Michigan, Mississippi, Missouri, North Carolina, Oklahoma, Tennessee, Utah, West Virginia, and Wisconsin). In 13 of these states, all applicants for public assistance are screened for drug use, while other states require a reason to believe the person is engaging in illegal drug activity or has a substance use disorder prior to testing. Some states offer treatment programs to those who test positive, but in most, positive results mean disqualification for benefits. This practice is not new: The Personal Responsibility and Work Opportunity Reconciliation Act of 1996 gave states the power to bar Temporary Assistance for Needy Families (TANF) to persons convicted of a felony for possession, use, or distribution of illegal drugs.

In reaction to what was becoming a trend across states, some asked on social media: Shouldn't the wealthy have to prove their worth for government benefits as well? U.S. Representative Gwen Moore (D-WI) introduced legislation in 2016 that would have required drug testing for all tax filers claiming itemized deductions totaling over $150,000; the option was to take the standard tax deduction, which is considerably lower. While this legislation was not enacted, it highlights the privilege that higher-earning taxpayers have that may not be available to low-income persons seeking assistance from the government. It also points to the kinds of assumptions we regularly make in society. In this example, it was drug use and poverty. Race adds another dimension of privilege. For example, research shows that public opinion assumes that the poor are overwhelmingly persons of color or illegal immigrants, and that the public is less likely to support public benefits for this reason (Lanford & Quadagno, 2021).

OPPRESSION

Oppression is the opposite of privilege. With privilege, systems and institutions are built to benefit certain groups and exclude others. Oppression involves creating systems and institutions that disadvantage some groups and allows dominant groups to exert control over other groups by withholding resources and benefits (such as healthcare, education, employment, and housing opportunities) and violating human rights. Examples of these systems are racism, sexism, heterosexism, ableism, classism, ageism, anti-Semitism, anti-Muslim, and anti-Hinduism.

Young (1990) identified five types or faces of oppression: exploitation, marginalization, cultural imperialism, violence, and powerlessness. Each of these types of oppression is described below.

Exploitation can be the act of benefiting from people's labors or skills or using another's resources without fair compensation. An example of exploitation would be not fully compensating agricultural workers or persons who work in factories. A fair wage would reflect the benefits that their labors bring to a company or the owners. Likewise, when a company extracts precious minerals from the earth but doesn't fairly compensate a country or those who own the land, this too is exploitation. Exploitation creates a system that perpetuates differences in income and wealth that lead to other disparities as well.

Marginalization is the result of politically, economically, socially, or culturally excluding a group of people from participation in mainstream society. Marginalized persons or groups are treated as though they are insignificant or peripheral to society. Caste systems, tribes, persons of different abilities, minority religious sects and ethnicities, persons of color, women, the elderly, and children are among the groups who have historically experienced marginalization. Marginalization often results in the violation of human rights.

- When someone is marginalized *economically*, they may be unable to obtain well-paid employment that includes benefits. Instead, they are forced into poorly paying livelihoods that are informal, lack benefits, and involve irregular hours.

- *Political* marginalization occurs when people are unable to participate in the decision-making process in their society—whether it be voting, having their voice heard, or being penalized for expressing their opinions.
- *Social* marginalization is the relegation of individuals or groups to the fringes of society. It is discriminatory and generally occurs on more than one dimension simultaneously. For example, someone who is socially marginalized may be prohibited from attending mainstream schools, shops, or clubs or living in certain communities. Social marginalization can be passed on from one generation to the next.
- Like social marginalization, *cultural* marginalization occurs when the traditions, religion, rituals, music, values, foods, languages, dress, as well as other forms of culture are not accepted or recognized or may be devalued or alienated by the society at large.

Social and cultural marginalization can lead to other types of marginalization. Consider an immigrant group whose foods, attire, and places of worship confine them to a neighborhood that has little or poor public transportation. Poor public transportation may make if difficult or impossible for those living in a marginalized community to access better-paying jobs outside of their community. Safety too may be an issue—but because most of the community cannot vote since they are not citizens, the police and other authorities can easily ignore safety issues in the community, as well as the lack of sanitation, clean water, quality education and health facilities, electricity, or internet access.

Cultural imperialism is when the dominant culture—their language, beliefs, customs, wants, needs, dress, food preferences, religious practices, household composition, family roles, musical tastes, political views, and so forth—dominate the society at large and are accepted as the norm. The dominant culture consists of those who have power in a society and control how the people in that society interpret social situations and communicate. Therefore, the beliefs of that society are the most widely disseminated and express the experience, values, goals, and achievements of the dominant group(s).

Think about how your family saw certain people, places, or situations when you were growing up. Perhaps as an adult you interpreted people, places, and situations differently than your family did because you used a new frame to see these things. American culture is built upon the Judeo-Christian belief systems emanating from White culture. Speaking English is expected in the United States, a two-parent family with children is considered the norm (despite the steady decrease in the number of such families), idealized relationships involve a male and a female, there is resistance to accepting a range of gender identification and sexual preferences, women are considered better nurturers than men, and males continue to earn more money than females: These are all examples of cultural imperialism. People who do not conform to these norms may be ignored and alienated due to stereotypes and discrimination.

Another type of oppression is **violence**. Even the threat of violence can be as potent as acts of violence in limiting the movements, aspirations, and participation of individuals and groups who fear random, unprovoked attacks against themselves, their properties, and their reputations. Violence can be physical, sexual, and emotional. What starts out as a disagreement or conflict can escalate into aggression and produce serious damage.

Paulo Freire, a Brazilian educational philosopher, believes that the deepest form of oppression is **powerlessness**. Powerlessness turns inward the oppression from outside forces. Self-hate, self-loathing, and continual feelings of inadequacy, guilt, and low self-esteem characterize powerlessness. People may constantly compare themselves to others and perceive themselves as inadequate. Women who have left domestic violence situations, children who were abused, individuals who were persecuted, migrants, and individuals who have been trafficked or enslaved commonly report powerlessness. This type of oppression renders the oppressed silent. It leaves them without a voice and often without an understanding of the oppression they are experiencing. Freire described how the public dehumanization of the oppressed is then internalized.

Distinguishing the different types of oppression is an important way of better understanding it. These different types of oppression can occur at different levels (Thompson, 1997): structural, cultural, and personal (Figure 6.1). Each of these levels interacts with the others to reinforce and affect oppression:

- The *structural* level is where oppression is institutionalized in a society.
- Laws, social institutions, economic and political systems, policies, and practices reinforce the values represented at the *cultural* level of oppression.
- These in turn guide our *personal* interactions and attitudes toward others. At the personal level, our perception of others is based on how our beliefs have been shaped and is likely to lead to stereotyping and defining our interactions with others. This is influenced by the norms and values established by the dominant culture and how the dominant culture has portrayed subordinate groups in literature, history, movies, the media, humor, songs, and so forth.

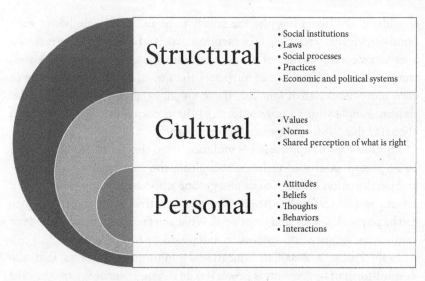

Structural	• Social institutions • Laws • Social processes • Practices • Economic and political systems
Cultural	• Values • Norms • Shared perception of what is right
Personal	• Attitudes • Beliefs • Thoughts • Behaviors • Interactions

Figure 6.1. Multiple levels of oppression.

Closely related to oppression is *prejudice*, which is defined as an opinion or judgment that is based on insufficient information or one that disregards knowledge that's contradictory to that opinion or judgment. Just as we can learn prejudices, we can unlearn them as well.

Stereotypes are biased, overgeneralized beliefs about a particular group or class of people. Stereotypes can be both positive and negative. Because stereotypes are biased and do not portray reality, most are negative and damaging. Stereotypes have been used by dominant groups to reinforce their position of power and oppress the targeted group(s). Dominant groups will impose stereotypes to undermine the abilities, skills, and qualities of the subordinated group in order to maintain the dominant group's position of power (Mullaly, 2009). As Thompson (1997) has noted, stereotypes can become ingrained in the dominant culture because it is difficult to refute conceptualizations that were not based on evidence. As stereotypes become absorbed by a culture, their ability to affect our actions and thoughts typically goes unnoticed.

Another concept associated with oppression is *discrimination*, which occurs when stereotypical assumptions are used to exclude persons, for instance by denying benefits or imposing burdens. Discrimination can be unintentional or intentional. For example, an older adult who has practiced good health and fitness throughout her life moves to a new community and applies for a position at the local gym as a fitness instructor. She has many years of experience in instructional fitness. At the interview, she impresses the staff with the innovative instructional techniques she has developed and her understanding of how to motivate clients. Later she is told that she didn't get the job because they hired someone who had more energy and who would better lead male fitness classes. It is possible that the person hired may have been equally qualified, but the assumptions that older adults have less energy and are less attractive are based on negative stereotypes of older persons. Acting on this is an example of age and gender discrimination. The interviewers may not have been aware that they held these views, in which case this would be unintentional. Discrimination is intentional when an individual uses stereotypes, biases, or unfounded attitudes toward others to treat people differently.

From a human rights-based perspective, persons should be judged on their individual attributes, skills, and capabilities rather than on stereotypes, prejudice, or assumptions. People with power tend to want to build and promulgate a society that maintains their power. This is something we all must keep in mind and in check. To support a diverse, pluralistic society we must make room for more than one gender, one race, one ethnicity, one religion, and one level of ability.

Much of the social work and interdisciplinary literature focuses on what we don't want: oppression, prejudice, marginalization, discrimination, misuse of stereotypes, cultural oppression, and exploitation. As social workers we strive to develop situations that enhance a sense of belonging. Social workers understand the importance of people being and feeling connected to families, friends, social supports, and decision-makers in communities and in governments. Belonging means having the right to contribute to and to seek support from one's communities and society. To do otherwise is to engage in "othering," or excluding individuals, groups, or communities. Othering is the foundation of conflicts, violence, the spread of disease, and inequities related to health, gender, nutrition, education, income, and wealth.

When persons or populations are intentionally or unintentionally excluded from full participation in a society, the whole society suffers— economically, socially, and politically. For example, gun violence in the United States, on average, claimed the lives of more than 110 persons each day between 2016 through 2020 (Everytown for Gun Safety Support Fund, n.d.). The U.S. homicide rate is 25 times than the average of other high-income countries (Johns Hopkins Center for Gun Violence Solutions, 2022). Since 2009, there have been 277 mass shootings in the United States, resulting in 1,565 people shot and killed and 1,000 people shot and wounded (Everytown for Gun Safety Support Fund, n.d.). The immediate causes often cited for the high rates of gun violence are easy access to guns and the mental well-being of shooters. Contrary to this belief, a John Jay study looking at the root causes of gun violence found that while individual behaviors contribute to gun violence, we also need to create communities that promote social bonds and anti-violence norms coming from key stakeholders (John Jay Research Advisory Group on Preventing and Reducing Community Violence, 2020). According to the John Jay Group (2020), in addition to confronting access to guns and increasing restrictions for individuals with violent backgrounds to guns, our focus should be on improving the physical environment, strengthening social norms and peer relationships that support anti-violence, engaging and supporting youth, mitigating financial stress and economic inequality, reducing substance abuse, and reforming the harmful effects of a racialized and biased justice process. In other words, making people feel part of the communities they live in, checking in on people by community members, getting people help before a crisis, reducing economic and mental stress, and treating all people fairly and with respect will help reduce the climbing rates of gun violence in the United States.

We know, too, that when older adults do not have adequate contact with others, their physical and emotional well-being deteriorates—too often resulting in the publicly funded institutionalization of an individual. Economic neglect is the main reason children are separated from parents and placed in alternative, publicly funded placements, causing further trauma and stress for children and parents. Rather than removing individuals from their homes, we could be looking to increasing their connections to and supports from the community where they reside.

USING HISTORY TO GUIDE OUR FUTURE

Throughout history, citizens have unknowingly ushered in totalitarian and oppressive regimes thinking the new leaders would set things right in times of great despair. Adolph Hitler used propaganda to marginalize groups that threatened his power and control over Germany. Propaganda helped Hitler introduce a new normative frame that villainized certain groups of people (with the intent to destroy) whom he blamed for Germany's social and economic problems. This is an extreme example of how one party sought to dominate all aspects of life and erase all other perspectives (Daniel & Sterphone, 2019).

With the onset of the Great Depression, millions of Germans were disillusioned by their political parties amid the failing economy in the early 1930s. No single party had been able to unite the different political parties in Germany to form a viable coalition government. Voters feared impoverishment, unemployment, and communism. Hitler acted on the fears of voters. He pledged to retake previously lost territories and appealed to young voters by promising to restore Germany's military might. He promised farmers that he would save their homesteads and promised jobs to the unemployed.

Anti-Semitism was a cornerstone of Hitler's agenda, and while it appealed to right-wing radicals, not all of Hitler's followers supported anti-Semitism (Daniel & Sterphone, 2019). Hitler trod lightly at first, careful not to alienate his supporters who did not support anti-Semitism, but he quietly forged ahead with his plans, collecting public opinions on Jewish people and using them to form a strategy.

When Hitler took control of Germany in 1933 (through a backroom political deal, not through an election), he established a Reich Ministry of Public Enlightenment and Propaganda. The Ministry's aim was to ensure that the Nazi message was successfully communicated through art, music, theater, films, books, radio, educational materials, and the press, and this was done on a regional basis. Hitler made sure that there was only one source of information for the German people (Herf, 2005). He outlawed other political parties and transformed Germany into a one-party dictatorship. Basic civil rights—such as the freedoms of expression, press, and assembly—were suspended. Those speaking out against the regime were treated as enemies of the State and imprisoned. No longer concerned with elections, the Nazi Party focused on winning over the 60 percent of Germans who had not supported Hitler and on building national consensus for Hitler's domestic and foreign policies (Herf, 2005).

Propaganda was key to winning over the public. Hitler used propaganda to encourage passivity and acceptance of the measures against the Jewish people by depicting the Nazi government as restoring order. Nazi propaganda sold the ideal of the "national community" to Germans; the regime made it increasingly clear that only those of the Aryan race would be permitted to be part of the new Germany (den Hertog, 2020). Aryans were a mythical, supposedly superior race. Many northern Europeans believed they had descended from the Aryan race. In the late 1800s, many European and American scientists created and divided humankind into smaller and smaller races. One of the races created was the "Semitic race," which they used to categorize Jews. The word *Semitic* is not a "race" but rather a linguistic term that refers to a group of languages traditionally spoken in the Middle East and parts of Africa, including Amharic, a language spoken in Ethiopia, as well as Hebrew and Arabic. The Nazis classified Jews, African Germans, and Roma as members of unacceptable races that had to be excluded. Others were to be excluded due to the presence of undesirable "biological" traits such as physical or mental disabilities, politics, sexual preferences, work attitudes, or nonconforming behaviors (den Hertog, 2020).

Propaganda campaigns created an atmosphere tolerant of violence against Jews. These propaganda campaigns created negative stereotypes of Jewish people and led to the passage of laws such as the Nuremberg Race Laws in 1935 (Herf, 2005). The Nuremberg Race Laws established Jewish people as a separate race rather than identifying people based on their religious preferences or cultural traditions. The laws embodied many of the racial theories underpinning Nazi ideology and provided the legal framework for the systematic persecution of Jews. Negative propaganda continued to escalate, leading to the enactment of laws in 1938 that barred Jewish people from working and stripping Jews of their homes, businesses, all assets, and livelihoods (den Hertog, 2020).

Propaganda created a climate of indifference, hate, and fear against Jewish people that tolerated the mass murder of six million Jews. Films and cartoons in State-controlled newspapers were used to create stereotypes of Jewish people as subhuman, wandering cultural parasites, consumed by sex and money. Later, as the Nazis advanced to occupy other countries, Jewish people were portrayed as dangerous enemies to the German Reich who needed to be eliminated (den Hertog, 2020).

During the implementation of the "Final Solution" (the mass murder of European Jews), Nazi guards forced Jewish prisoners in the concentration camps designated as killing centers to write postcards home saying they were being treated well and living in good conditions. In this way, propaganda was used to cover up atrocities and mass murder.

TIME FOR REFLECTION AND DISCUSSION

- The history of anti-Semitism is in part a story of rumors, lies, and myths that have persisted over the course of centuries. How do rumors get started? Why might lies and myths about people persist even after they have been proven wrong?
- How do you explain why people might believe such myths and stereotypes about Jews? What might it take to overcome false anti-Semitic beliefs?
- What rumors, lies, and myths do we propagate about other groups today?

CHAPTER 7

Social Identities, Positionality, and Intersectionality

TIME FOR REFLECTION AND DISCUSSION

WHO ARE YOU?

Take a few moments to answer these questions:

- Who are you? How do you identify yourself?
- Did you identify yourself by race/ethnicity? Gender? Sexual orientation? Age? Relationship status? Position? Height? Weight? Culture? Or some other characteristics?
- Who were you thinking would read your response?

We tend to identify ourselves in ways we think matter, depending on our audience. In the 1970s, two psychologists, Tajfel and Turner, developed social identity theory to explain the process of how we identify ourselves and how we develop prejudices and stereotypes. They observed that we identify who we are based on our group memberships because groups give us a sense of social belonging in the social world (Tajfel & Turner, 1979). According to social identity theory, we put people in groups or categories because we are taught to categorize knowledge. In doing so, we overstress the similarities of things or people in the same group (the in-group) and the differences between groups (out-group). Social identity theory says, we do this to enhance our own self-image.

Social identity theory suggests there are three mental processes involved in creating in-groups and out-groups. The first stage is *social categorization*, which is when we put people into groups, including ourselves, as a way of

A Human Rights-Based Approach to Justice in Social Work Practice. Shirley Gatenio Gabel, Oxford University Press.
© Oxford University Press 2024. DOI: 10.1093/oso/9780197570647.003.0007

understanding and identifying ourselves in society. The context in which we find ourselves affects the groups we select as a means of identification. Next is *social identification*. In this stage, we adopt the identity with the group we have categorized ourselves as belonging to, and our self-image becomes tied to the group membership. We then internalize the attitudes, values, social explanations, and identity of the group with which we identify. For example, if you identify as a student, you may find yourself taking on the behaviors, viewpoints, and opinions you believe students hold. In the final stage, *social comparison*, we tend to compare ourselves to other groups. Tajfel and Turner (1986) say that we do this to maintain our self-esteem. If we believe our interests are threatened by other groups, we will develop negative stereotypes and prejudices toward other groups. People have many social identities, and at times these identities can conflict with one another.

Critics of social identity theory argue that the theory does not fully account for all the factors affecting self-esteem/image, and that a fuller explanation of intergroup processes and group identification is needed (Brown, 2000). Social identity theory, however, does help us understand why we not only internalize group identities but also create negative identities for those in other groups.

How we see ourselves is context-bound. The dominant group's views of other groups become systematized in one's culture and are not only internalized by the dominant group but also affect how other groups see themselves. This ties to Young's description of internalized oppression (1988) and Freire's concept of powerlessness (Freire, 1994).

It is not one identity alone that contributes to privilege or oppression. Each of us is a synthesis of multiple identities that affect how we see ourselves, how others see and respond to us, and how we respond to others. There are some identities that are visible and others that are integral to how we see ourselves but not readily apparent to others. Your socioeconomic background, sexual preferences, religious views, or cultural background may or may not be visible to others, in contrast to your skin color, height, or age.

Positionality

Figure 7.1 is a depiction of power and oppression in the United States. Those who identify closest to the center of the wheel are the inner circle or dominant groups. They tend to have the most institutionalized privileges. Those farthest away from the center hold the fewest privileges. Wheels like this help us visualize the meaning of marginalization. People who are marginalized are farther from the center, from power. The farther from the center one finds oneself, the more marginalized one is.

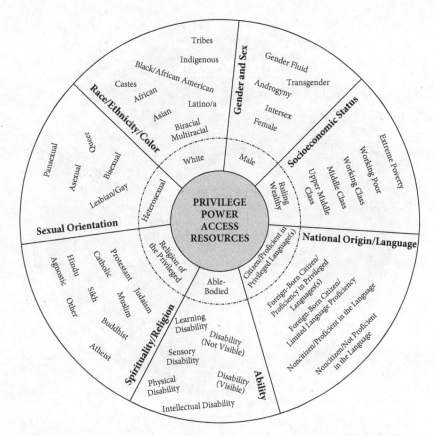

Figure 7.1. Wheel of privilege and power.
Adapted from Sloan, L., Joyner, M. C., Stakeman, C., & Schmitz, C. (2018). *Critical multiculturalism and intersectionality in a complex world* (2nd ed.). Oxford.

TIME TO EXERCISE

For each of the identities depicted in the wheel in Figure 7.1, such as race, gender, age, circle the category that best represents your position. Then draw lines to connect the circles in each of the identities to form your web. For many, the level of power/marginalization will likely shift between identities.

- Were you surprised to learn of your privilege and marginalization across the identities?
- What surprised you most?

Now think of someone you know, perhaps a friend from class or someone you work with. To the best of your knowledge, circle the categories for each identity that you think best describes them. How does their web compare to yours?

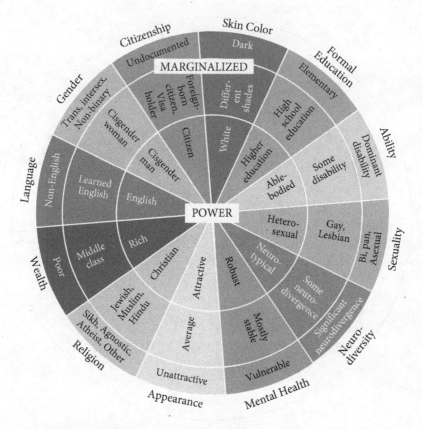

Figure 7.2. Revised wheel of privilege and oppression.

As noted earlier, identity, privilege, power, and oppression are context-bound. The wheel in Figure 7.1 reflects one view of privilege and power in the United States. What categories do you think are missing?

The wheel has been created by many different people to reflect the identities that matter to people and to their experiences. Figure 7.2 shows another version of the wheel of privilege/oppression. Students have contributed to this version over several years.

TIME TO EXERCISE

- How does your web shift in the revised wheel? Do you find yourself with more privileges or fewer?
- How did the revised wheel change the web drawn for your friend/colleague?

- What thoughts and feelings were evoked when completing the positionality assessment?

  Describe how your growing awareness of diversity, oppression, power, and privilege influenced your response.

Intersectionality

Intersectionality describes how our multiple identities combine, sometimes privileging us in certain identities and then marginalizing us in others. Intersectionality is a theoretical framework grounded in the idea that human experience and identity is shaped by multiple social positions (e.g., race, gender) and cannot be adequately understood by considering social positions independently (Bauer et al., 2021). The theoretical framework is most often credited to legal scholar Kimberlé Crenshaw (1989, pp. 139–168; 1991) and sociology professor Patricia Hill Collins (1990), who present it within Black feminist theory to better explain the experiences of Black women in the United States.

Brantley et al. (2021) trace the origins of intersectionality to the pioneering work done by the Combahee River Collective (CRC) (1977, 1983). The CRC was founded in 1974 by Black, lesbian, socialist feminist women, many of whom had been active in the Black Panthers, Students for a Democratic Society, and the Congress for Racial Equality (Collins & Bilge, 2016). The CRC challenged U.S. nationalism and its alliance to capitalism. According to Brantley et al. (2021), the CRC built on the legendary work of Anna Julia Cooper, who spoke to the compounding oppression of being Black and female among activists such as Sojourner Truth, Harriet Tubman, Frances E. W. Harper, Ida B. Wells-Barnett, and Mary Church Terrell. According to the CRC's Combahee River Collective Statement:

> We are actively committed to struggle against racial, sexual, heterosexual, and class oppression, and see as our particular task the development of integrated analysis and practice based upon the fact that the major systems of oppression are interlocking. The synthesis of these oppressions creates the conditions of our lives. (1977, p. 210)

The CRC in many ways was a reaction to the 1970s events around women's liberation, Black activism, and the growing gay rights movement. The National Organization for Women (NOW), founded in 1966, did not effectively address race, nor did it reflect the concerns of working-class Black women. At the same time, some Black advocacy organizations were silent on LGBTQI+ and women's rights in the 1960s into the early 1970s (BlackPast, 2018).As Brantley et al. (2021) note, it is important that we acknowledge this foundation of intersectionality and its evolution. Intersectionality was created by women who felt that their views and their life experiences were not fully embraced by existing activist organizations. This is often the reason new organizations and new perspectives on justice are launched.

Since Crenshaw and Collins introduced intersectionality to academia, it has been extended to apply to a wide range of intersections of race, ethnicity, gender, socioeconomic status, sexual orientation, and other social identities or positions (Bowleg, 2012; Hancock, 2007). These intersections are not merely overlapping or additive; rather, the intersections create dimensions that generate unique experiences (Bowleg, 2012).

Intersectionality is a widely used concept within social work. The interconnecting social identities such as race, gender, class, sexuality, and ability produce experiences of both privilege and marginalization. This forces us to recognize the differences that exist *among* groups, not only the differences *between* groups. For example, one's experience as a White female with cognitive disabilities may be different from that of a Black female with cognitive disabilities. Intersectionality encourages us to bring the complexities of group-based politics into social work practice by critically examining the variations in social location that exist within groups. We use intersectionality in social work to better understand ourselves as we prepare to practice, as well as to expand our understanding of the experiences of the populations we work with. We also use it as a theoretical research paradigm to understand the interaction of various social identities and how these interactions define personal experiences and power hierarchies in a society.

It is important to acknowledge that our understanding of human experience can be limited to how we conceptualize identity within the existing culture and within a period. We see our conceptualizations of race, ethnicity, gender identification and sexual preferences, religion, and income as key factors contributing to our experiences in the United States today. However, these were not always the categories used to understand social identity; our definitions of these categories have evolved. For example, until recently, officially, and commonly, gender and sex were thought of as binary concepts (e.g., sex and gender: male/female; sexual identity: heterosexual/homosexual). The emergence of queer theory in the 1990s challenged us to think differently. Queer theory originated from multiple critical and cultural contexts, including feminism, post-structuralist theory, radical movements of people of color, the gay and lesbian movements, AIDS activism, sexual subcultural practices, and postcolonialism. Queer theorists contend that there is no set normal, only changing norms that people may or may not fit into. For queer theorists, the main challenge is to disrupt binaries by tearing down the privilege built into our social infrastructure and society around gender and sex. One of the key concepts in queer theory is the idea of "heteronormativity." According to this theory, heterosexuality is promoted as the normal and preferred sexual orientation and is reinforced in society through the institutions of marriage, taxes, employment, and adoption rights, among many others.

As practicing social workers, we commonly ask individuals we are working with to identify themselves as male or female, or perhaps straight or gay. When we do this, we are reinforcing heteronormativity and existing power structures that oppress and marginalize groups that don't conform to the commonly used existing categories. Instead, we may consider *asking the individual how they prefer to be referred to* in relation to their gender and/or sexual identity (e.g., lesbian, gay, bisexual, transgender, queer, asexual, intersex) and which pronouns are preferred. We should also ask if there are any terms they request *not* be used in reference to them, and in what cases.

Crenshaw (1989) argues that many Americans believe that racism ceased to exist with the passage of the 1965 Civil Rights Act. It was believed that a law forbidding irrational bias would bring justice and end centuries of racism. In other words, the system only needed to be cleaned up, not rebuilt. We adopted "color-blind" standards and cheered the end of racism. Yet, if we are truly color-blind, why do wealth and income inequalities exist across races? In the 1980s and 1990s, theorists didn't offer the mechanisms for understanding how racism was embedded in our social and economic institutions. Crenshaw (1989) picked up on this and used it in the intersectionality framework she developed. This was further developed by critical race theorists in subsequent years.

SECTION 3
Justice

CHAPTER 8
What Is Justice?

Can you recall a day that the news did not report an injustice? Stories of injustice are prominent and frequent. Why? Are injustices occurring more frequently? Perhaps. We know that publicized incidences of injustice arise when our sense of justice is shifting, and a new paradigm is being shepherded in by the public. Whether they are stories about racial or gender injustice, growing health and economic disparities, treatment of immigrants or persons with disabilities, incarcerations, voting policies, access to reproductive services, police actions, or the uneven impacts of global warming—these stories dominate our media and affect our perspectives on these issues.

The U.S. Declaration of Independence presented a bold vision for a nation where there would be equal justice for all, yet nearly 250 years later, we continue to fight for justice. Without question, we have made substantial gains in legal, political, social, educational, and economic justice, and the lens we use to see issues has shifted over time. We can look to colonialism, slavery, racial segregation, treatment of workers, the role of women in the home and workplace, child labor, and much more to see how our understanding of these issues has evolved. Our sense of how we should treat one another and our policy goals constantly evolve as we understand more about the world we live in and the range of experiences for people.

Before defining justice, we must understand that our sense of justice today reflects our past and current culture. It is easy to think of justice as unwavering and differentiating good from bad, yet **societal concepts of justice change all the time**.

Women's role in the workplace is a good example of how our sense of justice is advancing. It was customary for women to leave their jobs, often as

A Human Rights-Based Approach to Justice in Social Work Practice. Shirley Gatenio Gabel, Oxford University Press.
© Oxford University Press 2024. DOI: 10.1093/oso/9780197570647.003.0008

secretaries or in the helping professions, once they married and most certainly when they became pregnant. It was considered good practice or fair to fire women when they married or became pregnant because women were expected to assume household and nurturing responsibilities. In the first half of the 20th century, many working women were treated as temporary workers by employers. During World War II, many women entered the workforce to support the war effort and many married women went to work to replace their husbands' salaries (their husbands were fighting in the war). Of course, for many women who were in households that had minimal resources, especially immigrants and women of color, work had always been a necessity.

After World War II, there were concerted efforts to remove women from the workforce to allow men to resume these positions. A significant number of women chose to remain in the labor force, however, and attitudes toward their employment slowly began to shift (Conway et al., 2003). Fueled by feminist advocacy in the 1970s, a growing number of women felt that barring women from the labor force or keeping women at home was unjust. Employers, too, weighed in on the need for policies and practices regarding pregnant women at work. The Pregnancy Discrimination Act of 1978 amended Title VII of the 1964 Civil Rights Act to prohibit discrimination based on pregnancy, childbirth, or related medical conditions. This legislation reinforced a change in how a growing number of people viewed the role of women and women's participation in the labor force.

Similarly, the paradigm we have used to guide our relationship with the environment has shifted. A century ago, far less thought was given to how people's current actions would affect the environment and people's lives in the future. We have since learned how many racialized and low-income communities bear the brunt of polluting industries and other environmental hazards, including oil and gas extraction, pipelines, refineries, mineral mining, and sewage dumping. The people living in toxic communities are least likely to benefit financially from these economic and industrial actions but are most likely to suffer the resulting health, economic, and social consequences. These communities often have little power to influence site placement, cleanup, and other decisions. We are more aware of the indirect consequences of industrialization on poor communities now than we were several decades ago, and we have reframed what we consider justice.

Can you name some situations where your sense of justice has shifted? Perhaps you can recall arguing with your parents or siblings when you were a child about what is fair or just—maybe referring to how snacks or privileges were being distributed. Perhaps you argued about how a cake is sliced, or you felt that doing more chores earned you greater privileges, like staying up later or more computer time. Thinking back, who made the decisions about what was fair? Probably it was your parents, teachers, camp counselors, or older or influential friends/siblings who controlled the culture of the home, classroom, camp, or group of friends. This is generally the pattern in governance as well. Those who have power to decide on the distribution of resources and opportunities also control social, political, and economic interactions and the culture.

History is replete with examples of rulers, politicians, and heads of state who sought to control culture as a means of building their power. For instance, in 1966, when China's Chairman Mao Zedong sought to re-assert his control of the Communist Party, he launched a mass Great Proletarian Cultural Revolution that went on for 10 years in China. Schools and universities closed, and shrines, churches, libraries, and stores were destroyed and ransacked to rid China of its feudal traditions. Mao introduced a new economic system, new ideas of justice, and new ways of living by changing the culture.

More recently, France was the first European country to ban the full-face Islamic veil in public places in April 2011. From the perspective of France's then-President Sarkozy, veils oppressed women and were not welcome in France. He and others like him saw veils as an injustice to women and society at large. Yet France is home to the largest Muslim population in Europe. For many Muslims, wearing a veil is a religious act—a way of demonstrating their submission to God and observing modesty in their dress and behavior. Full-face veils were subsequently banned in Belgium in 2011, Germany in 2016, and Austria in 2017 as well. Social commentators had a lot to say about the irony of mandating the wearing of masks during the 2020–21 COVID-19 pandemic in all of these countries. Nonetheless, the dominant culture in these countries did not respect face veils as a cultural and religious right. Banning face veils affected the way people viewed those who wore veils and influenced social, political, and economic interactions with women who wore veils. From the view of the dominant culture, wearing a face veil concealed an individual's identity and was un-just. The contrasting view was that wearing a face veil was a religious and cultural right, and imposing limitations or prohibitions was unjust.

TIME FOR REFLECTION AND DISCUSSION

In most cases, it is an elite group, rather than one person, who controls the culture. Think about who enforces the culture in the community you live in or where you may worship. What kinds of things do they seek to influence in your life?

Philosophers, scholars, politicians, clerics, and people in general have been writing about justice for a very long time. Ideas of justice have been explored by people in all parts of world and are influenced by time periods, cultural exchanges, traditions, history, political forces, and economics. More often than not, changes in the definition of justice come from a heightened sense of injustice, violence, abuse, war, or revolution that reflected an alternative view of the future. What rings of justice in one era and in one culture may reek of injustice in another era or culture.

There are multiple definitions of justice, as each definition is relevant to a time and culture. That said, certain elements of justice transcend culture and time. For one, justice is relational. In all issues of justice, it is an interpretation that a resource, right, or opportunity that is available to some should be available to others. An injustice comes about when there is a scarcity or limitation imposed on resources. Issues of justice arise when people can advance claims to rights, opportunities, and resources that others have and they have been denied. We appeal to justice to resolve such conflicts by settling what each person or group is entitled to have in accordance with the prevailing interpretation of justice.

Another common element of justice is that justice is to be delivered. Unlike human rights, which are inherent for all humans, justice obligates an agent to deliver it. We are entitled to our human rights, but we demand justice from an authority or decision-maker when our human rights are violated (i.e., not fulfilled). The agent might be a divine being, an individual person, a group of people, or an institution such as a government or an employer.

We expect the administration of justice to be consistent. There are generally rules, laws, practices, and processes to actualize justice, and the expectation is that changes to procedures, laws, and rules must be agreed upon and not dispensed in an arbitrary manner. In the United States, we hold our civil and political rights dear. In 2021, dozens of states enacted wide-ranging laws overhauling their election systems to impose restrictions on voting (particularly mail-in votes) and to give state legislatures greater control over the administration of elections, such as limiting absentee-ballot drop boxes, tightening identification requirements for voting by mail, barring election officials from proactively sending out ballot applications, or shortening the timeframe during which absentee ballots can be requested. Some legislatures went farther and conducted partisan reviews of election results, removing some powers from election officials like secretaries of state, or exerting pressure on county and local election officials about how elections were managed. These changes are likely to affect voters of color disproportionately, echoing the country's long history of racial discrimination at the polls such as barring Black citizens from voting by imposing poll taxes or literacy tests or intimidating voters. This is an example of how inconsistent rules that benefit some and exclude others contribute to an injustice.

Views on justice are typically codified in law, but this is not always the case: Justice may be defined by common practice within a culture, community, or country. For example, should offspring decide for themselves who their life partners will be? In many cultures, parents negotiate who their children will marry and when. In other cultures, parent's negotiating a marriage for their child would be considered unjust and beyond parental authority. In many cultures up through most of the 18th century, monarchs ruled, male domination over women was expected, slavery was widely practiced, and discrimination was common (Lauren, 2013).

Figure 8.1 summarizes the factors that affect a society's view and practice of justice and how it evolves.

Differing Views of Justice

An extensive literature on the meaning of justice exists across disciplines and going back millennia. Conceptions of justice can vary widely, even within the same time period. In social work we tend to gravitate toward conceptions of justice that posit justice as equality or equity, suggesting that

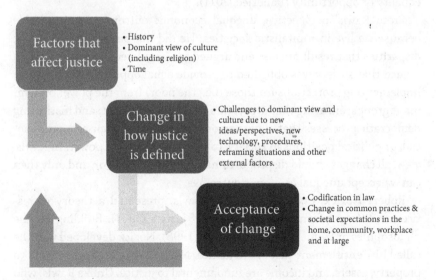

Figure 8.1. Evolving justice.

an ideal type of distribution exists. This is in contrast to other definitions of justice that emphasize laws or processes more than outcomes.

John Rawls' theory of justice is widely cited in social work and beyond. His theory envisions an egalitarian society and provides two principles of justice that governments should apply to all decisions (1999, 2001). The first principle, known as the *equal liberty principle*, guarantees to all equal basic political and civil liberties such as freedom of speech, assembly, and religion; property ownership; and political participation. This corresponds to the political and civil human rights we learned about in a previous chapter. The second principle has two parts:

- The first part, known as the *fair equality of opportunity principle*, guarantees fair access to education and work for all citizens with equal ability and talent, irrespective of their socioeconomic background (Banerjee, 2011).
- The second part, known as the *difference principle*, accepts some inequalities in social and economic institutions as fair but requires social and economic inequalities to be regulated so that they work to the greatest benefit of the least advantaged members of society.

In later years, Rawls strengthened the importance of the first principle by presenting equal civil and political freedoms as givens; they cannot be annulled or taken away. He also revised the notion that the first principle must be fulfilled before the second one by giving greater importance to fair equality of opportunity (Banerjee, 2011).

From Rawls' perspective, unequal economic outcomes are inevitable because we live in capitalistic societies. He did not believe the economic disparities that result are just and argued for "regulated inequality." Rawls argued that society was obligated to provide equal opportunities for all by implementing protections for those (i.e., the poor) from the power of dominant groups; ensuring that everyone's basic needs are met; and instituting democratic processes that allow persons, regardless of their economic, social, or political positions in society, to rise to positions of power. In Rawls' view, all changes should disproportionately benefit the poor, and only then can we accept unequal economic outcomes.

Robert Nozick, once a student of Rawls, presented a theory of justice far different from Rawls' concept of justice (1974). Building off the philosophies of Hume (1740) and Hayek (1998), Nozick developed what he called his "entitlement theory" to justice. Nozick argued that the rights to property, assets, and income are fundamental to justice. Unlike Rawls, who saw the role of government as key to delivering justice by redistributing wealth and income through its tax system, Nozick argued that justice was about a fair process. To be a just process, the transaction must adhere to three principles: justice in acquisition, transfer (i.e., must be a voluntary transfer of assets), and rectification (correcting improper means of acquisition and transfer). As long as an individual or entity has followed these three principles, there are no grounds for grievance of injustice. Those who worked the hardest or are most deserving will acquire greater wealth. This requires a minimal state, according to Novick, and is the only way that justice and freedom can thrive. Novick acknowledged that patterns of wealth (distribution) emerge over time according to hard work, luck, investments, or even gifts. He did not see this as an injustice because it may reflect people's laziness or inability to sell their labor at a high price and is among the quirks of the free market because the market does not discriminate.

Types of Justice

Issues of justice arise in different spheres of our lives and in different ways. Injustice may reflect unjust institutions, procedures, allocations, decisions, or punishment. There are different types and concepts of justice: distributive, procedural, retributive, and restorative. These types of justice have important implications for socioeconomic, political, civil, and criminal justice and are discussed below.

Distributive justice is about members of society receiving a "fair share" of the benefits and resources available. Fair allocation typically considers the total amount of goods or services to be distributed, how they will be allocated, and the pattern of distribution that results. Should benefits and services be distributed according to need, equality, or equity? The scarcer a benefit or service, the more contentious the debates will be over deciding fairness. The focus may be on economic distribution or health, education, or social benefits and services. Distributive justice considers both the outcome and the process for achieving the outcomes. Rawls' *Theory of Social Justice* is about distributive justice (1999).

MEETING NEEDS, EQUALITY, AND EQUITY—WHICH LEADS TO JUSTICE?

Need is generally something that would improve a situation or an element lacking in a situation. For example, we need to eat food for survival, so food is a need. Without access to and availability of food, our survival will be jeopardized.

Equality involves giving all people the same support to meet their needs. Everyone is given the same access to equal resources, even though some individuals or groups need greater assistance than others to access the resource available to them. The focus is on providing the same opportunities, not on outcomes.

Equity recognizes that people have different needs to achieve similar outcomes. The emphasis is on what individuals need to achieve outcomes. For instance, making accommodations for people with disabilities is based on the concept of equity.

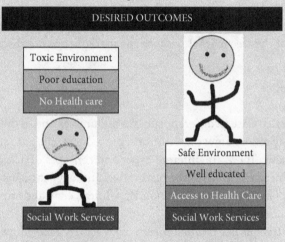

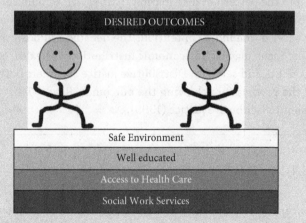

When we integrate our understanding of intersectionality into concepts of equality and equity, we must acknowledge that some individuals may have privileges that others do not. For example, if we were to provide social work services (e.g., counseling, therapy, advocacy, information, and referral) to all individuals, the services would not have the same effect for all. If you live in a safe and stable environment, are well educated, and have access to healthcare services, social work services alone may be what is needed to help you achieve the desired outcomes, such as living independently, happiness, and satisfaction in personal relationships. But if you live in a polluted community, lack access to quality healthcare, and did not complete high school, social work services alone would most likely not be enough to help you achieve the desired outcomes. The equity approach argues that we should embrace differences and provide the resources necessary for all individuals to achieve desired outcomes.

Focusing on the fairness of the process is known as **procedural justice**. Procedural justice is about whether the process for making or implementing decisions was fair. For example, procedural justice might look at whether courts make rulings without bias, the criteria for receiving benefits, or whether those affected by a policy were able to voice their opinions as the policy was being developed. Another example would be access to information—was it readily available to all affected by the decision?

Another type of justice is **retributive justice**—are people getting what they deserve (their "just deserts")? Retributive justice is generally retroactive, meaning that it typically looks at wrongdoing or past transgressions and societal responses such as punishment or penalties. Retributive justice seeks to make penalties or a punishment harsh enough as to deter actions that violate the rights of others or are against the state. Though not the intention, retributive justice can be harsher than needed, at times mimicking revenge for crimes committed. Critics have noted that this approach does not contribute to the well-being of society because both the victims and perpetrators of crimes are left with a void or anger, and sometimes are unable to contribute to society in meaningful ways.

An alternative approach to retributive justice is **restorative justice**. Whereas retributive justice sees wrongdoings as crimes against the state and its laws, restorative justice focuses on the effects of transgressions against individuals and attempts to restore wholeness to both those who have been violated and those who have committed the violation. This approach seeks to heal the wounds of those who were violated, to have offenders understand the harm they caused and take responsibility for it, and to restore the functioning of a community or individual that was harmed. It is an interactive process during which offenders, victims, and communities share their feelings and expectations to one another. This can happen on personal levels or at macro levels through victim–offender mediation programs, or truth and reconciliation commissions.

Social Work's Definition of Justice

There is no shortage of stories related to justice, particularly social justice. Curiously, social work lacks an official definition of social justice. Different social work professional associations and organizations have similar but differing definitions, and the same is generally true in the scholarly social work literature. Justice seems to be a broad concept, with social justice occupying a large portion of concern within social work. Within social work, there are also those who specialize in juvenile justice, criminal justice, racial justice, global justice, food justice, and much more.

The educational policies of the Council on Social Work Education (CSWE) specifically direct institutions of higher education in social work to develop social worker students' competency in human rights and social, economic, and environmental justice. Some see economic and environmental justice as subsets of social justice, but not all would agree. Figure 8.2 summarizes the interrelatedness of some of the types of justice.

Here are the definitions of the different types of justice offered by social work organizations.

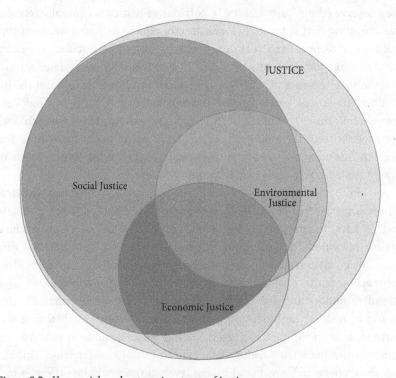

Figure 8.2. How social work categorizes types of justice.

The National Association of Social Workers (NASW) defines **social justice** as "the view that everyone deserves equal economic, political and social rights and opportunities. Social workers aim to open the doors of access and opportunity for everyone, particularly those in greatest need" (n.d., p. 2).

Environmental justice occurs when all people equally experience high levels of environmental protection and no group or community is excluded from the environmental policy decision-making process or experiences a disproportionate impact from environmental hazards. Environmental justice affirms the ecological unity and the interdependence of all species, respect for cultural and biological diversity, and the right to be free from ecological destruction. This includes responsible use of ecological resources, including land, water, air, and food (CSWE, 2022).

According to *The Social Work Dictionary* (Barker, 2013), **social justice** is "an ideal condition in which all members of society have the same basic rights, protection, opportunities, obligations, and social benefits." The Center for Economic and Social Justice (n.d.) states:

> **Social justice** encompasses **economic justice**. Social justice is the virtue which guides us in creating those organized human interactions we call institutions. In turn, social institutions, when justly organized, provide us with access to what is good for the person, both individually and in our associations with others. Social justice also imposes on each of us a personal responsibility to work with others to design and continually perfect our institutions as tools for personal and social development . . . Economic justice, which touches the individual person as well as the social order, encompasses the moral principles which guide us in designing our economic institutions. These institutions determine how each person earns a living, enters into contracts, exchanges goods and services with others and otherwise produces an independent material foundation for his or her economic sustenance. The ultimate purpose of economic justice is to free each person to engage creatively in the unlimited work beyond economics, that of the mind and the spirit.

Challenges of Defining Justice

Why is it so important that we define justice and the types of justice? Social justice is a core value of social work, and justice-oriented social work practice has roots in the early history of the profession. Without a clear sense of what social work strives to achieve, the profession runs the risk of ambiguous and conflicting translations of the conceptualizations of social justice into practice. How we define social justice also affects the type of social welfare system we build.

Social work was founded in reaction to the harsh conditions that people lived in over 100 years ago. Walter Trattner, a social welfare historian, describes the social environment of the time:

American cities were disorderly, filthy, foul-smelling, disease-ridden places. Narrow, unpaved streets became transformed into quagmires when it rained. Rickety tenements, swarming with unwashed humanity, leaned upon one another for support. Inadequate drainage systems failed to carry away sewage. Pigs roamed streets that were cluttered with manure, years of accumulated garbage, and other litter. Outside privies bordered almost every thoroughfare. Slaughterhouses and fertilizing plants contaminated the air with an indescribable stench. Ancient plagues like smallpox, cholera, and typhus threw the population into a state of terror from time to time while less sensational but equally deadly killers like tuberculosis, diphtheria, and scarlet fever were ceaselessly at work. (Trattner, 2007, p. 57)

In reaction to this situation, early social workers were drawn to the profession from a moral obligation to improve lives. They focused on changing the behavior of individuals. Others viewed the squalid living conditions as a call to reform the socioeconomic structures in the society that left the majority of people living in survival mode while only a few profited from the labor and toil of the working class and poor.

Inherent in the history of social work are these dual definitions of social justice. One approach emphasized giving individuals the opportunity and assistance to improve themselves, while the latter definition sought to change the systems and structures within our society to produce more equitable outcomes. Over the years, we have grown to understand that the social and economic problems of an individual often reflect the problems of not just one individual but also of those in similar circumstances. For example, an individual whose children are being removed by the authorities due to neglect is most likely to be someone who needs financial assistance, emotional and social support, and perhaps shelter and food for their family. To help this person, we need to change the system so that parents are not threatened by the removal of their children due to insufficient resources by advocating for affordable housing, preventing eviction, developing employment programs and job opportunities, and providing affordable childcare, child support, and tax credits.

If we advocate to access benefits only for those with whom we work within the existing system, then we are perpetuating current systems. Many within social work may argue that this is not social justice. More often, though, social justice in social work calls for systemic reallocation of resources within a society toward the realization of equitable outcomes. This has pitted social workers who utilize micro approaches (e.g., working with individuals, families, and small groups to help manage mental, emotional, social, behavioral, and financial challenges that are negatively affecting their well-being and quality of life) against those who use macro approaches (e.g., addressing the challenge of alleviating societal problems to improve the quality of life locally, nationally, and internationally through advocacy, community organizing, program development, and policymaking). In a rights-based approach to social work practice, there is no dichotomy, because all social workers strive for the realization of human rights for all, regardless of the main method utilized.

TIME FOR REFLECTION AND DISCUSSION

1. What is your concept of justice? Do you know someone who has a different concept of justice? How do your differing views of justice affect your views on politics and current events?
2. How do different concepts of justice affect contemporary U.S. society? What about societies outside of the United States?
3. Should we work toward a common concept of justice or learn to live with alternative definitions in our society? Why?
4. How do concepts of justice affect social work practice in an increasingly diverse society?

Defining Justice

This book helps learners understand how we can integrate a human rights-based approach to achieve justice. **Justice is defined as the fulfilment of human rights**. When governments protect, respect, and fulfill the human rights of people, justice is served. Throughout the ensuing chapters, readers will learn how to apply a rights-based approach to current social issues and to understand what makes a social issue just or unjust. Readers will learn to apply rights, as articulated in international human rights instruments, to social issues.

Social Workers and the Fight for Justice

At the core of social work is the fight for justice. The NASW, the CSWE, the International Federation of Social Workers, and the International

Association of Schools of Social Work all highlight justice as a primary value and function of social work. The NASW's most recent Code of Ethics (2021) states, "Social workers promote social justice and social change" (Preamble, Par. 2), particularly with and on behalf of vulnerable and oppressed individuals and groups of people.

From its inception, the social work profession sought to introduce a revision of societal resources to serve justice. The settlement house movement, one of the predecessors to the social work profession, viewed charity-based methods as perpetuating the status quo. Charity-based approaches come from a tradition of acting to fulfill God's commandments and acts of kindness. Charity-based approaches were criticized as paternalistic and preaching morals. In time, however, the settlement house movement came to appreciate the importance of working directly with individuals as well as fighting for structural reforms. Likewise, the other half of the social work ancestry, the charity organization societies, came to understand the limitations of the charity-based approach and began to advocate for structural changes. Merging the two movements formed the social work profession.

Social work pioneers such as Ellen Gates Staff, Lillian Wald, Florence Kelley, Grace Abbott, and Jane Addams fought for the social and economic reforms that they deemed necessary to stop further economic inequality and dissolution of community from occurring (Reisch & Garvin, 2016). Much of their work focused on specific social issues, such as child welfare, juvenile justice, public health, sanitation, housing, and consumer safety, and they allied with feminists, trade unionists, civil rights activists, and radicals outside of social work (Reisch & Andrews, 2002). The accomplishments of these and other pioneers were plentiful in the first few decades of the 20th century. Yet, to a certain extent, the tensions between the charity-based and rights-based approaches were not fully resolved within the profession. Were social workers professional extensions of the philanthropists who sought to help the deserving among the needy? Or were social workers advocates for justice in a society that left too many people without adequate food, security, income, and shelter, while others accumulated assets far beyond their needs? Should social workers be reforming individuals or society?

While social work pioneers wrestled with these issues and the social problems of the day, they had a blind eye when it came to racial, gender, and ethnic marginalization. According to Foner, social work emerged during the most "thoroughly racialized . . . point in American history" (1999, pp. 12–13). Yet social work's pioneers largely ignored the exclusion and denial of rights to a significant portion of the U.S. population (Reisch & Garvin, 2016). While social workers advocated equal opportunities for all, they did not address the barring of people by color, gender, or ethnic stereotyping that was embedded in U.S. institutions by then. The focus was on specific issues rather than on class or race.

Given our heightened awareness of racism and oppression in recent years (including violence and other actions against others, particularly against Black, Indigenous peoples, and other people of color [BIPOC]), NASW strengthened its Code of Ethics (2021) to read "Social workers **must** [emphasis added] take action against oppression, racism, discrimination, and inequities, and acknowledge personal privilege" (Standard 1.05(b)). This is the only standard in the Code of Ethics that is mandated. This revision makes clear that it is not optional or normative but a required responsibility for social workers to act against oppression, racism, discrimination, and inequities and to acknowledge personal privilege. It also makes clear that being non-racist is no longer enough. Social workers must also be anti-racist and committed to take actions that will restructure society in ways that make the society anti-racist.

NASW went further and issued a statement on June 17, 2021, apologizing for past practices in American social work:

WASHINGTON, D.C.—As the nation looks at its long, cruel history of systemic racism, the National Association of Social Workers (NASW) acknowledges that our profession and this association have not always lived up to our mission of pursuing social justice for all. NASW apologizes for supporting policies and activities that have harmed people of color.

"The murder of George Floyd at the hands of police in the early months of the pandemic spurred our country and NASW to directly address the effects of racism in our social institutions and among social workers," said NASW CEO Angelo McClain, PhD, LICSW. "While NASW continues to offer anti-racist training in communities, publicly denounces violence and advocates tirelessly for anti-racist policy changes, we must also acknowledge the role the social work profession has played in supporting discriminatory systems and programs for decades."

For instance:
- Progressive Era social workers built and ran segregated settlement houses
- Social worker suffragists blocked African Americans from gaining the right to vote
- Prominent social workers supported eugenics theories and programs
- Social workers helped recruit Black men into the infamous Tuskegee Experiment
- Social workers participated in the removal of Native American children from their families and placement in boarding schools

- Social workers also took part in intake teams at Japanese internment camps during World War II
- And since the founding of the profession, bias among some social workers has limited delivery of healthcare, mental health treatment and social services to people of color.

These and other examples are uncomfortable truths. But they also reinforce our commitment to ending racism in the social work field and working with strong coalition partners to dismantle oppressive and racist policies, systems, and practices across our country. Social workers are called by our Code of Ethics to fight injustice in all its forms and to honor the dignity and worth of all people. While we at times have fallen short of this ideal, our profession has recently reinvigorated and expanded its racial equity mandate. Details of this work are included in the newly released report, *Undoing Racism through Social Work: NASW Report to the Profession on Racial Justice Priorities and Action*.

"NASW, the social work profession, and our society have made much progress on achieving racial equity in the last few generations, but there is still a long, challenging road ahead," NASW President Mildred "Mit" Joyner, DPS, MSW, LCSW, said. "Be assured that NASW will not tire in our quest to help our nation eliminate racism and achieve justice and liberation for all Americans."[1]Around the world, history is full of stories of social workers who stood up for what was right, but there also are too many times that social workers failed to serve justice. In part, this is because as social workers, we often work for governments or for agencies that are funded by governments. Or perhaps we work for programs that are funded by wealthy, influential people. To please employers, social workers may take on their boss' vision of how society should look, ignoring the disrespect or harm it may cause to the well-being of the population we are trying to assist. Many times, this is because social workers, at all levels of practice, seek to implement public policies and programs (whether they are working in public and private organizations) that seek to maintain the status quo. At times, the best interests of the populations served may conflict with the existing public policy goals. And as a result, despite the best intentions of social workers to help others, social workers also have a record of being on the wrong side of justice in history.

Below are two examples of times when social workers did not stand up for justice. There are many others. These examples are provided to give you an opportunity to reflect on the conflicting roles social workers sometimes find themselves in and to think about how you may have acted in the situations described.

BEING JUST IN SOCIAL WORK PRACTICE

After reading these two examples, consider:

- What kinds of similar conflicts might social workers find themselves in today?
- What do you think you would do: Would you serve the population you are working with by following the law? Would you serve justice? Or . . .?
- What human rights were violated in each case example?

EXAMPLE 1: MCCARTHYISM AND SOCIAL WORK

McCarthyism, named after its founder, Senator Joseph McCarthy, was a vociferous campaign against communism in the United States that began in the mid-1940s and lasted through 1960. Fearing that the growth in government-sponsored social welfare would lead the United States to adopt communism, people in many professions, including social work, reported to the FBI the names of colleagues they suspected of being communists. The accused were blacklisted or lost their jobs, even though most did **not** belong to the Communist Party.

McCarthyism was a reaction to President Franklin Roosevelt's New Deal in 1935, which ushered in a large expansion of publicly funded social services. Social workers were among those who enthusiastically supported the New Deal, but others saw the growth in government as an invasion into private lives and livelihoods (Andrews & Reisch, 1997). The expansion of public social services brought many job opportunities for social workers and drove the growth of the profession. After World War II and the start of the Cold War, social welfare expansion became equated with the growth of communism. McCarthyism grew from these fears.

The shadow of the Great Depression accentuated worries of losing one's job as McCarthyism spread. Social workers' fear of becoming unemployed and the newness of social work as a profession during this postwar period led to a general passivity by social workers and social work associations on the key social issues of the day (Andrews & Reisch, 1997). Promoting a professional identity took precedence over advocating for welfare benefits and civil rights and planted the seeds for direct social work practice to dominate other forms of social practice such as activism, community work, group work, and policy (Gatenio Gabel et al., 2022). Social workers felt that pursuing social reform and advocacy could easily be mistaken as supporting socialism and communism during this period.

During McCarthyism, many social workers refused to sign so-called loyalty oaths and lost their jobs. Social workers who were active in labor unions found themselves removed from leadership positions. Social workers who had been prominent members of the New Deal coalition or the rank-and-file movement of the 1930s were particularly vulnerable (Fisher, 1936). Social workers were fired from university faculties and major nonprofit social service organizations. Several social work scholars had their work censored or rejected for publication by leading journals because they were believed to be or to support communists. Bertha Capen Reynolds, the Associate Dean of the School of Social Work at Smith College and one of the most influential social work scholars of the period, lost her position and was backlisted into the 1960s for her left-leaning politics (Leighninger, 2004). Both the NASW and the CSWE assisted the FBI in its investigation of social workers suspected of supporting communism.

And so, during this period when human rights were seriously threatened in the United States, the profession that names the pursuit of justice as core to its mission largely looked away. As a former colleague of mine reminds us, "Social work's progressive roots only seem to flourish in the sunlight. When darkness overtakes the land, we hunker down and neither curse that darkness nor light a candle" (Newdom, 1994, p. 75).

EXAMPLE 2: CHILD WELFARE WORKERS AND AMERICAN INDIAN CHILDREN

Beginning in late 1800s, state and federal policies sought to weaken American Indian tribal and family structures. Tribal and family structures were destabilized and many families became impoverished because reservations were frequently located far from hunting grounds or were unsuitable for agriculture (Thiebeault & Spencer, 2019). During the 1890s the federal government began to remove American Indian children from their families to attend boarding schools. The intent was for them to assimilate into White culture. Social workers and church personnel were typically the ones who removed the children and placed them in the boarding schools.

Resistance eventually made boarding school placements less popular, so a new effort to assimilate American Indian children into White culture was introduced in 1958. The Child Welfare League of American contracted with the U.S. Bureau of Indian Affairs (BIA) to carry out the Indian Adoption Project (IAP). Concerned about the rising rates of unmarried Native American women who were giving birth to children but lacked the resources to care for them (Jacobs, 2013), the IAP was an effort to "rescue" Native American children by placing them for adoption by White families. Social workers in conjunction with the BIA identified mothers and mothers-to-be, arranged for them to surrender their children, and then placed the children with White adoptive parents (Jacobs, 2013).

Placing children in boarding schools or with White adoptive families all too often resulted in permanently severing the connection between American Indian children and their families and tribes. In the boarding schools, the American Indian children had their long hair cut, were punished for speaking their native languages, were forbidden from using the names they were given at birth, and were taught to reject their tribal beliefs, identity, culture, and families. Many families struggled for years to regain their children, and too many were unable to regain custody (Jacobs, 2013). In adolescence, the Native American children experienced alarming rates of chemical dependency, suicide, and mental illness. As adults, many were unable to return to their Native American communities because they no longer felt they belonged, nor were they able to live in White society. The removed children, their families, and their tribes have never fully recovered from the severed relationships, broken ties to their culture, and lost years. And yet, the practice seems to continue: In 2016, American Indian children were over three times more likely to be in an out-of-home placement than White children (Landers, 2016).

Social workers were the ones implementing these colonialist policies. Relatively little resistance was heard from social workers and social work institutions on the traumatic and tragic removal of children from their families and culture (Thiebeault & Spencer, 2019). In fact, research has shown that social workers, believing they knew what was best for the children, promulgated negative and hurtful stereotypes of American Indians as alcoholics and dysfunctional people who were unable to care for their children (Jacobs, 2013).

In response to the unwarranted removal of Indian children from their families and tribal communities, in 1978 Congress enacted the **Indian Child Welfare Act** (ICWA). The ICWA recognized tribal sovereignty and acknowledged that tribal courts were in the best position to make decisions regarding the interests of American Indian children. ICWA required that efforts be made to keep Indian families together, including providing at-risk families with social supports; when it was deemed necessary to remove an American Indian child from the home, the child must be placed with extended family or tribal members whenever possible (Thiebeault & Spencer, 2019).

Despite the protections of the ICWA, a disproportionate number of Indian children continued to be removed from their homes and placed in non-Indian homes. One of the reasons for this is that child welfare workers, who are often social workers, are unfamiliar with the ICWA and do not know about the requirement that children be placed with extended family or tribal members. If we are committed to pursuing justice, then we must seek the knowledge needed to understand situations beyond what is readily available to us.

TIME FOR EXERCISE

- Identify an issue of justice being debated today. Explore the social work position on the issue.
- Have different social work organizations taken the same position, or does it vary?
- What type(s) of justice is being pursued, and by whom?
- What theory of justice or method of justice rests behind the justice pursued?
- How do you feel about the social work position?

CHAPTER 9

Social Justice

Since the beginning of the profession, social work has claimed social justice as an organizing value and guide for practice (Marsh, 2005). Even before social work became a profession, the prominence of social justice as a concern and impetus for social work can be traced to the settlement house movement in the late 1800s and early 20th century, one of the forebearers of the profession. The centrality of social justice in social work was reinforced by the emergence of social justice as a critical concern in American life more generally during the Progressive Era. Social justice often counters humankind's unfortunate propensities for greed, power, and physical and economic violence. It is a reaction to exploitation and oppression. Like all forms of justice, social justice is contextualized within history, culture, time, and human social relations.

The National Association of Social Workers (NASW)'s Code of Ethics prominently situates social justice within social work. The significance of social justice in the framing of social work professional standards and practices distinguishes social work from other helping professions and guides social work goals and practices. The preamble to the 2021 Code of Ethics establishes that social workers are responsible for promoting social justice and identifies it as one of the six core values driving the profession's mission (National Association of Social Workers, 2021). Social justice is again identified three times under social workers' ethical responsibility to the broader society—one of the six ethical standards relevant to the professional activities of all social workers (National Association of Social Workers, 2021, Ethical Standards). Social workers are charged with advocating for living conditions "that are compatible with the realization

A Human Rights-Based Approach to Justice in Social Work Practice. Shirley Gatenio Gabel, Oxford University Press.
© Oxford University Press 2024. DOI: 10.1093/oso/9780197570647.003.0009

of social justice" and promoting policies and practices "that safeguard the rights of and confirm equity and social justice for all people" (National Association of Social Workers, 2021, Ethical Standards, 6).

Despite the distinction of social justice in the Code, social justice is not defined in the document. The ambiguity of the term is common throughout most of the social work literature (Morgraine, 2014; Nicotera, 2019). As discussed in our previous chapter, it is not uncommon for multiple concepts of justice to coexist. However, the meaning of social justice varies widely within the profession. Some feel that because social justice is a driving goal in social work, this ambiguity of its meaning can be problematic.

Social justice is also a key concept in the Council on Social Work Education (CSWE)'s Educational Policy and Accreditation Standards (EPAS). The most recent EPAS version grounds social justice, along with economic and environmental justice, as central to the profession and practice: "Social workers understand that ethics are informed by principles of human rights and apply them toward realizing social, racial, economic, and environmental justice in their practice" (Council on Social Work Education, 2022, EPAS, Competency 1). The 2022 EPAS version includes nine competencies (competencies are the knowledge, values, skills, and cognitive and affective processes social work students must be able to integrate and apply in practice).

To be accredited, social work educational programs must provide evidence that students have demonstrated the level of competence necessary for professional practice. The second EPAS competency requires social work programs to advance human rights and social, racial, economic, and environmental justice in their curriculum. Social work educational programs must train students to "critically evaluate the distribution of power and privilege in society to promote social, racial, economic, and environmental justice by reducing inequities and ensuring dignity and respect for all" (Council on Social Work Education, 2022, EPAS, Competency 2). Competency 5 requires programs to prepare students to "use social justice, anti-racist, and anti-oppressive lenses to assess how social welfare policies affect the delivery of and access to social services" and to "apply critical thinking to analyze, formulate, and advocate for policies that advance human rights and social, racial, economic, and environmental justice" (Council on Social Work Education, 2022, EPAS, Competency 5).

Both the NASW Code of Ethics and the CSWE EPAS drive social work practice and responsibilities. The CSWE EPAS differentiates the concept of social justice from economic and environmental justice, and it also links human rights to justice. In the CSWE EPAS, the promotion and realization of human rights are identified as a vehicle to achieve justice in our society.

Defining Social Justice

In this book, we define social justice as the realization of social rights. Social rights are defined and protected in the International Covenant on Economic, Social and Cultural Rights (ICESCR). They include the rights to social security, protection of the family, an adequate standard of living (including freedom from hunger, access to clean water, adequate housing, and protection of property), and mental and physical health.

SOCIAL RIGHTS IN THE ICESCR

According to the ICESCR, everyone has the right "to social security, including social insurance" (ICESCR, Article 9). The right to social security includes the right to access and maintain benefits without discrimination to help secure protection from lack of work-related income, unaffordable access to healthcare, and insufficient family support (in the case of children and adult dependents) (ICESCR, 2008, General Comment No. 19, para. 2). Governments have an obligation to develop a national strategy to fully implement the right to social security (ICESCR, General Comment No. 19, 2008, para. 2).

The ICESCR specifies that the following rights must be guaranteed for an individual or community to have an adequate standard of living:

The Right to Food (Article 11(2)) means that food must be available in a quantity and quality sufficient to satisfy dietary needs, must be safe and culturally appropriate, and must be accessible without interfering with other human rights.

The Right to Water (Articles 11 and 12) is not explicitly mentioned in the ICESCR but is generally interpreted as necessary to fulfill the rights to an adequate standard of living and health (ICESCR, General Comment No. 15, 2008, para. 3). Individuals and communities have a right to safe, affordable, clean, and physically accessible water for personal and domestic uses. States have an obligation to make water available for personal and domestic use to prevent starvation and disease as needed for one's health. A related duty of governments is to ensure that everyone has access to **adequate sanitation**, which is crucial to protecting the quality of the water supply.

The Right to Housing (Article 11) goes beyond the right to have a roof over one's head and includes the right to live in peace and dignity, with security from outside. Housing is considered adequate if (1) it protects from forced eviction and harassment; (2) provides access to facilities essential for health, safety, comfort, and nutrition; (3) is affordable without compromising other basic needs; (4) is habitable; (5) is in a location allowing access to social services; and (6) allows individuals to express their cultural identity.

The Right to Health (Article 12(1)) is implied by the right to "the enjoyment of the highest attainable standard of physical and mental health." The ICESCR identifies the following four steps for governments to take to realize the right to health: (1) reduce the stillbirth rate and infant mortality and provide for the healthy development of children; (2) improve all aspects of environmental and industrial hygiene; (3) prevent, treat, and control disease; and (4) develop resources needed to provide all with medical attention in the event of sickness.

The ICESCR obliges governments to provide "the widest possible protection and assistance" to the family, especially when the family is "responsible for the care and education of dependent children" (ICESCR, Article 10). This allows for varied interpretations of government responsibility, which most often includes ensuring the safety and well-being of families and children. This often includes special protection for mothers for a reasonable time before and after childbirth by providing maternity leave with pay or adequate social security benefits (ICESCR, Article 8(2)).

In addition to the ICESCR, social rights are upheld by a strong stand against discrimination articulated across the international human rights legal documents. Beginning with the Universal Declaration of Human Rights (UDHR), freedom from discrimination (Article 2) resonates throughout all major human rights treaties to ensure that the equality of all human beings is secured, as stated in Article 1 of the UDHR. Non-discrimination is the central theme of two core instruments: the International Convention on the Elimination of All Forms of Racial Discrimination (CERD) and the Convention on the Elimination of All Forms of Discrimination against Women (CEDAW). The CERD treaty prohibits policies that have a discriminatory impact on people of color, even where there is no intent to discriminate. CERD embodies an obligation to affirmatively address racial disparities in outcomes for people of color, both within government programs at all levels of government—federal, state, and local—and in society at large, and to redress past discriminatory practices and current outcomes. CEDAW has similar provisions regarding gender discrimination.

The Human Rights Committee on the International Covenant on Civil and Political Rights (ICCPR) states that discrimination

as used in the Covenant should be understood to imply any distinction, exclusion, restriction or preference which is based on any ground such as race, colour, sex, language, religion, political or other opinion, national or social origin, property, birth or other status, and which has the purpose or effect of nullifying or impairing the recognition, enjoyment or exercise by all persons, on an equal footing, of all rights and freedoms. (United Nations Compilation of General Comments, p. 134, para. 1)

The Committee notes that "the enjoyment of rights and freedoms on an equal footing . . . does not mean identical treatment in every instance" (United Nations Compilation of General Comments, p. 134, para. 1), referring to circumstances, for example, when women and children should be treated differently.

Other major human rights instruments that reinforce non-discrimination are:

- International Covenant on Civil and Political Rights (1966)
- Convention against Torture and other Cruel, Inhuman or Degrading Treatment or Punishment (1984)
- Convention on the Rights of the Child (1989)
- International Convention on the Protection of the Rights of All Migrant Workers and Members of Their Families (1990)
- UN Declaration on the Rights of Persons belonging to National or Ethnic, Religious and Linguistic Minorities (1992)
- Convention on the Rights of Persons with Disabilities (2006)
- UN Declaration on the Rights of Indigenous Peoples (2007)

Similar provisions are part of the European Social Charter (Article 12) and the American Declaration (Article XVI).

We cite human rights in international, regional, and domestic laws and demonstrate how shortcomings to achieving human rights are violations. As social work practitioners, we should know how to find the laws documenting our rights and be able to explain the laws and rights to the people whose rights may be compromised. We engage in social justice efforts by achieving social rights, whether working with individuals, families, groups, communities, or institutions or at the policy level or conducting research.

SOCIAL JUSTICE AND SOCIAL WORK

Social justice should drive the work we do as social workers. To achieve social justice, we work alongside service users, colleagues, and partners beyond social work, such as community members, community organizers, nonprofit organizations, elected officials, and activists. Although social justice has been an integral part of social work since the inception of the profession, many have argued that in the latter part of the 20th century, an emphasis on clinical social work mitigated the importance of social justice in practice (Specht and Courtney, 1994; Asakura & Maurer, 2018). Several scholars have accused the profession of historical amnesia concerning the rich history of social workers as political actors, ethical resisters, activists, and organizers from critics within the profession (Specht, 1991; Abramovitz, 1998; Reisch & Andrews, 2002; Bowles & Hopps, 2014). Neglecting the role of social justice in our social work practice threatens to steer the profession further away from the course of social justice.

Social Justice Issues Today

Unlike the situation in many other related helping professions, social justice sits conspicuously at the center of social work, regardless of who we are working with and what level of practice we are engaged in. New social justice issues arise all the time depending on events around the world and as we grow in our understanding of the causes and implications of social issues.

COVID-19 and Social Justice

COVID-19 affected all of us but brought greater suffering and hardship for some. As of 2022, there were more than 270 million reported cases of COVID-19 worldwide and many more unreported cases. Over 5 million people died from COVID-19, and the actual death toll is believed to be much higher than reported. COVID-19 affected all people, at all income levels, in all places, and of all ages, but it hit hardest in those with access to fewer resources, in countries with fewer resources, and among those whose health was less robust. People of color, low-income individuals, older adults, and persons with compromising health conditions were the most vulnerable. Sadly, access to vaccines penalized rather than prioritized the most vulnerable populations.

The pandemic offered opportunities for global solidarity led by science but instead gave rise to geopolitical infighting and fragmented action favoring the educated, those with resources, and those with good health. People who had the least voice bore the heaviest repercussions of the pandemic. Although talks are under way to better prepare for future pandemics and health crises, much more should be happening to strengthen collective capacities for prevention of, preparedness for, and response to future health threats through new financing instruments, surveillance and detection, and new partnerships to battle disinformation and misinformation.

The disparities in terms of who got sick, who died, who was vaccinated, and who had access to information about prevention, causes, and treatment were notable around the globe and within the United States (Figure 9.1). The highest percentage of COVID-19 cases occurred among non-Hispanic White people. However, racial and ethnic minority groups were disproportionately infected with COVID-19. Among non-Hispanic White people, the average percentage of those testing positive for COVID-19 was 7 percent, compared to 13.8 percent for Blacks, 11.9 percent for Latinx, and 7.2 percent for Asians. Black, Latinx, American Indian, and Alaska Native persons in the United States were also more likely to have higher COVID-19-related hospitalization and death rates than non-Hispanic White populations (Centers for Disease Control and Prevention, 2021).

Why were Blacks and Latinx almost twice as likely than Whites to experience COVID and more vulnerable to hospitalization and death than Whites? The COVID-19 pandemic disproportionately affected many racial and ethnic minority groups because of the conditions in which people are born, grow, live, work, and age. These circumstances, also known as social determinants of health, are largely shaped by the distribution of money, power, and resources at global, national, and local levels. Social determinants of health contribute to most health inequities within and between countries, which could be remedied if resources were made available.

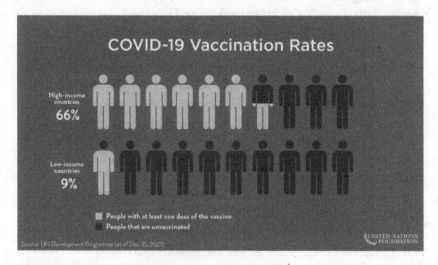

Figure 9.1. Differences in COVID-19 vaccination rates.
Material courtesy of the United Nations Foundation. © 2021 United Nations Foundation.

For example, several studies have shown that people in racial and ethnic minority groups are more likely to live in areas with high rates of COVID-19 infection (Millet et al., 2020; Lewis et al., 2020). The likelihood of transmission is affected by the conditions that people live in. Crowded conditions and unstable housing can hinder COVID-19 prevention strategies like hygiene measures, self-isolation, or self-quarantine, thus increasing the likelihood of infection.

During the COVID-19 pandemic, the unemployment rate was highest for racial and ethnic minorities and persons living in households earning less than $40,000 annually (Galea & Abdalla, 2020). The unemployment rates of Black and Latino workers were higher than those of Whites and Asian employees before and during the pandemic. For example, in the third quarter of 2020, the unemployment rate for Black men 16+ years old was 13.8 percent compared to 7.4 percent for White men. Moreover, job losses during the first half of 2020 occurred disproportionately among Black, Latino, and Asian groups (Goldman et al., 2021). Unemployment increases the risk of eviction, homelessness, or living in crowded spaces with a friend or family—factors that raise transmission rates.

Another factor contributing to higher transmission rates among some groups is the disproportionate representation of racial and ethnic minority groups in essential work settings such as healthcare facilities, farms, factories, warehouses, food processing plants, accommodation and food services, retail services, grocery stores, and public transportation (Centers for Disease Control and Prevention, 2021). Individuals in such essential work settings are more likely to become infected because they have close contact with the public or other workers and use public transportation to commute to work. They are also more likely to work when sick because they do not have paid sick days (Economic Policy Institute, 2020).

Latino and Black workers are also overrepresented in less skilled, frontline occupations associated with high risk, are less likely to be able to work from home, and are more likely to be exposed to COVID-19 without adequate protections (Goldman et al., 2021). Non-Hispanic Black adults were 60 percent more likely than non-Hispanic White adults to live in households with healthcare workers, and 64 percent of Hispanic workers lived in households with at least one worker who was unable to work from home (compared with 56.5 percent among non-Hispanic Black adults and 46.6 percent among non-Hispanic White adults) (Alobuia et al., 2020).

Once infected, members of racial and minority groups were more likely to be hospitalized for COVID-19 than non-Hispanic Whites. Non-Hispanic American Indians or Alaska Natives were 3.1 times more likely to be hospitalized than non-Hispanic Whites, Blacks were 2.4 times more likely, and Hispanics were 2.3 times more likely (Centers for Disease Control and Prevention, 2022). The increased hospitalization rates in racial and minority groups may also reflect limited access to preventive health measures because of lack of transportation or childcare, inability to take time off work, communication and language barriers, cultural differences between patients and providers, lack of a usual source of care, and discrimination in healthcare systems. Another factor contributing to higher rates of infections and hospitalizations are underlying medical conditions that increase the risk for severe illness from COVID-19, which may be more common among people from racial and ethnic minority groups (Centers for Disease Control and Prevention, 2022).

Adding to this are the lower and slower vaccination rates among racial and ethnic minorities that increased the risk of COVID infection. Bayati et al. (2021) identified three themes that affected inequities in the uptake of the COVID-19 vaccine: (1) the pervasive mistreatment of Black and Latinx communities; (2) distrust due to historical experiences and lack of trusted messengers and messages, choice, social support, and diversity; and (3) structural barriers to vaccination access. Vaccine hesitancy, defined as the delay in accepting or refusing immunization despite availability, is highest among Black and Latinx people (Bazan & Akgun, 2021). Much of this is based on the mistrust of the healthcare system and clinical research on the part of Black and other minority communities. You may be familiar with the Tuskegee study, in which, to study the natural progression of syphilis, scientists withheld curative treatment from hundreds of Black men for decades after penicillin was discovered. This is just one example of how the exploitation of the Black community in science has resulted in distrust of government health directives.

Another factor contributing to lower vaccine rates is the longstanding systemic disparities in access to technology and literacy. Vaccine scheduling heavily relied on mobile apps and internet portals. Inequitable access to technology and lower technological literacy augmented the existing inequities for lower-income, older, and immigrant populations.

Using a rights-based approach to social justice, we seek to better understand the effects of COVID-19 policies on different populations. A human rights approach directs us to understand how the rights of different people were furthered or violated because of the policies and actions implemented during the pandemic. Of course, all rights are interrelated, but we begin by identifying which human rights are most pertinent to this issue.

The right to health is a fundamental human right. We begin by looking at the UDHR. The right to health is mentioned as part of the right to an adequate standard of living (Article 25). Two other human rights articulated in the UDHR are also essential in understanding COVID's effects and disparate outcomes: the right to life (Article 3) and the right to social security (Article 22). The right to social security focuses on the responsibility of a government to fulfill the economic, social, and cultural rights that are indispensable for its members to live in dignity and the free development of their personalities.

We also must consider the ICESCR because it specifies our social, economic, and cultural rights. Unlike the UDHR, which is a non-binding declaration, countries have chosen to ratify the ICESCR and ratification gives the force of law to our social, economic, and cultural rights. The United States has not ratified the ICESCR for reasons discussed in Chapter 5.

USING A RIGHTS-BASED FRAME TO JUSTICE IN SOCIAL WORK

1. Identify the social issue, who is affected, the scope, and how people are affected.
2. What are the most relevant human rights related to this issue that are not being upheld?
3. What international human rights instruments specifically address human rights violations? Start with the UDHR and then explore relevant treaties that have been ratified, such as the ICESCR, ICPPR, International Conference on Population and Development (ICPD), Convention on the Rights of the Child (CRC), and CEDAW.
4. Reframe the social issue as a social rights issue—for instance, denying girls an education that is equal to one offered to boys violates the human rights of girls as specified in the ICESCR (Article x), ICPPR (Article x), ICPD, and the CRC (Article x).
5. Advocate for a change!

Which articles of the ICESCR do you think are most relevant to better understanding the effects of COVID-19? Article 12, the right to health, and Article 9, the right to social security, are key. Depending on your interests, you may want to include other articles as well. ICESCR includes other articles critical to our understanding of justice from a rights-based approach. Article 2 asserts that social, economic, and cultural rights must be achieved without discrimination regarding race, color, sex, language, religion, political or other opinions, national or social origin, property, birth, or other status. Article 10 states that governments need to be particularly protective and responsible for the well-being of children and youth, regardless of a child's background.

The difference in health outcomes by race and ethnicity lead us to question whether discriminatory practices led to these disparate outcomes. Could the U.S. government have done more? Did it act in discriminatory ways, knowingly or unknowingly? The emphasis on non-discrimination is a strong feature of the ICCPR. Governments are called upon to prevent, protect against, and punish discriminatory actions. As stated in Article 26 of the ICCPR:

> All persons are equal before the law and are entitled without any discrimination to the equal protection of the law. In this respect, the law shall prohibit any discrimination and guarantee to all persons equal and effective protection against discrimination on any grounds such as race, colour, sex, language, religion, political or other opinion, national or social origin, property, birth, or other status.

The ICCPR and the International Convention on the Elimination of All Forms of Racial Discrimination (CERD) are two of the three international human rights conventions the United States has ratified. The Convention regulates in some detail the obligations of States to eliminate racial discrimination. Listed in Article 5 are the principal civil, political, economic, social, and cultural rights that must be enjoyed "without distinction as to race, colour, or national or ethnic origin" (CERD, 1965). CERD is important in the United States because it is one of the few human rights treaties the United States has ratified. If discriminatory practices are demonstrated, CERD can be applied to social rights (the United States has not ratified ICESCR). Regarding COVID-19, centuries of systemic inequities have created vast disparities in infection rates, access to health services, and outcomes.

This is important to our analysis of COVID-19 policies and practices because the resulting disparities in health, access to vaccines, and information about COVID-19 reflect the systematic violation of social rights of racial and ethnic minority populations in the United States. Governments have the responsibility to ensure everyone's rights to health, life, and social security. Many U.S. policies perpetuate racial and ethnic inequities. By not addressing these inequities, the government failed to protect and promote the rights of all Americans. Knowing this and not acting to remedy the situation perpetuates discrimination, which is a violation of rights as articulated in Article 26 of the ICCPR, Articles 2 and 5 of the CERD, and Articles 3, 22, and 25 of the UDHR. Not addressing these inequities is a human rights violation and a social justice issue that, as social workers, we choose to challenge.

Having identified the human rights violated, our next step would be to advocate for the changes needed for our rights to be realized. COVID-19 shined a light on the disparate outcomes that result from the discrimination embedded in our systems in the United States. It took hundreds of years to develop this complex system, meaning that efforts to rebuild a just system will need to drill deep; at the same time, other interdependent systems will need to change as well. In other words, changing the health-care system will not get at the root of the problem without simultaneous changes in education, economic, policing, child welfare, social welfare, and other systems.

Where would you begin?

Poverty

The global pandemic also wreaked havoc on our collective efforts to erad-icate poverty and create a more prosperous and healthier planet for all. Around the world, we have been making good progress on reducing the number of people who live in poverty, particularly in extreme poverty. COVID-19 reversed that trend. It is projected that nearly 150 million individuals were pushed back into extreme poverty in 2021 due to the compounding effects of COVID-19 (Sanchez-Paramo et al., 2021). Many of these people live in fragile, conflict-prone, climate-risk environments, making the challenge even harder. Countries bearing the greatest burdens and setbacks are those least able to respond due to their limited domestic resources and high debt burdens. In the United States and worldwide, pov-erty is concentrated among people of color. The intersectionality of race and ethnicity, plus poverty, is critical to informing social work practice.

Sex and Gender

The international human rights legal framework contains instruments to combat discrimination, including discrimination against indigenous peo-ples, migrants, minorities, people with disabilities, women, race and reli-gion, and sexual orientation and gender identity. Discrimination based on gender is common despite the progress made in many countries. Laws still exist that deny women the right to inherit marital property, the right to inherit as men do, and the right to work and travel without their husbands' permission—along with many others. Women continue to be subject to violent and abusive practices, which are unabated in many countries, and they thus often suffer intersectional discrimination because of their race or origin and because they are women.

In the United States, gender equality related to compensation at work is a significant issue. Despite progress, women who work full time in the United States are still paid just 83 cents to every dollar earned by men, and the consequences of this gap affect women throughout their lives. The pay gap persists into retirement. As a result of lower lifetime earnings, women, on average, receive 70 percent of what men do in Social Security and pensions (AAUW, 2021).

We have all learned how sex, sexuality, and gender are far more nuanced and complicated than the binary designations we used for centuries. Lesbian, gay, bisexual, transgender, queer, and intersex (LGBTQI) persons face specific obstacles to accessing many of their rights, including their right to social protection.

Sex refers to the physical differences between male, female, or intersex people. A person typically has their sex assigned at birth based on physiological characteristics, including their genitalia and chromosome composition. **Intersex** persons are born with reproductive or sexual anatomy that doesn't fit male or female binary categories. Healthcare professionals typically assign intersex babies one of the binary categories at birth.

Sexuality typically refers to one's sexual orientation—that is, to whom someone is sexually attracted. The terms **lesbian**, **gay**, **bisexual**, and **pansexual** refer to people's sexual orientation.

Gender, on the other hand, involves how a person identifies. For centuries, gender was typically a binary category as well, but today we understand it differently as a broad spectrum. A person may identify at any point within this spectrum or outside of it entirely. People may identify with genders different from their sex at birth or with none at all. These identities may include transgender, nonbinary, genderqueer, or genderneutral. **Transgender** means identifying with a gender different from the sex assigned at birth. Terms like **genderqueer** and **non-binary** refer to people who fall outside the construction of gender as male or female. There are many other ways a person may define their gender. Gender is a social construct that reflects the socially constructed roles, behaviors, and attributes at a particular time.

This is not an exhaustive list of terms: Different cultures, both historically and today, have used diverse language that expresses the wide range of sexual orientations and gender expressions. For instance, "Two-Spirit" refers to Native American and First Nations people who fall outside Western gender norms, and "hijra" typically refers to South Asian individuals who are assigned as male at birth but identify as women or as a third gender.

LGBTQI people are entitled to enjoy all the rights outlined in international, regional, and domestic human rights law. Yet, due to strongly held cultural and social norms surrounding gender expression and sexuality, they are often excluded, discriminated against, and denied their rights. Recently, some nations have passed legislation to help protect and promote the rights of LGBTQI communities and individuals. Depriving a person of the right to choose their identity works against making all societies inclusive ones in which all members fully participate and no one is left behind. It is a violation of rights that can be alleviated by changing laws, practices, and cultural attitudes and is therefore viewed as a social justice issue.

TIME FOR EXERCISE: GENDER

In recent years, gender has morphed into a complicated topic that goes beyond male and female binary designations. Below are a few questions to help you explore how these issues can affect someone's life and the people we serve as social workers.

- When it comes to oppression and human rights, members of the LGBTQI community face several forms of social injustice and oppression. For example, same-sex marriages are outlawed in some countries. Additionally, trans students often face discrimination and bullying at school. What are some practices and policies in your community that you would consider oppressive to the LGBTQI community? Why?
- Globally, steps are being made to close the education gap between boys and girls. However, in some parts of the world girls may never set foot in a classroom. Do all children have a right to education? What are some of the reasons why children might not attend school? Why are girls less likely to attend school? How would you frame this as a rights-based issue of a social injustice?

Age

Discrimination occurs between groups and within groups. Ageism means discriminating against someone because of their age. Older people might be stereotyped as feeble, weak, or unable to keep up with changes in the workplace. This may become a reason not to hire or promote someone or even to push someone out of the workforce. An older individual might also be seen as a burden by their family and society. We create these ageist stereotypes consciously and unconsciously in our communities all the time. Think about how communities market themselves as places for young families, with playgrounds and new trendy restaurants, rather than talking about retirees' supports or interests. Instead, retired persons are directed to retirement communities, which are segregated from others. Research repeatedly shows that persons of all ages benefit from interacting with one another.

TIME FOR EXERCISE: AGEISM

- In what ways would the community you work or live in benefit from including persons of all ages?
- Identify ways in which your workplace or community may marginalize older persons.
- How might your community welcome persons of all ages? How would that messaging differ from what currently exists?

Race and Social Justice

What is race, and why does it matter? Race is not a fixed biological concept. Most people belong to more than one "race." Some of you may understand race as a focus on "otherness" or groups that have been continually marginalized. Race is a social construct that has been used to advantage some groups of people over others throughout history. A person of any race can be prejudiced or discriminatory, but only those who have sufficient resources to oppress other groups can be racist (drworksbook, n.d.). A racist is someone who is prejudiced against people based on their perceived membership in a particular racial or ethnic group, typically a group that is marginalized. An individual can be a racist, but racism reflects larger societal actions and practices. An individual may lead efforts to systematically institutionalize racism, but racism goes beyond the actions of any individual alone. Racism is the systematic discrimination implemented and institutionalized throughout a society's policies and practices to produce inequitable outcomes (e.g., in health, income, education, livelihoods). Racism reinforces racist policies and practices (drworksbook, n.d.). Dismantling racism requires commitment from many people at all positions in a society.

Our human history is filled with horrific stories of racism. Racism stems from discrimination against a group of people based on the idea that some inherited characteristic, such as skin color, head size and shape, or other physical characteristics, makes them inferior. Race has been used repeatedly in history to justify oppressive acts and abusive policies against less powerful groups. Race figured prominently in efforts to justify the continuation of slavery around the world. During the 1830s and 1840s, phrenology was popular in the United States. This pseudo-science, founded by German physiologist Franz Joseph Gall, considers skull shapes to indicate mental abilities. Physicians such as Charles Caldwell used phrenology to attempt to justify the perpetuation of slavery in the face of a growing abolitionist movement. Similarly, Samuel Morton, a physiologist, used skull configurations to help justify removing Native Americans from their land. Characterizing Native Americans as having fewer cognitive abilities than Whites, Morton declared Native Americans a hindrance to progress and argued for federal land removal policies.

Around the same time, Adolf Hitler in Germany used the racist ideology known as eugenics to rationalize his plans to exterminate Jews living in Europe. By casting Jews as a different, inferior, and dangerous race, Nazi propaganda was able to create distance between Jews and their neighbors who had coexisted for centuries. The world was shocked by the racist atrocities committed by the Nazis, but racism did not end. Racial segregation laws, restrictive voting rights, and biased judgments and punishments continued in the Southern United States. In South Africa, laws were enacted banning sexual relations and marriage between different population groups and requiring separate residential areas for Africans from people of mixed race. These Apartheid policies were enforced for much of the 20th century until 1994, when, with the enfranchisement of Black Africans and people of color, a new constitution was instituted and the old government was overthrown.

That same year in Rwanda, the racially motivated slaughtering of 800,000 people occurred in just 100 days. Under Belgian rule in the 1930s, Rwandans were divided into racial/ethnic categories favoring the Tutsis over the Hutus. About 85 percent of Rwandans are Hutus, but the Tutsi minority dominated the country. Physically, Hutus and Tutsis appear similar, but a long history of political tensions gave rise to the racial genocide.

Ethnicism

Similar conflicts continue around the world. Rather than being labeled as racial, it is common for ethnicity to be used as the rationale for discrimination and violence. Similar to racism, one ethnic group (identified perhaps by its religion, culture, or language) views itself as superior to others. The conflict is usually not about ethnic differences but political, economic, social, cultural, or territorial matters. In some disputes, the desire of one ethnic group to dominate or destroy another is known as "ethnic cleansing." Ethnic cleansing generally refers to the efforts of a group that holds power to marginalize or eliminate an identified ethnic group or groups through deportation, displacement, or mass killing in an attempt to create an ethnically homogeneous society. Ethnic cleansing campaigns have existed throughout history, and the rise of extreme nationalist movements in the 20th century led to atrocious and malicious massacres and human displacements, such as the Turkish massacre of Armenians during the first World War and the forced displacement and mass killings carried out in the former Yugoslavia at the end of the 20th century.

Ethnic conflicts and cleansing campaigns have continued into the 21st century. Some of you may recall the longstanding ethnic tensions between Arab nomads and sedentary Fur and other agriculturalists that escalated in Darfur in 2003, when rebels among the agriculturalist population began attacking government installations in protest of perceived neglect of non-Arabs and of the country's western region. The government responded with the creation of the Janjaweed militia, which attacked sedentary groups in Darfur. Despite a 2004 ceasefire and the subsequent presence of international peacekeeping troops, by 2007 hundreds of thousands of people had been killed and more than 2 million displaced.

Much of the conflict in Afghanistan traces back to deeply rooted structural discrimination against a group known as the Hazaras. For more than a century, the Hazaras have experienced ethnic cleansing, slavery, land grabbing, targeted taxes, and pillaging of homes, and they have been systematically excluded from government and political positions, economic opportunities, and social settings. The Pashtun ethnicity has ruled the country for centuries. In large part, the discrimination and violence against the Hazaras stems from religious differences: The Hazaras are Shi'a and the Pashtuns are Sunnis. The Hazaras are the targets of violence by extremist groups, including the Taliban (who are Pashtuns) and the Islamic State. Since 2021, when the Taliban retook Kabul, they have re-institutionalized sectarian and ethnic discrimination.

In another part of Asia, Myanmar (formerly known as Burma), ethnicism is at the base of the conflict. Since gaining its independence decades ago, Myanmar has struggled with military rule, civil war, poor governance, and widespread poverty. In August 2017 over 700,000 people—half of them children—fled from Myanmar to Bangladesh to escape terrifying violence. Those fleeing were the Rohingya, who numbered around 1 million in Myanmar at the start of 2017 and were one of the many ethnic minorities in the country. Rohingya Muslims represent the largest percentage of Muslims in Myanmar. The government of Myanmar, a predominantly Buddhist country, denied the Rohingya citizenship and even excluded them from the 2014 census, refusing to recognize them as a people. The Rohingyas' exodus in 2017 was spurred by escalated and violent tensions, with 6,700 Rohingyas dying. About 1 million Rohingyas continue to live in refugee camps in Bangladesh. That and other heightened tensions between different ethnic groups in the country led to the military coup that took place in February 2021. The conflict has largely been ethnic-based, with several ethnic armed groups fighting Myanmar's military, calling for increased autonomy or federalization of the country.

Other ethnic tensions fuel the denial of human rights to certain groups around the world in the 21st century, including but not limited to the Uyghur genocide in China, the war in Tigray in Ethiopia, the wars in Iraq, the Syrian war, and the Boko Haram insurgency that began in 2009 to assert Islamic ways over Christians in Nigeria.

Racism and ethnicism are similar in that they construct rationales for treating others groups as inferior, denying groups their human rights, and fueling hatred (Kandaswamy, 2007). While it is important to understand the cultures of others, it is not enough: We must also understand racial and ethnic privilege, race relations, and White supremacy. If we continue to judge the lifestyles of all groups against the norms for one group (Whites), racism, ethnicism, and all other "isms" will be perpetuated. We need to roll up our sleeves and stop avoiding the complex institutional, cultural, and macro-social processes that can create racial inequality and injustice (Bonilla-Silva, 1997).

TIME FOR REFLECTION AND DISCUSSION: CREATING A JUST SOCIETY

This exercise will help deepen your understanding of racial injustice and its history.

Each of our personal and professional experiences of racial and other types of injustice is unique. Our experiences are affected by when we were born; where we have lived; the income of our households; who we are racially, ethnically, and in other ways; our perspective of normality; and much more. One thing that we all have in common, however, is that we all need to learn more about people's experiences (our own and that of others), history, and current struggles, regardless of our race, ethnicity, abilities, immigration status, gender, sexual orientation, age, and all the other factors that help define who we are.

A few years ago, the *New York Times* launched "The 1619 Project," followed by a podcast and public forums. Its originator, Nikole Hannah-Jones, was awarded a Pulitzer Prize for her work. The 1619 Project is a wide-ranging summary of the Black experience in America. It explores aspects of slavery, its continuing legacy, and how being White or Black affects everything from how you fare in courts, hospitals, and schools to the odds that your neighborhood will be bulldozed for a freeway. According to The 1619 Project, U.S. history should begin with the arrival of the first African slaves in 1619 in Virginia, not with the arrival of the *Mayflower* in 1620. The Project was controversial when it was launched; in fact, several state lawmakers introduced bills to strip funds from schools that used it in their curriculum.

Read some chapters from *The 1619 Project: A New Origin Story* by Nikole Hannah-Jones. Excerpts are available online (https://www.nytimes.com/interactive/2019/12/20/magazine/1619-intro.html), or you can listen to the podcast (https://www.nytimes.com/2019/08/23/podcasts/the-daily/1619-project.html?searchResultPosition=18).

The following questions can be used for reflection or to stimulate classroom discussions:

- How do the societal structures developed to support the enslavement of Black people, and the anti-Black racism cultivated in the United States to justify slavery, influence many aspects of modern laws, policies, systems, and culture?
- How have resistance, innovation, and advocacy by Black Americans over the course of American history contributed to the nation's wealth and the strengthening of its democracy?
- What does it mean to be an American? How does The 1619 Project challenge your definition?
- In what ways has capitalism fueled racism?

Another important book is *Caste: The Origins of Our Discontents* by Isabel Wilkerson. *Caste* describes inequity in the United States from the arrival of the first enslaved people in 1619 to the COVID-19 pandemic. Wilkerson explains how long-buried injustices affect our lives and public choices and are structurally embedded in our society, creating an unspoken caste system based on skin color. The book is divided into seven parts, and students can be assigned different parts of the book for class discussions. The following questions might be used to stimulate discussions:

- At the beginning of *Caste*, American racial hierarchy is compared to a dormant virus. Given our recent experiences with COVID-19, what are the strengths of this metaphor? How does this comparison help combat the pervasive myth that racism has been eradicated in America?

- Caste and race are not the same thing. What is the difference between the two? How do casteism and racism support each other? Discuss how class is also different from caste.
- Wilkerson discusses three major caste systems throughout the book: India, Nazi Germany, and America. What are some of the differences that stood out to you among these three systems? What are the similarities? How did learning about one help you understand the others? For instance, did the fact that the Nazis actually studied America's segregation practices and Jim Crow laws help underscore the breadth of our own system?
- According to Wilkerson, "Evil asks little of the dominant caste other than to sit back and do nothing." What are some of the ways that each of us, personally, can stand up to the caste system?
- Wilkerson writes about the "construction of Whiteness," describing the way immigrants went from being Czech or Hungarian or Polish (the "others") to "White"—a political designation that only has meaning when set against something "not White." Add to this the Irish and Italians. What does this "construction of Whiteness" tell us about the structure of caste? How does the caste system take people who would otherwise be allies and turn them against one other? What are some of the steps that society, and each of us, can take toward dismantling the caste system?
- Wilkerson uses a caste system to explain how racism is embedded in U.S. social, economic, and political systems. Critics of her book claim that Wilkerson confuses caste and racism, and in doing so ascribes negative attributes to caste, Hinduism, and Indian culture. What is your opinion?

HATE CRIMES AGAINST ASIAN AMERICANS

During the first year of the COVID-19 pandemic, hate crimes against Asian Americans and businesses owned by Asian Americans rose by 77 percent. This includes the spa shooting in Atlanta, Georgia, in March 2021 that killed eight Americans, six of whom were of Asian descent. From March 2020 to June 2021, more than 9,000 anti-Asian hate crimes were reported; the actual number may be much higher because hate crimes typically are vastly underreported. Negative bias and microaggressions against Asian Americans grew during this period as well.

COVID-19 is believed to have emerged in Wuhan, China, in December 2019. It spread rapidly throughout the globe during the spring of 2020. During the pandemic, China and more generally Asians were blamed for the relentless virus. Then President Trump himself publicly blamed China for the pandemic by referring to it as the "Chinese virus" or "China virus." White House staff perpetuated this, calling it the "Wuhan virus" (Rogers, 2020) and "kung flu" (Boyer, 2020).

Stigmatizing people of Asian descent is not new. History shows that beginning in the late 1700s, when Asians began arriving in the United States, they have been subject to xenophobia, stigmatization, and "othering" (Gover et al., 2020).

Anti-Asian violence has affected the mental well-being of many Asian Americans. More than 35 percent of Asian Americans reported that their mental health worsened in 2020 and 2021(Findling et al., 2022). Almost 60 percent of Asian Americans reported that learning about the acts of discrimination and violence against Asian people negatively affected their mental well-being (Findling et al., 2022).

- From a rights-based approach, describe how hate crimes against Asian Americans represent a social justice issue, and explain why.
- What should social workers being doing to promote justice for persons of Asian American descent?

Racism, Justice, and Policing in the United States

Did you know that the greatest democracy in the world, the United States, also has the world's highest incarceration rate? And that each year, U.S. police kill civilians far more often than police do in other wealthy countries (Bailey et al., 2021)? This is in contrast to the sense of police as upholders of justice in our society. We now have a large body of research from different disciplines that documents racial bias and racism in all aspects of the judicial system. Blacks are more likely to receive harsher treatment than Whites in terms of encounters with police, bail amounts, sentence lengths, and capital punishment (Bailey et al., 2021).

One of the ways we can address this injustice is by changing police interactions. Contemporary U.S. policing has roots in slave patrols, which were first established in 18th-century colonial Virginia in an effort to capture runaways and quell uprisings. After the abolition of slavery and the short-lived progress of the Reconstruction Era, police and prisons served as key institutions for reasserting White dominance, especially in the South. In the decades that followed, police sanctioned, enabled, and participated in the lynching of Black persons. In the South, White people used police, prison-enforced vagrancy laws, and sharecropping systems to force formerly enslaved people back to the fields (Bailey et al., 2021). Police killings of Black men rose sharply in the late 1960s. By the 1970s, President Nixon's "War on

Drugs" expanded the size of the incarcerated population sevenfold and accelerated incarceration rates for Blacks to five times the rate for White people.

Policing and incarceration have profoundly adverse consequences on health and communities. Police violence harms the mental health for entire communities because of continual and constant surveillance and threat of violence. Policing practices need to be revamped, but this alone will not solve the racism pervasive in policing. Racism is part of all our institutions and part of our practices. We can begin to understand the pervasiveness and manifestation of structural racism when we look critically at the disparate outcomes. Policing and prisons have been one of the vehicles American society has used to exert control over the Black and Brown populations. We need to look at how other public sectors reinforce structural racism, such as policies and practices in education, housing, social services, and mental health and health services. The systems are intertwined and reflect the values and priorities of our dominant culture. Calls for justice, as we discussed in the previous chapter, come at a time when the dominant paradigm is being challenged because cultural values and priorities are changing. We are living in a such a moment now.

TIME FOR REFLECTION AND DISCUSSION
—————————————————————————————————————

- If you wanted to address issues related to racial injustice and structural racism in your community, where would you start? What current actions or behaviors might need to change?
- What is at stake if communities do not take steps to change structural racism?

CHAPTER 10
Economic Justice

For decades, the legacy of the civil rights era has bound our vision of justice (Bannan, 2019). During the civil rights era, we fought for non-discrimination primarily related to public accommodations, education, housing, and employment. The goals were equal access and equal opportunity to public accommodations, education, housing, and employment—which are not the same as equity. Equality looks at whether everyone has the same to begin with, whereas equity focuses on outcomes. Both are important, but equitable outcomes were neglected for decades in favor of equal access. Our definition of justice for decades was framed by equality of access and opportunity. We failed to take a hard look at how the institutions and processes we built reinforced discriminatory success. The results are the disparities created throughout our society.

The disparities created are particularly important when we talk about economic justice. Economic justice is the outcome of intersectionality—it reflects the differential realization of economic rights for different people and groups and is bound by societal structures. Some examples of economic injustice are the wage and salary gaps between men and women, the growing unequal distribution of wealth in the United States, discrimination and exploitation of immigrant workers, and the disproportionate number of low-income households that do not have paid coverage for family or sick leave.

We want to better understand why economic disparities exist for people of different skin colors and why differences exist among genders, immigrant groups, ages, and other groups. What are the consequences of economic disparities? How can we reduce economic inequities? Abilities, education, and skills may account for some of the differences among groups. Still, when we explore this further, we understand that many economic disparities exist due to factors that have less to do with an individual's or group's ability, education, or skill set. Black households, for example, have far less access to tax-advantaged forms of savings, due in part to a long history of employment discrimination and other oppressive practices (Hanks et al., 2018). Research shows that Blacks are less likely to be homeowners than Whites, and therefore have less access to the savings and tax benefits that come with owning a home. Also, the toll of persistent employment discrimination has left many Black individuals in less advantageous jobs than White persons. The result is less access to stable jobs, good wages, and retirement benefits from work—all key drivers to building savings for American families. While an employer may knowingly or unknowingly discriminate against workers by race, or a mortgage broker intentionally or unintentionally perpetuates discriminatory lending practices, the result is that persistent housing and labor market discrimination continues and widens disparities between Black and White persons (Figure 10.1). The wealth and median incomes of Latinx, Native American/American Indian, and some Asian American and Pacific Islander households fall far below White counterparts' as well.

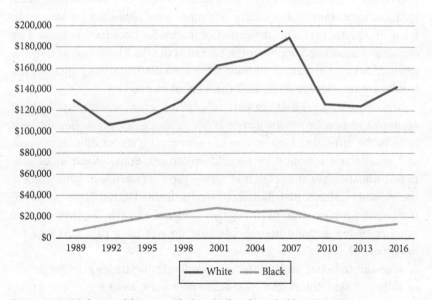

Figure 10.1. Median wealth among Black and White households, 1989–2016.
This material was published by the Center for American Progress in the following article: Hanks, A., Solomon, D., & Weller, C.E. (2018). Systematic inequality: How America's structural racism helped create the Black-White wealth gap. American Progress, CAP. https://www.americanprogress.org/article/systematic-inequality/

Defining Economic Justice and Economic Rights

Economic justice is defined here as the realization of economic rights. What are economic rights? Remember, all human rights are interrelated and overlap. Without political and civil rights we cannot achieve economic, social, environmental, and cultural rights. Social rights often overlap with economic, environmental, and cultural rights and sometimes it is difficult to differentiate one right from another.

This is evident in how the United Nations Office of High Commissioner for Human Rights (OHCHR) simultaneously defines economic, social, and cultural rights. OHCHR states:

> Economic, social and cultural rights are those human rights relating to the workplace, social security, family life, participation in cultural life, and access to housing, food, water, healthcare and education. (OHCHR, n.d., p. 1)

Economic rights generally consist of:

- **Workers' rights**, including the right to fair wages and equal pay for equal work, the right to decide freely to accept or choose work, freedom from forced labor, the right to leisure and reasonable limitation of working hours, the right to safe and healthy working conditions, the right to join and form trade unions, and the right to strike
- **Social security and social protection** for individuals due to contributions or need, and the right not to be denied assistance arbitrarily or unreasonably. This includes the right to equal and adequate protection due to unemployment, sickness, old age, or other lack of livelihood in circumstances beyond one's control.
- **Protection of and assistance to the family**, which includes the right to marriage by free consent; the right to maternity, paternity, and parental leave coverage and protection; and the right to protect children from economic and social exploitation
- **The right to an adequate standard of living**, including the rights to food, adequate housing, water, sanitation, and clothing
- **The right to health** as it relates to healthy occupational conditions, access to health facilities, services and goods without loss of employment, and protection against diseases
- **The right to education**, because education and vocational training are highly associated with livelihood options, including the right to free and compulsory primary education and to available and accessible secondary and higher education

These rights are articulated in the Universal Declaration of Human Rights (UDHR) and in the International Covenant of Economic, Social and Cultural Rights (ICESCR). Economic rights are referenced in the UDHR as follows:

> **Article 22** makes clear that everyone is entitled to economic, social, and cultural rights necessary for one's dignity.
>
> **Article 23** articulates the right to work, to choose employment, and to form labor unions.
>
> **Article 24** sets forth the right to rest and leisure and to reasonable limitation of working hours.
>
> **Article 25** includes the right to a standard of living adequate for health and well-being of one's self and of one's family, including food, clothing, housing and medical care and necessary social services.
>
> **Article 26** states that individuals have the right to education, free and compulsory at the elementary level, with technical and professional education generally available, and higher education equally accessible on the basis of merit.

The ICESCR aims to ensure the protection of economic, social, and cultural rights. Economic rights, though intertwined with other rights, are highlighted in the following articles of the ICESCR:

> **Article 2** asserts the right to non-discrimination based on race, color, sex, language, religion, political or other opinion, national or social origin, property, birth or other status.
>
> **Articles 6** proclaims the right to work, which is the opportunity to gain a living by work that one freely chooses or accepts.
>
> **Article 7** presents the right to a fair wage and safe working conditions.
>
> **Article 8** affirms the right to form and join unions.
>
> **Article 9** upholds the right to social security.
>
> **Article 10** endorses protection and assistance to the family.
>
> **Article 11** sustains the right to an adequate standard of living.

Social and economic rights are also articulated in specialized human rights treaties such as the Convention on the Rights of the Child (CRC), the Convention on the Elimination of All Forms of Discrimination against Women (CEDAW), the International Convention on the Protection of the Rights of All Migrant Workers and Members of Their Families (ICPRMWM), and the Convention on the Rights of Persons with Disabilities (CRPD), treaties that focus on the needs of marginalized groups around the world.

Another treaty, the International Convention on the Elimination of All Forms of Racial Discrimination (ICRD), must also be considered when discussing economic disparities because many such disparities result from conscious or unconscious individual and systemic discriminatory practices.

Social and economic rights are included in national, regional, and global legal systems through laws and regulations, and in national and state/provincial constitutions. By securing these rights into legal systems, governments are obligated to ensure that these rights are upheld and to act if they are violated. When governments live up to their obligations, justice is served, but when they neglect or violate our rights, injustice occurs.

In countries such as the United States, civil and political rights receive more attention than economic rights, and economic freedom is the priority when we speak of economic justice. According to the Cato Institute (2022), a U.S. thinktank founded on libertarian principles, the foundations of economic freedom are personal choice, voluntary exchange, and open markets. From the libertarian perspective, progress in all aspects of life is dependent on economic freedom, which can only occur when property rights are secure, the rule of law is followed, political and economic stability exists, and there is sound money (money that is not prone to sudden appreciation or depreciation in purchasing power). Libertarians believe that limiting government interference in the market process increases the robustness of and growth opportunities for markets. From the libertarian point of view, economic justice is about freedom, the protection of one's freedoms and rights, and following the rules of law. Income and wealth inequality is not of concern unless the process by which one's income or wealth is begotten violates the rules of justice. The focus is not on outcomes but rather on procedural justice.

In general, libertarians don't see anything wrong with growing inequality. They oppose redistribution of income and wealth, which is seen as a violation of the individual's right to property. Nozick, for example, would argue that all individuals are entitled to earn and amass as much wealth as they are capable of, if they follow the laws. From the libertarian point of view, an economic injustice would be forcing people to pay high taxes to redistribute income to the poor (violating one's right to property) or allowing someone to secure assets unjustly.

Those on the political left, such as progressives, social democrats, and others, tend to see economic justice very differently. They contend that redistribution is not only morally right but necessary in a world of stark inequalities of wealth and income. From the progressive perspective, most wealth was achieved by exploiting workers, usurping property and resources from marginalized groups, and redistributing the assets among those in power to perpetuate the structures that allowed this to happen in the first place. Redistribution is viewed as a necessary remedial measure, a way to correct concrete injustices of the past that have resulted in growing and jarring economic disparities. Progressives focus on outcomes, whereas libertarians concentrate on ensuring that the process maximizes individuals' freedoms.

MARTIN LUTHER KING JR. AND THE POOR PEOPLE'S CAMPAIGN

President Lyndon B. Johnson launched a War on Poverty soon after assuming office. Johnson's strategy for ending poverty was to equalize opportunities for people to succeed through early childhood education, job training, and fair employment policies. He instituted other important supports, such as publicly funded health programs and community development programs. However, the U.S. involvement in the Vietnam War redirected funds away from the War on Poverty. Three years after Johnson's ambitious plan was launched, many of the programs remained underfunded and the programs did not have the intended impact.

Rev. Dr. Martin Luther King, Jr., dismayed by this limited success, concluded that a dramatic effort was needed to get the government to rededicate itself to fighting poverty (Mantler, 2013). In his "I Have a Dream" speech in Washington, D.C., in 1963 Dr. King laid out a broad economic struggle that Black Americans had faced and would continue to face without adequate redress of civil and economic rights. He told the audience, "One hundred years later, the Negro lives on a lonely island of poverty in the midst of a vast ocean of material prosperity. . . . In a sense we've come to our nation's capital to cash a check . . . that will give us upon demand the riches of freedom and the security of justice" (King, 1963).

Dr. King argued that the U.S. Constitution should be amended to add an economic bill of rights that enumerates a human right to be free from economic poverty. His criticism of capitalism grew as he became convinced that the capitalist system deprived Americans of spiritual wealth and genuine justice. In a 1967 speech he called for an alternative system to capitalism and communism, one that tackled the fact that "the problem of racism, the problem of economic exploitation, and the problem of war are all tied together. These are the triple evils that are interrelated" (King, 1967). He felt there should be more focus on jobs, unemployment, and poverty.

Together with the Southern Christian Leadership Conference (SCLC), Dr. King created the Poor People's Campaign. It sought to bring together a diverse coalition of White, Latino, Black, and Native Americans because systemic poverty was a national problem affecting all people. The Poor People's Campaign had five core goals: (1) a job with a living wage for every employable citizen; (2) a guaranteed minimum income for all who cannot work; (3) access to land as a means to income and livelihood; (4) access to capital as a means of full participation in the economic life of America; and (5) legal recognition of the right of people to participate in developing policies that affect them.

Dr. King recruited activists to join the Campaign throughout 1967. The launch of the Campaign was scheduled for May 1968. The idea was that the participants would camp out on the National Mall until the federal government committed to an economic bill of rights.

Tragically, Dr. King was assassinated in April 1968 in Memphis and never lived to see the launch of the Poor People's Campaign. Rev. Ralph Abernathy stepped in to lead the SCLC and Rev. Jesse Jackson led the planned protest in Washington, D.C. The Campaign went forward without Dr. King.

In May 1968, around 3,000 demonstrators huddled in the plywood huts across the over 15 acres between the Lincoln Memorial and the Washington Monument in a gathering dubbed "Resurrection City." For nearly six weeks, activists endured rain and mud, clashes with police, and, sometimes, chaos. High heat and heavy rains turned the encampment into mud city, and tensions grew with police and among participants. Protestors left each day. A crowning moment of the Campaign was on June 19, 1968 (Juneteenth), when nearly 50,000 people met on the National Mall for Solidarity Day. Coretta Scott King and Rev. Abernathy were among the many speakers.

Resurrection City ended on June 24. By that time, only 500 protestors were left, yet 1,000 police officers with tear gas were brought in to break up the encampment. Two hundred eighty-eight people, including Rev. Abernathy, had been arrested the previous day.

The protest was later described as "the biggest protest on the Mall that nobody's ever heard of" (Massimo, 2018). While the Campaign did achieve a few notable successes—such as changes in food stamps and nutrition programs—it did not accomplish what King had envisioned. Looking back, many people, including the Campaign's leaders, were still in mourning for Dr. King, and the public did not show interest in galvanizing around the issue. Mantler (2013), however, reminds us that the Campaign helped to forge a generation of activists through the 1970s and 1980s by bringing together diverse people on a common cause.

ECONOMIC BILL OF RIGHTS

Twenty-four years before Dr. King and his Poor People's Campaign called for an economic bill of rights, President Franklin Delano Roosevelt (FDR) had introduced one to Congress and the nation in his State of the Union Address on January 11, 1944. Roosevelt argued that the "political rights" guaranteed by the Constitution and the original Bill of Rights had "proved inadequate to assure us equality in the pursuit of happiness." He declared the need for an economic bill of rights. In his words, "people who are hungry and out of a job are the stuff of which dictatorships are made."

FDR encountered criticism from conservatives and libertarians for his economic policies, which were perceived to shift from individualism to collectivism by expanding the welfare state, and interventions such as regulating the economy (Powers, 1998). At the other end of the spectrum, FDR was accused of racism for incarcerating Japanese Americans on the West Coast in concentration camps after the bombing of Pearl Harbor (Robinson, 2001), failing to help the Jews in Europe (Breitman & Lichtman, 2013), opposing anti-lynching legislation (Katznelson, 2013), and inviting only White Olympic medal winners to the White House, thus excluding Jesse Owens, who had won four gold medals. Other critics have noted that people of color, including domestic and agricultural workers, were excluded from New Deal initiatives as part of a strategy to win the support of Southern Democrats in Congress (Katznelson, 2013).

The Economic Bill of Rights, also referred to as the Second Bill of Rights, put forth by FDR (1944) stated the following:

> In our day these economic truths have become accepted as self-evident. We have accepted, so to speak, a second Bill of Rights under which a new basis of security and prosperity can be established for all—regardless of station, race, or creed. Among these are:
> - The right to a useful and remunerative job in the industries or shops or farms or mines of the nation;
> - The right to earn enough to provide adequate food and clothing and recreation;
> - The right of every farmer to raise and sell his products at a return which will give him and his family a decent living;
> - The right of every businessman, large and small, to trade in an atmosphere of freedom from unfair competition and domination by monopolies at home or abroad;
> - The right of every family to a decent home;
> - The right to adequate medical care and the opportunity to achieve and enjoy good health;

- The right to adequate protection from the economic fears of old age, sickness, accident, and unemployment;
- The right to a good education.

The Committee of 100 presented the following version of an economic bill of rights to President Johnson and Congress in 1968 following King's death:

The Southern Christian Leadership Conference, architects of the Poor People's Campaign (Stanford University, n.d.), have outlined 5 requirements of the bill of economic & social rights that will set poverty on the road to extinction:

1. A meaningful job at a living wage for every employable citizen.
2. A secure and adequate income for all who cannot find jobs or for whom employment is inappropriate.
3. Access to land as a means to income and livelihood.
4. Access to capital as a means of full participation in the economic life of America.
5. Recognition by law of the right of people affected by government programs to play a truly significant role in determining how they are designed and carried out.

GROWING ECONOMIC INEQUALITIES

Why this focus on growing disparities? A key reason is that equality is viewed as essential to democracy. Houle (2009) explains that while the road to democracy may take different paths and equality may not be essential, growing income and wealth inequalities create the conditions that allow elites to amass power and resources and increase the likelihood that the elites will wage coups against democracies. This has been proven empirically (Houle, 2009).

Those on the lower rungs of the economic ladder are more likely to experience diminished economic opportunities and economic mobility. Inequality also tends to reduce the political influence of those at the lower end of the income and wealth spectrum (Hacker & Pierson, 2010). Widening disparities increase geographic segregation by income (Reardon & Bischoff, 2011), and some believe it hampers economic growth as well (Ostry et al., 2018). Increased economic inequalities will also raise the likelihood that higher education and the job opportunities that result from it will be restricted to those who can afford higher education as affordable higher education venues diminish (Jackson & Holzman, 2020).

Over the last few decades, income and wealth inequalities have exploded in the United States and around the world (Horowitz et al., 2020). In contrast, in the years following the end of World War II through the 1970s, there was substantial economic growth and broadly shared prosperity. Incomes, for all income groups, grew rapidly and at roughly the same rate, roughly doubling between the late 1940s and early 1970s. Beginning in the 1970s, however, economic growth decelerated and the income gap between those with high incomes and those with low incomes widened (Stone et al., 2020). As Figure 10.2 demonstrates, income growth for low- and middle-income households slowed sharply, while incomes at the top continued to grow strongly. Income growth is increasingly concentrated among high-income households, and the unequal income distribution patterns mimic those from a century ago during the 1920s, before the stock market crashed.

While income distribution grew more skewed, wealth—the value of a household's property and financial assets, minus the value of its debts—grew more highly concentrated than income (Stone et al., 2020). In 1989, the top 1 percent of households held 30 percent of the wealth in the United States; this grew to 39 percent by 2016. Horowitz et al. (2020) found that the wealth gap between upper-income families and middle- and lower-income families grew more sharply than the income gap and is growing more rapidly. Figure 10.3 shows that while wealth has grown across all income groups since 1983, it is increasingly concentrated in upper-income families. Middle- and lower-income families have a smaller share of wealth in the United States over time. Seventy-nine percent of household wealth is now concentrated in upper-income households (up from 60 percent in 1983).

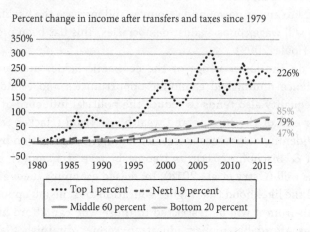

Percent change in income after transfers and taxes since 1979

Figure 10.2. Income gains at the top dwarf those of low- and middle-income households. Congressional Budget Office. This material was created by the Center on Budget and Policy Priorities (www.cbpp.org; Stone, Trisi, Sherman & Beltrán, 2020).

The gaps in wealth between upper-income and middle- and lower-income families
are rising, and the share held by middle-income families is falling

Median family wealth, in 2018 dollars, and share of U.S. aggregate family, by income tier

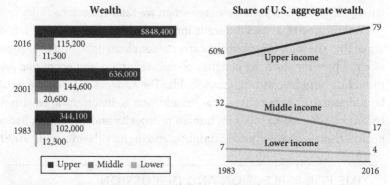

Note: Families are assigned to income tiers based on their size-adjusted income.
Source: Pew Research Center analysis of the Survey of Consumer Finances.
"Most Americans Say There is Too Much Economic Inequality in the U.S., but Fewer Than
Half Call it a Top Priority"

PEW RESEARCH CENTER

Figure 10.3. Incomes of upper-income families are rising, while those of middle- and low-
income families are declining.
Stone, C., Trisi, D., Sherman, A. & Beltrán, J. (2020). A Guide to Statistics on Historical Trends in Income
Inequality. Center on Budget and Policy Priorities. https://www.cbpp.org/research/poverty-and-inequality/
a-guide-to-statistics-on-historical-trends-in-income-inequality

Middle-income families now hold only a bit more than half of the wealth they
did in 1983 (a drop from 32 percent to 17 percent). Lower-income families,
who held 7 percent of the wealth in 1983, now hold only 4 percent.

Why income has grown unequally across income groups is subject to
extensive debate. The income stratification in the United States did not
occur because of a single action or policy; rather, it is the result of many
policies and decisions that, over time, have intersected and contributed
to inequitable income growth in the United States. The tax systems
and regulatory systems we have put into place have often benefited
corporations and the wealthy rather than individuals on the lower rungs
of the economic ladder. Such policies have allowed power to concentrate
in few corporations while simultaneously weakening unions, stagnating
wages, underfunding innovation, and lowering productivity—factors
believed to contribute to widening disparities. Adding to this is the
growth of punitive, restrictive, and highly monitored social welfare
programs that have not adequately reached those needing assistance;
instead, they often redirect families and individuals into menial and unstable employment.

Redistribution of resources such as income may help lift people out of poverty but by itself will not keep an economy growing. Economic growth is the priority for many people in the United States across the political spectrum. Different viewpoints emerge when we raise questions regarding the pattern of growth across different income groups. Those on the left often argue that the high cost of healthcare, student loan debt, and consequences of child poverty slow the benefits of redistribution and economic growth to middle- and low-income households. They advocate for these issues to be addressed. Others believe that, in addition to income and wealth redistribution, we need to focus on human prosperity and outcomes, including health, climate change, political rights, and dignity (Naidu et al., 2020).

TIME FOR REFLECTION AND DISCUSSION

- How should income and wealth be distributed? Should those who are more skilled earn more? Should there be limits to how much wealth one can accumulate?
- Identify an example of economic injustice today. Why is it an injustice? What economic rights are being violated? Other rights?

OCCUPY WALL STREET

Kalle Lasn and others from Adbusters, a Canadian anti-consumerist publication, were fed up with the growing power and influence of corporations on democracy and the lack of legal consequences for those whose actions brought on the Great Recession and global crisis of monetary insolvency, as well as the increasing disparities in wealth around the world. They proposed a peaceful occupation of Wall Street, with income and wealth inequality and corporate corruption as their main focal points.

The protest began on September 17, 2011, in Zuccotti Park in Manhattan's financial district. About 2,000 people gathered in lower Manhattan, many of whom camped out or slept in nearby churches. The protest movement against economic inequality and injustice mushroomed to approximately 1,000 similar protests in 28 other U.S. cities; European capitals and financial centers, including London, Paris, and Berlin; and parts of South America and the Far East.

Due to allegedly unsanitary and hazardous conditions, the police forced the protesters out of Zuccotti Park on November 15, 2011. Protesters then turned their focus to occupying banks, corporate headquarters, board meetings, foreclosed homes, and college and university campuses. Subsequent attempts to re-occupy Zuccotti Park were unsuccessful, and protestors continued their campaign through a variety of media, including social media, print magazines, newspapers, film, radio, and livestreaming.

Occupy Wall Street was collectively led. "We are the 99%" was the political slogan that they widely used, a reference to an May 2011 article titled "Of the 1%, by the 1%, for the 1%" by Nobel Prize-winning economist Joseph Stiglitz. According to Stiglitz, 1 percent of the population controls more than 40 percent of the wealth and receives more than 20 percent of the income.

The lasting effects of the Occupy movement are debated. Some argue that it was a transformative uprising against the power of corporate America that ignited a leftward shift of the Democratic Party and served as a model for the #MeToo and Black Lives Matter movements. Others claim it had little effect at all.

- What are your impressions of the Occupy Wall Street movement?
- Do you think it has affected public opinion?
- Why do you think more protests against economic inequality haven't been launched?

THE FUTURE OF ECONOMIC JUSTICE

About six in ten U.S. adults say there's too much economic inequality in the country today, and among that group, most say addressing it will require significant changes to the country's economic system, according to a Pew Research Center survey (Horowitz et al., 2020). Still, reducing economic inequality doesn't rank high on the public's list of priorities for the federal government to address. Only four in ten people rank this as a top priority, far less than those who say affordable healthcare, terrorism, or reducing gun violence should be a top priority.

The United States, like many parts of the world today, is deeply divided. Pulls to the right and left run deep in many nations, as does the inability to compromise. Without a shared vision of economic justice, our efforts will swing like a pendulum from one opposing view to another depending on who has power. For many social workers, economic justice is inevitably about shifting the power structures to empower low-income workers to take control over their labor, earnings, and wealth generation. Inequity is embedded within our infrastructure, which prioritizes some groups over others. It reminds us that rules favor those who make the rules. We cannot move forward without addressing the systemic racism, ageism, sexism, ableism, and other oppressions that are deeply rooted in our political, economic, and social infrastructure. It begs us all to think hard about how we, as social workers, can advance human rights to support economic justice.

CHAPTER 11

Environmental Justice

SHIRLEY GATENIO GABEL AND CATHRYNE SCHMITZ

W e seem to be living in a time when environment-related disasters occur more frequently and cause greater damage. These disasters have heightened our awareness of climate change, degrading acts against our environment, and the unsustainability of continuing to ignore the potential impact of our human actions. Rising temperatures create changes in the landscape and weather patterns. These changes are not borne equally by all and deepen inequities among communities and individuals. Those who have the least resources, live in communities of color, and have less power carry a disproportionate burden, which is an injustice related to the environment.

EARLY ROOTS OF SOCIAL WORK AND ENVIRONMENTAL JUSTICE

The "friendly visitors" of the charity organization societies and settlement house workers conducted social research to document environmental conditions in urban communities. They used it to advocate for changes at the community level and beyond. In the late 19th and early 20th centuries, charity organization societies and aid groups documented the living and working conditions and then used this information to design social innovations and usher in new social policies at local, state, and national levels. For example, investigations into the appalling conditions in tenement buildings led to local regulations governing the health and safety of

A Human Rights-Based Approach to Justice in Social Work Practice. Shirley Gatenio Gabel, Oxford University Press.
© Oxford University Press 2024. DOI: 10.1093/oso/9780197570647.003.0011

privately owned rental housing in densely populated urban areas (Lubove, 1963).

These social work pioneers made connections between the environment, poverty, and health. They observed how poor ventilation and lighting, unsanitary sewage and garbage disposal, and contaminated water supply contributed to insect-borne diseases and communicable diseases, such as tuberculosis. Social workers advocated for better sanitation and housing laws "because it was an intolerable injustice for any community to permit its working classes to live under such miserable conditions" (Hopkins, 1926).

The survey data revealed a high percentage of infant and maternal deaths due to environmental conditions. This information was one of the factors motivating the establishment of the national Children's Bureau. The Children's Bureau's first major initiative was to reduce maternal and infant mortality, which at the time was epidemic across all social classes but particularly among the poor (Lindenmeyer, 1997). The director, Julia Lathrop, and her colleagues successfully advocated for community-level interventions to raise awareness and to promote sanitation and education, which halved the number of infant deaths in the United States in the first decades of the 20th century (Almgren et al., 2000; Sable et al., 2012).

Growing Awareness of Environmental Justice

A resurgence in how the environment affected the well-being of individuals and communities occurred in the mid-20th century. Researchers like Aldo Leopold in the early 1940s and Rachel Carson in the 1960s drew our attention to the connections between humans and the ecology. In the 1940s, Leopold (2020), seen by many as the father of wildlife ecology, explored the links among conservation, economics, and the wilderness. Carson (2002) drew attention to the dangers of pesticides for humans and the ecology with her 1962 book *Silent Spring*. It was an instant bestseller and was the most talked-about book in decades. Carson spent over six years documenting her hypothesis that humans were misusing potent chemical pesticides before knowing the harm they could cause to humans, wildlife, domestic animals, and the Earth. She encouraged humans to act responsibly and carefully and as stewards of the living Earth by calling for sweeping policy changes. *Silent Spring* made us all more aware of the toxicity in our environments.

As our understanding of the harms resulting from environmental policies such as resource extraction, hazardous waste, and other land uses grew, so did our awareness of how lower-income, non-White communities often bore the heaviest impact (Environmental Protection Agency [EPA], 2022). The civil rights movement of the 1960s sensitized us to the different impacts of policies on different communities, including environmental impacts. The fight for equal treatment of all people, regardless of race, color, national origin, or income, regarding environmental policies and laws became known as environmental justice. As noted by the EPA, "Whether by conscious design or institutional neglect, communities of color in urban ghettos, in rural 'poverty pockets', or on economically impoverished Native-American reservations face some of the worst environmental devastation in the nation" (EPA, 2021, para. 5).

The linkages among economic, social, and environmental justice grew in the 1960s (McGurty, 1997). Organized by Cesar Chavez, Latino farmworkers in the early 1960s fought for workplace rights, including protection from harmful pesticides in the farm fields of California's San Joaquin Valley (McGurty, 1997). In 1967, Black students took to the streets of Houston to oppose a city garbage dump in their community that was held responsible for the death of a child. In 1968, a sanitation strike took place in Memphis, Tennessee. Objecting to the poor pay and treatment of sanitation workers who were Black and the lack of public sanitation services in their community, the Black community mobilized for better working and living conditions and increased pay (EPA, 2022). Also in 1968, residents of West Harlem in New York City fought against a sewage treatment plant planned for their community (McGurty, 1997).

The following year, the intersectionality of race, the environment, and justice gained national attention. Homeowners in Houston, Texas, resisted the placement of a waste management facility in their community after learning "about the public health dangers for their families, their communities and themselves" (EPA, 2022, para. 3). Residents formed the Northeast Community Action Group, and their attorney, Linda McKeever Bullard, filed a class-action lawsuit to block the landfill from being built. The 1979 lawsuit, *Bean v. Southwestern Waste Management, Inc.*, was the first lawsuit to challenge the location of a waste facility under civil rights law by explicitly linking environmental injustice and systemic racism (Ahmed, 2021).

The environmental justice movement came into its own in the 1980s. In 1982 Black activists in Warren County, North Carolina, opposed the dumping of PCB-contaminated soil into the landfill in a community where primarily Black and poor persons resided (EPA, 2022). Working with the Warren County community, the National Association for the Advancement of Colored People (NAACP) and others staged a massive protest. Although the Warren County protest failed to prevent the disposal facility, it is considered the start of the national environmental justice movement (EPA, 2022). Warren County residents met with people in other low-income communities of color to help them fight against toxic dumping and to demand accountability for the illnesses that resulted.

The Warren County protest spawned several studies exploring the relationship between race and the sites chosen for hazardous wastes. The General Accounting Office studied four hazardous waste sites in the southeastern United States and found that most of the people in those communities were Black; one-fourth of the residents had incomes below the poverty level (McGurty, 1997). An 1987 study conducted by the United Church of Christ found that race was the most significant factor in the placement of hazardous waste facilities and that three out of every five African Americans and Hispanics were living in a community where there was a toxic waste site (McGurty, 1997).

The environmental justice movement focuses on the overlapping issues of the environment, human rights, and ecological sustainability (Bullard et al., 2005). Income, race, ethnicity, education, language, ability, and culture reinforce power imbalances that give rise to oppression. People with less power and resources are more likely to live near waste or industrial facilities and suffer from air or noise pollution from traffic, crowded living conditions that compromise health, and other environmental hazards.

Defining Environmental Justice

Throughout this book, we have identified the different kinds of justice (social, economic, and environmental) as the realization of the most relevant human rights affecting that type of justice. The challenge of defining environmental justice in this manner is that international law's relationship between human rights and environmental protection is not straightforward. International human rights instruments lack an explicit recognition of a human right to a safe, clean, healthy, and sustainable environment, even though this right has been recognized in regional agreements and most national constitutions. The right to a healthy environment is part of over 100 constitutions (UN Environment, 2019).

A safe, clean, healthy, and sustainable environment is necessary for the full enjoyment of human rights, such as the rights to life, the highest attainable standard of physical and mental health, a satisfactory standard of living, adequate food, and safe drinking water and sanitation, housing, self-determination, and participation in cultural life (Lewis, 2012). Environmental issues such as pollution, deforestation, or the misuse of resources limit an individual's or a community's ability to enjoy a specific right that is guaranteed to them. A poor environment may also impede a government's ability to protect and fulfill the rights of its citizens (Lewis, 2012).

Article 25 of the Universal Declaration of Human Rights states that everyone has the right to a standard of living adequate for the health and well-being of oneself and one's family. Living in a safe, nontoxic environment is essential to one's health and well-being. This can mean that governments have an obligation to ensure that we live and work in environments that support our health and well-being. In this same vein, the need to live and work in a healthy environment is closely linked to the right to life. The right to life appears in Article 6 of the International Covenant on Civil and Political Rights (UN General Assembly, 1966a).

An environment that fosters good health can also be interpreted as being part of one's right to health. Under Article 12 of the International Covenant on Economic, Social and Cultural Rights (ICESCR; UN General Assembly, 1966b), all people have the right to the highest attainable standard of health. The UN General Comment 14 on Article 12 (UN Committee on Economic, Social and Cultural Rights, 2000) makes explicit that preventing and reducing exposure to a toxic environment (radiation, chemicals, or other conditions) is necessary for one's health. This right is also reinforced in the Convention on the Rights of the Child (1989), the Convention on the Elimination of All Forms of Discrimination against Women (1979), and the International Convention on the Elimination of All Forms of Racial Discrimination (1965). Article 11 of the ICESCR guarantees all individuals the right to an adequate standard of living, including adequate food, clothing, and housing, and the continuous improvement of living standards. Environmental situations that affect the availability of clean, safe, and secure water supplies or limit a community's ability to food and nourishment violate one's right to an adequate standard of living.

In 2010, the UN General Assembly Resolution 64/292 declared safe and clean drinking water "as a human right essential for the full enjoyment of life and all human rights" (UN General Assembly, 2010). The tight interconnection between climate change, environmental justice, environmental degradation, and basic human rights has since been repeated in UN documents. In 2012, the United Nations Human Rights Council (UNHRC) passed Resolution 19/10, creating a Special Rapporteur explicitly dedicated to human rights and environmental justice (UNHRC, 2012). The Special Rapporteur was renewed for the third time in 2021. Then, in October 2021, the UN officially voted that a clean, healthy, and sustainable environment is a human right (UN General Assembly, 2021). Groundbreaking as this acknowledgment is, the right to a clean, healthy, and sustainable environment does not exist in any international treaty to date.

Recognizing the right to a clean, healthy, and sustainable environment moves us toward environmental justice for all. When governments or people violate human rights by causing or allowing environmental harm, failing to protect people from toxins, or allowing some groups but not all to realize rights, our human rights are violated and an environmental injustice occurs (UN Environment, 2019). The obligations of States to prohibit discrimination and ensure equal and adequate protection against discrimination apply to the equal enjoyment of human rights relating to a safe, clean, healthy, and sustainable environment. Governments and others are obliged to protect against environmental harm that results from or contributes to discrimination, provide for equal access to environmental benefits, and ensure that their actions relating to the environment do not themselves discriminate.

Human rights are intertwined with the natural and built environment. Human rights cannot be enjoyed without a safe, clean, and healthy environment; sustainable environmental governance cannot exist without establishing and respecting human rights. When human rights are not upheld—or not upheld for all—it is an injustice.

The Council on Social Work Education (CSWE)'s description of environmental justice in the 2015 Educational Policy and Accreditation Standards (EPAS) recognizes the complexity:

> Environmental justice occurs when all people equally experience high levels of environmental protection, and no group or community is excluded from the environmental policy decision-making process nor is affected by a disproportionate impact from environmental hazards. Environmental justice affirms the ecological unity and the interdependence of all species, respect for cultural and biological diversity, and the right to be free from ecological destruction. This includes responsible use of ecological resources, including land, water, air, and food. (Adapted from CSWE Commission for Diversity and Social and Economic Justice and Commission on Global Social Work Education Committee on Environmental Justice, 2015, p. 20)

Defining the Ecological Context

Although "environmental justice" and "ecological justice" are often used interchangeably, they are distinct. Ecological justice is more expansive and inclusive than environmental justice. Ecological justice encompasses humanity living within natural limits, connected to all creation, and not harming other species. As presented in Figure 11.1, the ecological environment is broader; it is the context for all existence and survival. The ecological justice framework provides the context for human social, political, and economic systems that enhance lives or place lives at risk. The decisions humans make affect human lives and all other forms of life. Environmental justice is about how the social, political, and economic systems humans develop affect the lives of humans, particularly when the burdens are distributed inequitably.

Human survival cannot be separated from a healthy ecological environment (Gilliam et al., in press). As humans, we rely on other life forms and should respect other forms of life. "Biodiversity is essential for the processes that support all life on Earth, including humans. Without a wide range of animals, plants, and microorganisms, we cannot have the healthy ecosystems that we rely on to provide us with the air we breathe and the food we eat. And people also value nature of itself" (The Royal Society, 2022, para. 1). Maintaining a rich ecosystem is vital for supporting crop pollination, water purity, soil integrity, and the interactions between water and land (Intergovernmental Science-Policy Platform on Biodiversity and Ecosystem Services [IPBES], 2018; The Royal Society, 2022). The field of eco-social work recognizes the centrality of nature for human and planetary well-being (Boetto, 2017; Powers et al., 2019).

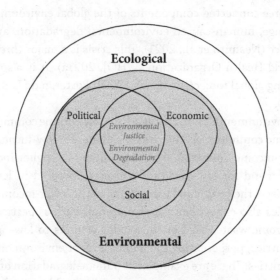

Figure 11.1. Interaction of ecological and environmental systems.
Adapted from Schmitz et al., 2013.

We are all exposed to pollution and toxic chemicals, but the burden of contamination falls disproportionately upon the shoulders of individuals, groups, and communities already challenged by poverty, discrimination, and systemic marginalization (Boyd, 2022). Environmental justice is an example of distributive justice, meaning that just outcomes are evaluated according to equity and fairness. The toxins in our environment are more likely to be borne by women, children, persons of color, migrants, Indigenous peoples, older persons, and persons with disabilities for various economic, social, cultural, and biological reasons. Laborers are at higher risk because they are more likely to be exposed to contamination on the job, are more likely to have poor working conditions, may have limited knowledge about chemical hazards, and may lack access to healthcare. So too are child laborers. Despite the reductions in child labor worldwide, millions of children work in potentially hazardous sectors, including agriculture, mining, and tanning. Likewise, those who live in low-income housing are more likely to be exposed to asbestos, lead, formaldehyde, and other toxic substances (Boyd, 2022).

The Global Environmental Crisis

To address local environmental inequities, we must first acknowledge the complexity of the global environmental crisis (Nesmith et al., 2021). There are three connected components of the global environmental crisis: climate change, human-caused environmental degradation, and environmental justice (Nesmith et al., 2021). This crisis is a major threat to public health (World Health Organization [WHO], 2021a). It is also a factor in the expanding global food crisis (Faiola, 2021; Porter, n.d.; United Nations News, 2021).

Just as environmental risks are higher for low-income communities than higher-income communities, the risks are higher for low-income countries than higher-income countries. For those living in higher-income countries, the demand for low-cost products manufactured in lower-income countries affects the health and ecosystems in the lower-income countries. Rich countries also export hazardous materials such as pesticides, plastic waste, electronic waste, used oil, and older vehicles to low- and middle-income countries, perpetuating the higher level of environmental hazards in other countries. These are examples of human degradation of our planet. Environmental justice cannot be achieved without addressing how humans degrade our ecological systems.

We must also confront how our actions lead to climate change. The rise in the temperature of our planet is destabilizing the Earth's poles and endangering the planet (Kaplan, 2021). In the last 40 years, the temperature has increased twice as fast as in the previous 100 years (Lindsey & Dahlman, 2021; United Nations Framework Convention on Climate Change [UNFCCC], 2021). If the warming continues at this rate, by the end of the 21st century, the average global temperature will increase 5 to 10 degrees Celsius (Lindsey & Dahlman, 2021).

Climate change threatens public health (National Public Radio, 2021). People in low- and middle-income countries are affected the most. Climate change has forced millions of people from their homes. People living in sinking small island states are threatened by rising sea levels caused by climate change. At the other extreme, severe drought endangers lives and livelihoods. By limiting access to needed resources, droughts may force migration and violent conflict (Intergovernmental Panel on Climate Change [IPCC], 2018).

OUR CHANGING ENVIRONMENT

- What changes in your environment have you noticed?
- How have the changes affected the way people live their lives?
- Who is most affected?
- What can you do or are you doing in response to the environmental changes you see happening?
- What are your thoughts about how social workers can be involved?

Environmental Justice Is a Social Work Issue

In social work, the embrace of environmental justice "requires practitioners to tackle structural and individual forms of oppression that impact upon people and destroy the environment in the process of creating a privileged life for the few" (Dominelli, 2013, p. 432). We all depend upon a healthy environment to fully enjoy the range of human rights. Without a safe and clean environment, we cannot expect to have human dignity for all (Daly & May, 2019).

As social workers, we work with individuals, families, groups, organizations, and communities. We are policymakers, advocates, and organizers. Our commitment to justice—social, economic, and environmental justice—provides a broad lens for analyzing issues. In shifting to an eco-social lens, eco-social workers make explicit the significance of the eco-logical environment for human existence (Powers et al., 2019).

Addressing Health

The environment can have devastating effects on health and morbidity. People in low-income and marginalized communities are more likely to be exposed to environmental hazards such as toxic substances, polluted water, or dangerously high levels of air or noise pollution (Cusick, 2020; Liu et al., 2021; WHO, 2021a). People living or working in impacted communities can develop many diseases, such as asthma, decreased lung function, emphysema, skin diseases, cancers, immune deficiencies, nerve disorders, and liver and kidney damage (WHO, 2021b). Exposure to toxic substances and air pollutants is also linked to early deaths. Pollution is now the leading global cause of premature death and disease (Landrigan et al., 2018). According to a WHO report, 24 percent of all global deaths, roughly 13.7 million deaths a year, are linked to environmental risks such as air pollution and chemical exposure (Prüss-Ustün et al., 2018).

Environmental degradation is a food justice issue for farmworkers who regularly work in fields sprayed with pesticides and people living in food deserts whose access to nutritional foods is limited (Kaiser et al., 2015). As agriculture became more industrialized, the farming sector consolidated, forcing smaller farmers out. Industrialized farming has replaced diverse, sometimes wild, crops with large blocks of homogeneous crops (Kaiser et al., 2015). Absent are the ecological systems that naturally provide sustenance for crops and wildlife and the diversity of food cultures. The result is mass production of genetically modified food products made widely available. Access to natural and minimally processed foods is limited because of their higher prices and select availability. Less affluent communities and communities of color are less likely to have access to healthy food products, have fewer food options, and are more likely to consume foods that will impair their health (e.g., foods with high levels of sodium and fat and with less nutritional value).

There are lessons to be learned by exploring the experience of the Flint, Michigan, community (see Nesmith et al., 2021). Despite years of persistence, advocacy, action, and organizing to make the systemic changes to restore safe and healthy drinking water to the community, the work of community members and others continues (Gilliam et al., in press).

WATER IN FLINT, MICHIGAN

The loss of industry in Flint, Michigan, was followed by years of White flight, and those who remained living in Flint were poorer and primarily persons of color (Highsmith, 2009). Poor economic prospects meant a loss of power and left remaining residents with fewer resources. Local and state officials looked for ways to save money and, unfortunately, chose solutions that endangered the health of the community (Butler et al., 2016; Denchak, 2018; Kennedy, 2016).

As Flint's social and economic infrastructure slowly crumbled, officials allowed the water supply to be poisoned and lied to residents about the dangers of their water supply. Dr. Hannah-Attisha, a lead researcher and advocate, persisted in fighting for the right of the people of Flint to know the truth about their water. City and state leaders rebuffed the evidence she presented, which showed that Flint children's blood lead levels had doubled after the water supply was switched from the Detroit River to the Flint River (Denchak, 2018). Despite the public officials' efforts to ridicule her work, Hannah-Attisha urged Flint residents, particularly children, to stop drinking the water, officials to stop using the Flint River as a water source as soon as possible, and the city to issue a health advisory. As public health officials and water experts joined Hannah-Attisha, officials eventually agreed that the data Hannah-Attisha presented were legitimate (Denchak, 2018; Hannah-Attisha, 2019). The change would not have occurred without years of organizing, advocacy, and lobbying (Nesmith et al., 2021; Gilliam et al., in press).

Residents won some battles but still continue their work for infrastructure change. Despite investigations and criminal and civil suits, many of those in power continue to sidestep accountability (Nesmith et al., 2021; Gilliam et al., in press). Residents of Flint have expanded their focus through the Environmental Transformation Movement of Flint (n.d.) to promote environmentally friendly solutions and a healthy living environment in their community.

- Identify three actions social workers can take to help the people living in Flint.
- Relate the Flint experience to other communities or your own experiences. What role did social workers play in these other communities?

Increasing Awareness of the Interconnections Between Mental Health and the Environment

Environmental issues also affect emotional well-being. As we become more aware of environmental injustices, we are also learning more about increasing mental health risks associated with environmental issues (WHO, 2021b). Climate change leads to physical losses and harm as well as the loss of security, stability, and predictability. The global environmental crisis can feel overwhelming (Turns, 2019). This contributes to mental and behavioral health concerns, including post-traumatic stress, depression, anxiety, and substance abuse (American Psychiatric Association, 2022; Climate Psychiatry Alliance, 2022).

People's experiences of climate change and environmental loss directly related to mental health are increasingly referred to as ecological grief (or eco-grief). It is the grief felt in relation to experienced or anticipated ecological losses, including the loss of species, ecosystems, and meaningful landscapes due to environmental change. Eco-grief is a natural response to ecological losses and is felt hardest by people who maintain close relationships with the natural environment (Cunsolo & Ellis, 2018).

Grief is a natural human response to loss. To grieve the loss of a loved one is a common human experience, yet we are far less familiar with how humans grieve losses in the natural world. We know that climate change is driving grief associated with the physical disappearance, degradation, and death of species, ecosystems, and landscapes (Cunsolo & Ellis, 2018). As in grieving the loss of another human, each of us experiences eco-grief differently. Feelings of grief and loss related to the environment vary in duration and intensity across humans and cultures. Depending on the meanings attached to the physical environment, gradual and cumulative losses in the physical environment may evoke complex grief responses for some people and mild, less visible experiences for others.

For many Indigenous peoples, the land and natural resources on which they depend for life are inextricably linked to their identities, cultures, livelihoods, and physical and spiritual well-being (Gilio-Whitaker, 2019; Nesmith et al., 2021). The forced removal and relocation of Indigenous peoples from their ancestral lands have often been accompanied by the loss of culture, language, livelihood, and well-being (Martinez & Irfan, 2021). Indigenous peoples often lack formal recognition over their lands, territories, and natural resources. They are often the last to receive public investments in essential services and infrastructure. They face multiple barriers to participating fully in the formal economy, enjoying access to justice, and taking part in political processes and decision-making. These traumas and forced migrations have left scars on their emotional well-being, which often go unrecorded and untreated. In the Western Hemisphere, Oceania, northern Russia, and China, Indigenous peoples experience high rates of alcoholism and suicide (WHO, 1999). Researchers estimate that nearly one out of three Aboriginal people in Australia suffer from psychological distress (Korff, 2022).

The history of inequality and exclusion has made Indigenous peoples more vulnerable to climate change, natural hazards, and disease. Indigenous peoples make up about 6 percent, or about 500 million, of the world's population, but one out of five people living in extreme poverty is an Indigenous person (Department of Economic and Social Affairs [DESA], 2009). The life expectancy of Indigenous peoples is nearly 20 years lower than the life expectancy of non-Indigenous people worldwide (DESA, 2009).

Another way climate change can increase ecological grief is through the loss of knowledge about how to respond to environmental changes. The loss of local knowledge, or traditional ecological knowledge, may affect those who have a close relationship to the immediate environment and may also affect society at large. For example, climate changes have led to a loss of confidence among Australian farmers in their ability to "know" the seasonal rhythms of the weather. Such loss is associated with heightened anxieties related to their livelihood's long-term future and viability. The loss of knowing can trigger feelings of loss around land-based knowledge passed on through generations (Cave 2020a, 2020b; Vernick, 2020).

TIME FOR REFLECTION AND DISCUSSION

- When you think about climate change, what do you feel?
- In what ways have you experienced climate change? What emotions have your experiences around climate change made you feel?
- What do you love and appreciate about the Earth?
- How does your environment affect your emotional well-being?
- Does eco-grief merit further study in social work? Why or why not?

Community Action

Social workers have a longstanding legacy of community action that we bring to practice in addressing the fallout from the global environmental crisis. While environmental justice frames our understanding of inequity and inequality, embracing eco-social practice frames how we understand the impact of climate change, environmental injustice, and systemically supported degradation. The community is a site for building relationships, acquiring skills, sharing knowledge, and developing collaborations. As our environment continues to change, communities will need to organize and develop the skills to adapt to new conditions while remediating dangerous conditions and their impact on individuals and communities.

TIME FOR DISCUSSION AND REFLECTION

As temperatures increase, weather extremes will increase, causing changes to the land, the oceans, vegetation, and wildlife. How do you think this will impact your community?

As temperatures rise with climate change, the impact of racist policy becomes more evident. Research in urban areas finds that temperatures are up to 13 degrees warmer in communities that were historically redlined (Hoffman et al., 2020). From 1990 to 2010, air pollution in the United States decreased, yet predominantly Black communities experienced increased exposure to air pollution (Liu et al., 2021). "Air pollution and extreme heat are killing inner-city residents at a higher rate than almost all other causes" (Cusick, 2020, para. 4).

The community provides a site for local organizing. The process of reclaiming the ecological environment by local residents can raise awareness about environmental justice while increasing cohesion, empowerment, and sustainability. Encouraging greater individual and collective understanding of climate change and injustice and engaging in action can increase commitment to valued community spaces (Groulx, 2017).

LESSONS FROM THE GREEN BELT MOVEMENT CASE STUDY

Wangari Maathai grew up in a village in Kenya that was lush, with a thriving ecosystem. When she returned after her undergraduate and a first graduate degree in the United States, she found that the village ecosystem had been decimated. Having received her first two degrees in the biological sciences and the third in veterinary anatomy, she turned her energy toward healing the ecology and the community. Her experience also informed her work as a woman marginalized in the political and economic systems. (See Sloan & Schmitz, 2019, for further discussion.)

Maathai engaged the women of the village in germinating and planting trees. As they worked together, they built relationships and the skills for creating social and ecological change. As the trees grew, a lush ecosystem returned. The women began to train women in other villages while creating revenue sources for themselves through their work with the land and animals. Their work led to the development of the Greenbelt Movement, which is now a global model (Green Belt Movement, 2018; Maathai, 2003, 2006; Merton & Dater, 2008; Strides in Development, 2010).

The Green Belt Movement expanded, taking a leadership role in educating people on the skills needed for creating environmental, political, and social change through political action. Participants learn the skills for facilitating change and engaging in nonviolent political action. Explore the website for the Green Belt Movement (https://www.greenb eltmovement.org/wangari-maathai) to see the connections between ecological change, the empowerment of women, advocacy, political action, and climate change.

Environmental and ecological justice can also be engaged at the neighborhood level. Organizing to "rewild" neighborhoods (facilitating the return of indigenous plants and animals) helps mitigate climate change (Tallamy, 2020). Engaging neighborhoods in the process of change can be a source of individual growth and community empowerment. Among the more common models for local action are community gardens, urban farming, rewilding, and organizing to plant trees.

Rising Incidences of Environmental Disasters

If the increase of emissions from greenhouse gasses continues at the current rate, disasters will continue to increase in frequency and unpredictability, and, combined with environmental degradation, we will see the continued pattern of too much or too little water (Kaplan & Dennis, 2021). According to *Environmental Health News*, "The common denominator of these disasters is their role in exacerbating social and health inequities, from negative health outcomes to increasing wealth gaps. Many communities, particularly Indigenous communities, have been dealing with similar challenges for decades" (Martinez & Irfan, 2021, para. 4).

We need to respond in layers, first addressing the immediate crisis and then rebuilding, which involves both adaptation and remediation. Studies show that community response is key to both the immediate and recovery response (van Heugten, 2014). Preparing for disasters, supporting the development of social networks, and engaging in actions to prevent and mitigate the effects of the climate crisis can help lower stress and anxiety for community members (American Psychiatric Association, 2022).

FIRE CASE STUDY

Devastating fires are ravaging multiple countries as they face drought related to the increase in planetary temperatures. Across the Amazon, Australia, and the western United States, fires have resulted in the loss of millions of acres of land (Ivanovich, 2018). Western and Southern states in the United States are experiencing a multi-year drought. Record-setting fires have raged across California, Colorado, Texas, Arizona, and Oregon over the last few years. In spring 2022, New Mexico experienced a new record of wildfires raging across the state (Cappucci & Samenow, 2022). The extensive devastation caused by these fires is causing people to flee their homes (Astor, 2022). Abnormally high temperatures, severe drought, unusually low humidity, and high winds set the stage for increasing danger. As Astor notes, "Wildfires are a natural part of the ecosystems of the West, but human activity has made them far worse" (Astor, 2022, para. 6).

When homes and businesses are burned to the ground, communities are destroyed. Fires ravage vegetation and wildlife, leaving ecosystems stressed (Cave, 2020a). Some communities are working to lower the danger by changing the natural and built environment, including reintroducing indigenous plants (Betigeri, 2020).

Indigenous people living in a close relationship with the land have developed a knowledge of nature and the land that can be informative (McLean, 2012). The knowledge gained through traditional practices leads to incorporating nature to protect and heal the environment (Betigeri, 2020). In 2019 in Australia, areas experienced devastating fires that destroyed millions of acres and killed more than 3 billion animals. Residents came to recognize there would not be a return to normal (Cave 2020a, 2020b; Vernick, 2020). Consequently, some communities have hired Indigenous fire experts to reduce risk (Vernick, 2020). Those communities that used traditional cultural burning methods to adapt did better (Cave, 2020b).

From the early days of the social work profession, social work pioneers understood the importance of environmental justice in solving societal ills. Over the years, social work emphasized social relations over physical conditions when considering the environmental context. Regardless, inequities in the physical environment manifested the oppressions of racism and classism.

Our awareness about the dimensions and interactions of the environment with human well-being has grown. The global environmental crisis highlights the interactive juncture of environmental justice, environmental degradation, and climate change. As the degradation of our resources continues, the levels of toxins we release rise and the temperatures and disasters increase. Marginalized communities and those with less voice repeatedly suffer the most.

We are also increasingly aware of the vulnerability of the land, plants, and wildlife around us that are struggling and, at the same time, vital for our well-being. An ecological frame embraces all forms of life and our shared existence, including our social, economic, and political human systems. As social workers, we need to understand how these systems interact and interact for different groups. This knowledge facilitates our ability to help others. Areas intersecting social work practice are wide-ranging. The topics discussed in this chapter—physical and mental well-being, disaster response and remediation, and community building—are just a few areas affected by environmental justice. Social workers bring their knowledge and skills to practice at these junctures.

Understanding the strengths of diversity and the need to build off those strengths in developing coordinated responses provides a base for engaging in transformative change. The community offers a context for healing as we work to heal our human communities within the ecology and nature.

Integrating a Human Rights Approach to Justice in Social Work Practice

CHAPTER 12

Applying a Rights-Based Approach to Justice in Social Work

You have learned about human rights, oppression and power, and social, economic, and environmental justice. Each of these concepts is powerful, and together they have the potential to transform social work practice and people's lives. The foundation of a rights-based approach to social work practice rests on a simple yet critical principle—respect for one another. A rights-based approach asks us to respect whomever we work with, whether we agree or don't agree with someone else's opinions, positions, actions, or goals. Helping people better their lives has always been at the core of social work practice, and doing this while showing respect for and giving dignity to the people we work with was an essential aspect of the profession at its founding. Over the years, though, we've strayed as a profession. History has shown us that social workers confused their professional expertise as a license to wield their perspectives on how people should live their lives. As social workers, our foremost guide should be the people we are serving. All too often, social workers became the enforcers of the dominant group's vision rather than advocating for the rights of the people they were serving. When social workers prioritize enforcing the dominant group's view, we may intentionally or unintentionally violate the human rights of the people. In doing so, social workers run the risk of perpetuating the injustices in our society.

This book aims to "right" social work practice (Gatenio Gabel et al., 2022). By introducing social work students to human rights and related concepts early on in their social work education, the book hopes to shape

A Human Rights-Based Approach to Justice in Social Work Practice. Shirley Gatenio Gabel, Oxford University Press.
© Oxford University Press 2024. DOI: 10.1093/oso/9780197570647.003.0012

how social workers will see social issues to further justice. Seeking justice is the basis of our professional ethics and values in social work.

Throughout the text, you've been practicing how to identify human rights, where to locate human rights treaties and laws, and how to apply them. When we don't protect and promote human rights, we inadvertently can further situations that concentrate power in the hands of a few and oppress people's lives, livelihoods, and choices. You've learned how to take on different perspectives by understanding your own position in society and the positionality of the people with whom you are working. We've explored intersectionality in all our lives to learn how many of us can simultaneously be privileged and oppressed. We then learned about the different ways we can understand justice. We differentiated and explored social, economic, and environmental justice and learned why each of them is important in social work practice.

In this chapter, we put it all together. In short, we will learn how to integrate a rights-based approach to justice in social work practice, whether we're working on a one-to-one basis with individuals and families, in a community or organization, or with policymakers to change systems.

A RIGHTS-BASED APPROACH TO JUSTICE

International human rights instruments are based on universally recognized principles and provide a rich and distinct and, most times, a legal framework for approaching current social, economic, and environmental injustices that intersect with social work practice. Rights-based approaches in social work practice look to understand the root of the problem and how the different systems have hindered the delivery of justice that manifests as inequities, exclusion, and marginalization.

A rights-based approach means that with every right comes a corresponding responsibility. All of us, as human beings, have rights and responsibilities. The Universal Declaration of Human Rights (UDHR) recognizes that everyone is born free and is equal in dignity, worth, and freedom. It also acknowledges that we have responsibility for one another and our communities. Communities are important on a personal level because the right to free and full development of an individual's personality needs a supportive community for this to happen. We all are part of communities and are responsible for fostering communities that appreciate and promote human rights. It is our responsibility as rights-bearers.

As rights-bearers, we also have the responsibility of choosing governments and creating institutions that will respect and promote human rights. Governments and their institutions have the primary responsibility to respect, protect, and fulfill human rights by creating the infrastructure needed to advance human rights and uphold justice. Governments must hold individuals and organizations accountable if they violate the rights of others or fail to uphold rights. Yet, as social workers, we are responsible for supporting and empowering individuals and communities to claim their rights and encourage governments that respect and promote rights. As private individuals and professionals, we also have the responsibility to call governments out when they fall short of fulfilling their obligation to uphold human rights and justice.

A rights-based approach is different from the approach we came to rely on in social work practice. Social work adopted a needs-based approach, sometimes called the medical model. In a needs-based approach, professionals are trained to become experts who inform service users of their needs and decide the worthiness of the needs presented (Gatenio Gabel, 2016). Evaluating needs is couched in the dominant view and values of how people should live their lives, with little or no input from service users. The needs-based approach trains professionals to assess, diagnose, and treat according to standards and goals developed by experts. The emphasis is on what is wrong with an individual or situation, not the rights of individuals to self-determine how they want to live their lives and the responsibilities of the government to support them.

Think about going to a physician for a health problem you are experiencing. You would relate your symptoms to the physician, who would diagnose you and recommend a treatment. Suppose you don't want to take medications prescribed or undergo chemotherapy, preferring natural healing methods. The chances are that the same physician would not treat you, and perhaps would refer you to a different health provider. In a rights-based approach, the health provider would be guided by your desired treatment, helping you understand the likely consequences of your choices, not imposing a directive, and would be prepared to treat you according to your wishes.

Another critical difference between a rights-based and a needs-based approach is that in a needs-based approach, the outcomes are prioritized over the process (Gatenio Gabel et al., 2022; Gatenio Gabel, 2016). A rights-based approach values both outcomes and the process. Imagine, for example, that you are working with youth in a community-based organization. Your organization has a public grant to reduce teen pregnancies in the community. The grant measures your success by your organization's ability to reduce the number of teen pregnancies. In a needs-based approach, reducing the incidence of teenage pregnancies would be prioritized. By comparison, a

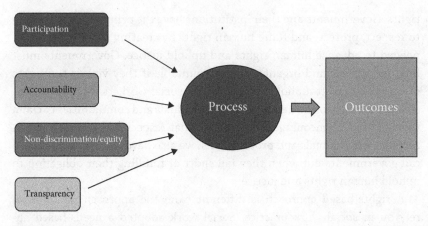

Figure 12.1. Rights-based approach to justice.

rights-based approach may have the same outcome but will also value the process of achieving and arriving at the outcome (Figures 12.1 and 12.2). For example, a rights-based approach would include youth discussing teen pregnancy, their feelings about it, their preferences, and their ideas about how teen pregnancies could or should be reduced. It might also include parent groups having similar discussions and input. This type of participation from the community increases the sustainability of the solutions. It also reduces the likelihood that discriminatory practices and outcomes will be chosen and increases the transparency and accountability of programs.

Participation in decision-making helps shift power from government officials and their agents to service users. A result of ongoing participation is that goals are not static in a rights-based approach. In a needs-based approach, goals are established for a program, usually for a set period. In a rights-based approach, goals are constantly changing because we learn things as we go along from experts, service users, community members, organizations, and other stakeholders. Learning from different perspectives leads us to understand things differently. As our knowledge is enhanced,

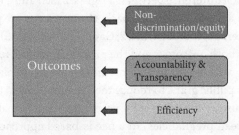

Figure 12.2. Needs-based approach to justice.

the goals we've established may need to be modified to reflect the change in our knowledge.

In a rights-based approach, goals are based on human rights standards, unlike needs-based goals that typically are grounded in economic efficiency or social control. Human rights-based normative standards are what we aspire to achieve. In reality, no one has wholly achieved these standards, though some countries are farther along than others. Countries where efforts are made to involve societal members in transparent, responsible, and inclusive decision-making tend to be farther along in realizing human rights and have created more economically, socially, and environmentally just societies.

PERSON-IN-ENVIRONMENT FRAMEWORK IN SOCIAL WORK PRACTICE

The founding of social work was an acknowledgment that individuals do not exist in vacuums and are very much influenced by their physical and social environments. The way we establish our social structures and the condition of the physical environment will affect the opportunities, dreams, and lived experiences of people. Unlike other helping professions that primarily look inward to the individual and try to help the individual fix what's not working on the inside, social work goes beyond the individual to consider how the individual's family, community, neighborhood, and public policies contribute to social problems and the kind of support needed. Considering how the individual's physical and the emotional environment influence the individual is referred to as the person-in-environment (PIE) perspective. We use this perspective to develop intervention strategies in social work practice.

The PIE perspective, sometimes referred to as a theory, is a crucial concept and philosophy in social work that states that a person's behavior can largely be understood by looking at their environment, including their background. For many people, a father who abused his children may not be someone we would want to help, but we would find empathy to work with this person as social workers. Unlike other helping professions, a social worker would look at the individual's history of environmental influences, including an alcoholic mother who neglected him as a child, an abusive father who beat him, and a violence-ridden neighborhood. This history would help us understand how the environment influenced his behavior. Understanding this does not condone the father's abuse, of course, but it allows us to see how the father is a product of the environment he grew up in. It also makes clear that if we want to help this family, we must focus on the well-being of the family and on the well-being of the communities that families live in.

The PIE perspective goes back to the founding of social work. Mary Richmond, one of the social work pioneers in the early 20th century, spearheaded the concept that people's problems were heavily influenced by their environment. In 1917, she wrote the first social work textbook, *Social Diagnosis*. Richmond urged social workers to consider a person's mental health issues within the context of the environment, including the policies that affected the individual's well-being. Richmond is best known for her contributions to establishing casework methods. She was also an advocate for social change and believed that social workers needed to be part of the larger political and legal worlds to help people.

The PIE perspective provides a holistic and comprehensive method for assessing clients. Social workers assess many environmental aspects, including religious, political, familial, community, socioeconomic, ecological, and educational, to best understand someone's behavior. Social workers identify these aspects of the environment to understand better how the environments contribute to the challenges an individual or family is facing. Sometimes, a social worker can help people by helping them access benefits or services that they could not access on their own, or by helping a family move to a safer neighborhood. Or, having heard that several people are experiencing a similar problem, a social worker may advocate for social change to address the problem by organizing the community and speaking to policymakers.

In her writings, Richmond included the physical environment as part of the PIE perspective. She viewed it as critical to understanding the social aspects of individual choices (Richmond, 1922). As social work developed over the years, the importance of the physical environment diminished, and greater emphasis was placed on social interactions.

Systems theories—explanations of how factors at different levels affected the whole system or individual—became very popular in the early 20th century among psychologists and natural scientists and were adapted as social system theories in social work. Social systems theories hold that who we are as individuals is a product of the groups, organizations, societies, and families surrounding us. These theories build upon the PIE perspective.

In the 1960s, biological scientists studying ecology coined the term *ecological perspective*, referring to the study of organisms and how they interact with their environments. In the 1970s, Gitterman and Germain (1976) applied this concept to social work to capture the transactional process between humans and their environments. People's needs were conceptualized into interrelated areas that transcended the methodological methods of practice, such as casework, family therapy, and group work. Both social systems theories and ecological perspectives heavily influenced Gitterman and Germain's life model theory of social work practice (Gitterman & Germain, 1976). The life model calls upon social workers to help individuals examine their environment and cope with the limitations and toxicity in the environment—whether it be at the level of interpersonal relationships, community, institutions, policies, or critical historical events and societal changes that influence generational cohorts.

Other theories have incorporated an ecological perspective and systems theories over time. The ecological perspective and systems theory is at the heart of social work practice. It distinguishes social work from other helping professions that may not account for how an individual's environment affects their well-being. This approach will generally differentiate three levels (sometimes four) of nested systems: microsystems, mezzo systems, and macrosystems (Figure 12.3).

Microsystems are the people, groups, and institutions that most directly influence an individual's well-being, from an individual's emotional and behavioral health to access to benefits. **Mezzosystems** are the communities, institutions, and organizations affecting individuals, such as schools, health centers, businesses, social services entities, public benefit centers, and community-based organizations. **Macrosystems** refer to the general culture, media representations, laws, policies, and public regulations affecting how individuals are perceived and their well-being.

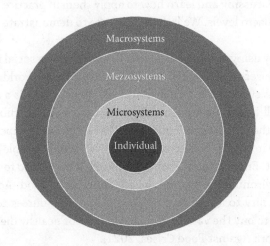

Figure 12.3. Micro-, mezzo-, and macrosystems in social work.

This approach trains social workers to look beyond the individual to understand factors at multiple systems levels that contribute to the challenges of service users. You'll be learning more about this in your social work studies.

What is neglected in the evolution of the PIE perspective is how the physical environment interacts with human beings and affects their well-being. As Zapf has noted (2009), a number of scholars have pointed out the shift from the environment to exclusively the social environment in the latter part of the 20th century. Today, however, social workers are eager to re-invite the effects of the physical environment on individuals (and vice versa) back into social work practice. The recognition of environmental justice in the Council on Social Work Education Educational Policy and Accreditation Standards (CSWE EPAS) is an important step forward in training future social workers to include the physical environment in their assessment and intervention plans at all levels of social work practice. Including the environment is not only about righting injustices. There are significant differences in access, availability, and use of services, benefits, employment, and inclusiveness depending on whether someone resides in a rural, suburban, or urban community. Place has powerful implications for one's sense of identity, perspective, and resources for problem-solving.

INTEGRATING THE HUMAN RIGHTS APPROACH TO JUSTICE IN SOCIAL WORK PRACTICE

It's time for us to pull together the many concepts, theories, and ideas we've been discussing and learn how to apply them in practice at the micro, mezzo, and macro levels. We'll then use a case to demonstrate how this can be applied.

We start by using a rights-based lens to understand a social issue. For example, food insecurity is one of the critical social issues worldwide, even in rich countries such as the United States. Food insecurity is a major threat to the overall health of humans, more so than malaria, tuberculosis, or HIV. During the COVID pandemic in 2020–21, the world experienced a severe increase in global food insecurity. Nearly 1 billion people did not have enough to eat. Enough food is being produced; it's access to food that is the problem. Environmental issues may affect access to food. Access to food includes inability to afford to buy food, a lack of resources to grow food, and inability to buy the variety of food we need for healthy diets (FSIN and Global Network Against Food Crises, 2021).

Step 1: Diagnose the Social Problem from a Rights-Based Perspective

Diagnosing the problem involves the following actions:

- Identify the social issue/problem and its results.
- Apply international human rights instruments and documents to explain the social problem. Whenever possible, cite national laws and policies that affirm the right in question or the absence of such law or policy.
- Frame the social issue from a rights-based perspective (e.g., human rights violation, partial realization of a human right, participatory process neglected).

From a rights-based framework, we would diagnose the social problem as the inaccessibility to food. The right to food and the right to be free from hunger stems from Article 25 of the UDHR, which lays out the right to a minimum standard of living (United Nations, 1948). The right to food is expanded upon in the International Covenant on Economic, Social and Cultural Rights (ICESCR, 1966). The right to food is presented as integral to the overall right to a minimum standard of living and is comprehensively defined in General Comment 12, written by the Special Rapporteur on the Right to Food (Ziegler, 2005):

> The right to adequate food is realized when every man, woman and child, alone or in community with others, has the physical and economic access at all times to adequate food or means for its procurement. (UN General Assembly, International Covenant on Economic, Social and Cultural Rights, 1966)

Several countries have created constitutional amendments, national laws, strategies, policies, and programs that aim to fulfill the right to food for all. The U.S. Department of Agriculture (2022) defines food security as "access by all people to enough food for an active and healthy life." In 2020, over 10 percent of U.S. households (13.8 million households) were food insecure. Food-insecure households (those with low and very low food security) are defined as those that had difficulty at some time during the year providing enough food for all their members because of a lack of resources. Maine is the only U.S. state that recognizes a right to food; voters there approved an amendment to the state constitution in November 2021 (Brennan, 2022). However, if access to food can be related to discriminatory practices in the United States, advocates can argue that it violates the

International Covenant on Civil and Political Rights (ICCPR), which was ratified by the United States in 1992.

Step 2: Demonstrate How Not Upholding a Human Right or Principle Is an Injustice

Demonstrating this involved the following actions:

- Describe how intersectionality has contributed to the social problem/issue identified. Have certain populations been oppressed as a result of discriminatory policies or practices? In what ways?
- Identify and explain the main social, economic, and environmental injustice(s) presented by the social problem/issue identified.

Again using food insecurity as an example, think about what populations in the United States may be more prone to food insecurity than others. Households with children are more likely to be food insecure than those without (U.S. Department of Agriculture, 2022). In more than half of these households, only the adults were food insecure (U.S. Department of Agriculture, 2022). Households with children headed by a single woman are nearly twice as likely as those headed by a single man to be food insecure. However, women living alone are at virtually equal risk as men living alone. Among Black, non-Hispanic households, 21.7 percent experience food insecurity, compared to 17.2 percent of Hispanic households and 7.1 percent of non-Hispanic White households. Lower-income households are more likely to be food insecure than those with higher incomes. Over 35 percent of households at or below the federal poverty level (FPL) are food insecure, compared to 5.1 percent of those earning 185 percent or more of the FPL. These statistics suggest that although everyone has the right to food, single-mother, low-income households headed by Black or Hispanic mothers are highly vulnerable. We would investigate whether statistics support this and look for research studies that have explored causal factors (e.g., affordability, availability) and whether policies have omitted or neglected the realities of low-income, Black and Brown single-mother households. For example, are food assistance policies targeted to only the very poor rather than poor and near-poor households? Is there sufficient funding? Are there affordable food stores in low-income communities? We should also consider the location of communities—geographic isolation may result in higher food prices, for instance, and this would disproportionately affect lower-income households.

Using existing data and research findings, we would determine if the food insecurity of low-income, Black and Hispanic single-mother households is due to social, economic, or environmental injustices.

Step 3: Develop Rights-Based Social Work Interventions for Justice

Developing interventions involves the following actions:

- Consider how your proposed intervention will address the root cause(s) of the social problem/issue.
- How will the proposed intervention promote and protect the human rights you've identified?
- How will the proposed intervention address the justice concerns you've identified?
- Specify whether the intervention proposed is at the micro, mezzo, or macro level, and why.

After doing our research, we may conclude that food insecurity among the single-mother households we identified may be due to poverty, chronic health issues, and lack of affordable housing. Households with limited incomes often have to face tradeoffs between food and other necessities such as shelter and medication (Wight et al., 2014). Yet not all poor households are food insecure, and households above the FPL can also be food insecure. Let's say we investigate this further and learn that affordable housing is scarce in communities with higher incidences of food insecurity. The scarcity of housing may force some mothers to accept lower-quality housing that compromises their health and their children's health. Perhaps the resulting poor health of the mothers or children compromises the ability of the mothers to work full time or at all, and therefore their household incomes are lower.

What could we do as social workers at the macro, mezzo, and micro levels?

In about half of the single-mother homes, the mothers were found to be food insecure but not the children. Perhaps this is because children are receiving school breakfasts and lunches, and mothers are using sparse funds to provide dinners and snacks at the expense of their own health. Possible responses at the macro level would be to advocate for dinners to be served at childcare centers or for higher food assistance levels. At the mezzo level, we may want to consider holding nutrition classes for parents if we believe they need more education about eating a healthy diet. Perhaps we could advocate for more affordable food stores in a community. At the micro level, we may want to work with parents on household budgeting or getting a parent the health services needed.

Food insecurity across the United States is correlated with an increased prevalence of chronic health conditions such as diabetes, hypertension, and arthritis (Seligman et al., 2010). These chronic conditions lead to higher healthcare costs and higher levels of healthcare utilization that negatively affect individuals, families, and society. For example, diabetics may be more likely to use the emergency department because of poor nutrition, resulting in lower cognitive functioning. The result of either of these scenarios is that a family is less likely to meet work and family demands and will need help. In other words, we all bear the costs of someone going hungry.

Using a rights-based approach, in addition to government statistics and research findings, we would want to speak with individuals who are food insecure to hear what they are experiencing and how they can be helped, regardless of whether our intervention was aimed at the micro, mezzo, or macro level.

PRACTICING TO PRACTICE

Near and dear to the social work profession since its founding has been protecting and promoting the well-being of children. Despite the efforts of social workers worldwide, children continue to be treated in ways that are harmful to their health and mental well-being. Such practices violate children's rights and are a social injustice that requires us to think innovatively to address its root causes.

The following case example is based on the New York City child welfare system. The case can help students develop practice skills from a rights-based approach to justice.

NARROWING THE FRONT DOOR TO NEW YORK CITY'S CHILD WELFARE SYSTEM

During the first year of the COVID-19 shutdowns in New York City, children could not attend school in person. Fears arose that without the eyes and ears of school personnel and childcare providers, the well-being of children would suffer. Instead, the number of reports to the system, investigations of families, families surveilled and supervised, and removals of children from their homes were cut in half (Arons, 2021).

Child welfare reports dropped, emergency department visits declined, and the number of hospitalizations was stable (Sege & Stevens, 2021). The near-shutdown of the system of reporting parents for not caring for their children appears not to have placed children at higher risk; instead, it seems children were safe and doing well. Rates of substantiated abuse did not rise—they dipped, rates of substantiated neglect remained unchanged, and children and families were not separated—they stayed in their homes.

Nationally, the total number of child abuse reports to state child welfare agencies plummeted by up to 70% during the pandemic (Swedo et al., 2020). Decreased reporting by educators due to school closures cannot explain the total decline. Yet, the reduced reporting by schools diminished the disproportionate reporting of families of color, one example of bias that has led to widely acknowledged racial disparities in child welfare reporting (Lukens et al., 2021). In New York City, neighborhoods with the highest rates of child poverty had rates of investigation four times higher than neighborhoods with the lowest child poverty rates. Even among neighborhoods with similar poverty rates, Black and Latino residents had higher rates of investigation (Arons, 2021).

What was happening during COVID-19 tells an essential story about prevention. The enhanced federal assistance available to families during the pandemic was protective, and the ability of a parent to spend more time in their homes with their children made children feel better and strengthened family relations. Establishing positive parenting practices appears to have substantially reduced risk factors for child physical abuse and corporal punishment (Sege & Stephens, 2021).

The biggest driver of families into the child welfare system (many families affected by the system believe the "family regulation system" is a better name) is poverty and related stressors. In New York City, hundreds of millions of tax dollars are spent on investigations, surveillance, policing families, court filings, family separation, and, all too often, the permanent dissolution of a family. These funds expended might be worth it if the system achieved its promises to safeguard children and families—but it does not. Research shows that foster youth are more likely than their peers to experience a host of troubling outcomes, including low academic achievement, grade retention, lower high school graduation rates, and higher risk for poor mental health (Gypen et al., 2017). Parents, too, undergo trauma that affects them for years and may interfere with their ability to lead self-sufficient lives. The family regulation system also has long played a key role in maintaining racial and class hierarchies through its policing of Black, Native, and immigrant families (Arons, 2021).

In sum, these results signal that we have failed to invest in what children need the most—*their families*. When families are under economic and emotional stress, children suffer. And yet, when families are genuinely in need of help at a time when a parent has left the family, or a parent has lost a job, has lost their childcare support, or is overwhelmed by the responsibilities of trying to earn an income and raise a family, often on their own—rather than rush in with supports, we do the opposite. We actually add to the burdens a parent is already struggling with by separating children from their families, causing further trauma and uncertainty in their lives. Investigations into family lives are more likely to add more stress and trauma to children and their families than positive outcomes. It is time for a new approach that helps children and families and supports rather than punishes them as they go through challenging periods in their lives.

Questions to consider:

- What is the social problem/issue in the case above?
- What human rights are violated or unrealized? Explain how.
- Which human rights instruments refer to the rights you have identified?

One of the issues highlighted by the case example is the racism existing in the child welfare or family regulation system and its devastating impact on children and families. We are learning that the system created to protect children and families is biased, often crushes family integrity and autonomy, and too often harms children. The families and children affected are disproportionately Black and other children of color. Most cases involve parents who cannot meet their children's basic needs due to poverty—only one out of four cases reported to protective services involves parental abuse of children. Over the years, policies and laws passed at the federal and state levels have reinforced punitive practices for families needing support, especially Black families. Authorities more frequently investigate Black parents than parents of other races. These investigations of families are often traumatic, intrusive, and disruptive and are more likely to result in children's removal from the home. Black parents are also more likely than other parents to have their parental rights terminated. Structural racism in child welfare is longstanding.

- How does this information affect your identification of the social problem?
- How do you think intersectionality has contributed to the social problem/issue identified?
- What is the main social, economic, and environmental injustice(s) presented in the case example?

As social workers, we are adept at taking issues from case to cause—from micro to macro perspectives. Read the case story below. Think about the perspective of child welfare caseworkers, parents, and children and how intersectionality comes into play.

- Is Sarah being oppressed? How?
- What intervention would you plan from a rights-based approach to justice as her social worker?
  - How would your proposed intervention address the root cause(s) of the social problem/issue?
  - Would you intervene at the micro, mezzo, or macro level? Why?
- How would the proposed intervention promote and protect Sarah's human rights?
- How would the proposed intervention address the justice concerns identified?

SARAH

As a child, I cried out for help, but the system didn't help me when I was a child, and it hasn't helped me as a parent.

When I was a teenager, I had enough of fighting off my mother's husband, who would come on to me sexually and kept trying to have sex with me. My mother wouldn't defend me. Instead, she accused me of wanting attention and lying when I complained. I called NYC Administration for Children's Services and ACS sided with my mother rather than me. Her husband had not penetrated me, so it was my word against theirs. I felt like I didn't matter, like my safety didn't matter, like my being a child didn't matter. I felt invalidated as a human being.

My mother shipped me off to Pakistan in response to the ACS investigation. I lived in Pakistan for a year with my stepfather's family. The values were so different, and I appreciated the good parts. Families sat together for meals; children respected their elders. But there were times when the family would beat me, and they arranged a marriage for me that I didn't want. My U.S. citizenship meant they could get a good dowry price. Again, I felt alone, abandoned, and unprotected.

Finally, I asked a friend to call the U.S. Embassy on my behalf. They sent a car for me, and I left Pakistan, but my mother said she could not protect me from her husband if I came to live with her again. With no place to live, I ended up on the streets and in the shelter system.

It was during this period that I met my oldest son's father. He abused me physically and emotionally, and I thought that was his way of showing love. I didn't know it could be different. I never for a second thought he would abuse our son. But he did.

One day our infant son was fussing, and in response, his father bit him on the back three times. He said he was playing, but the bites were serious. My son's father didn't care and took off. I was upset and scared but didn't know where to go. Living in a shelter with an infant, especially a fussy one, isn't easy. Everyone is in your business, and people called ACS on me two or three times when they heard my son crying at night. Shortly after the biting incident, someone called ACS again and wanted to know how my son got his bruises. I lied and said I got his skin caught in his stroller. I lied because I was scared that ACS would remove him and that his father would come after me. I didn't trust ACS because they didn't protect me as a child. Lying was the only way I knew to protect my son. I could have used some coaching to understand how to be safe and tell the truth. ACS concluded that I bit my son and removed him. My son went into care at a few months old and wasn't returned to me until he was nearly three years old.

I continue to live in constant fear of ACS, and so does my child. My son was diagnosed with ADHD and ODD and has separation anxiety. I can't help believing that his time away from me contributed to his problems. When I disagreed with the school about placing my son in a class for special education students, the school called ACS, and they placed him in foster care for two weeks. When my son came home, he was angry at me, and he started acting out. My past experiences with ACS seem to haunt me no matter how hard I try to be a good mother to my son. If my son has trouble in school, the first assumption is that I'm doing something wrong, and it becomes my responsibility to prove otherwise.

The system allowed me to get molested. Then it took my son. And no matter how hard I try, I can't get the system out of my life.

CHAPTER 13
Conclusion

Each of us comes to social work with a desire to make a social situation better. Our interests are diverse, and so are the people and communities we hope to help. Uniting us, however, is a belief that we can introduce change in the lives of people and communities that will improve lives for the better.

The founders of the social work profession seemed to understand that systemic changes were needed to bring justice to the lives of individuals and communities. Our social work pioneers were human rights defenders, challenging practices and the systems we were building. As the profession evolved and social workers worked with a range of social issues, people, and communities, we also became splintered. Arguing for increased professionalization, many social workers focused on developing theories and interventions that would distinguish social work as a profession. In doing so, the importance of seeking justice and fighting for human rights receded. Advocacy was left to macro-practitioners, those social workers who mainly practiced in communities, organizations, and policy arenas. The fissure created between micro-practitioners and macro-practitioners grew more profound over the years. As interest in clinical social work grew, the progressive nature of the social work profession also waned.

A human rights-based approach to justice in social work practice reverses this trend. In a rights-based approach, all social workers begin by interpreting social issues through a human rights lens. Is a situation violating or promoting human rights? Is it privileging some and oppressing others? Are those affected by the changes being discussed part of the

A Human Rights-Based Approach to Justice in Social Work Practice. Shirley Gatenio Gabel, Oxford University Press.
© Oxford University Press 2024. DOI: 10.1093/oso/9780197570647.003.0013

discussion? A rights-based approach looks at both outcomes and the process for arriving at the outcomes, just as we do in social work.

A rights-based approach appreciates the interrelatedness of social issues and individuals, groups, communities, the environment, and policies. Just as social issues cannot be siloed from one another, we cannot silo individuals from their families, communities, the environment, or the practices of the society at large.

When human rights are realized, justice is served. Upholding, promoting, and realizing human rights is a way to achieve justice. Today we focus on social, economic, and environmental justice in social work. Each area is differentiated by the human rights that should be upheld and are not. Nevertheless, in all three areas, discriminatory policies and practices are human rights violations, creating the injustices that we seek to rectify as social workers.

A human rights-based approach to justice in social work practice calls upon all social workers—whatever their preferred practice method may be—to reaffirm the role of social workers as human rights defenders. This approach reunifies all social work practitioners by insisting that we consider how global, regional, national, and local policies and actions affect the lives of individuals and communities and simultaneously appreciate that individuals' emotional and physical well-being is affected when their human rights are ignored or violated.

Our world today is complex and host to a myriad of social, economic, and political issues. Our views about racism, sexuality and gender identity, health and aging, and global interrelations have taught us that we hold many identities simultaneously. If we want to appreciate the whole of a person, we must understand how an individual's multiple identities come together and the position we assign an individual in our society. It brings us back to social work's foundation, the person in the environment, but at the same time requires us to be forward-thinking and appreciate the complexities of an individual's life and how it affects their livelihood, choices, and expectations in life.

This book has endeavored to bring these many concepts together and integrate them into social work practice by offering an approach, perspective, and guidance. To be true to who we are as social workers, each of us must reckon with issues of justice and bring these issues into our preferred method of practice. It is hoped that a rights-based approach will help burgeoning social workers frame the complex social issues they will confront as social workers and lead them to bring about greater justice in our worlds.

Universal Declaration of Human Rights

PREAMBLE

Whereas recognition of the inherent dignity and of the equal and inalienable rights of all members of the human family is the foundation of freedom, justice and peace in the world,

Whereas disregard and contempt for human rights have resulted in barbarous acts which have outraged the conscience of mankind, and the advent of a world in which human beings shall enjoy freedom of speech and belief and freedom from fear and want has been proclaimed as the highest aspiration of the common people,

Whereas it is essential, if man is not to be compelled to have recourse, as a last resort, to rebellion against tyranny and oppression, that human rights should be protected by the rule of law,

Whereas it is essential to promote the development of friendly relations between nations,

Whereas the peoples of the United Nations have in the Charter reaffirmed their faith in fundamental human rights, in the dignity and worth of the human person and in the equal rights of men and women and have determined to promote social progress and better standards of life in larger freedom,

Whereas Member States have pledged themselves to achieve, in cooperation with the United Nations, the promotion of universal respect for and observance of human rights and fundamental freedoms,

Whereas a common understanding of these rights and freedoms is of the greatest importance for the full realization of this pledge,

Now, therefore,

The General Assembly,

Proclaims this Universal Declaration of Human Rights as a common standard of achievement for all peoples and all nations, to the end that every individual and every organ of society, keeping this Declaration constantly in mind, shall strive by teaching and education to promote respect for these rights and freedoms and by progressive measures, national and international, to secure their universal and effective recognition and observance, both among the peoples of Member States themselves and among the peoples of territories under their jurisdiction.

ARTICLE 1

All human beings are born free and equal in dignity and rights. They are endowed with reason and conscience and should act towards one another in a spirit of brotherhood.

ARTICLE 2

Everyone is entitled to all the rights and freedoms set forth in this Declaration, without distinction of any kind, such as race, colour, sex, language, religion, political or other opinion, national or social origin, property, birth or other status.

Furthermore, no distinction shall be made on the basis of the political, jurisdictional or international status of the country or territory to which a person belongs, whether it be independent, trust, non-self-governing or under any other limitation of sovereignty.

ARTICLE 3

Everyone has the right to life, liberty and the security of person.

ARTICLE 4

No one shall be held in slavery or servitude; slavery and the slave trade shall be prohibited in all their forms.

ARTICLE 5

No one shall be subjected to torture or to cruel, inhuman or degrading treatment or punishment.

ARTICLE 6

Everyone has the right to recognition everywhere as a person before the law.

ARTICLE 7

All are equal before the law and are entitled without any discrimination to equal protection of the law. All are entitled to equal protection against any discrimination in violation of this Declaration and against any incitement to such discrimination.

ARTICLE 8

Everyone has the right to an effective remedy by the competent national tribunals for acts violating the fundamental rights granted him by the constitution or by law.

ARTICLE 9

No one shall be subjected to arbitrary arrest, detention or exile.

ARTICLE 10

Everyone is entitled in full equality to a fair and public hearing by an independent and impartial tribunal, in the determination of his rights and obligations and of any criminal charge against him.

ARTICLE 11

1. Everyone charged with a penal offence has the right to be presumed innocent until proved guilty according to law in a public trial at which he has had all the guarantees necessary for his defence.
2. No one shall be held guilty of any penal offence on account of any act or omission which did not constitute a penal offence, under national or international law, at the time when it was committed. Nor shall a heavier penalty be imposed than the one that was applicable at the time the penal offence was committed.

ARTICLE 12

No one shall be subjected to arbitrary interference with his privacy, family, home or correspondence, nor to attacks upon his honour and reputation. Everyone has the right to the protection of the law against such interference or attacks.

ARTICLE 13

1. Everyone has the right to freedom of movement and residence within the borders of each State.
2. Everyone has the right to leave any country, including his own, and to return to his country.

ARTICLE 14

1. Everyone has the right to seek and to enjoy in other countries asylum from persecution.
2. This right may not be invoked in the case of prosecutions genuinely arising from non-political crimes or from acts contrary to the purposes and principles of the United Nations.

ARTICLE 15

1. Everyone has the right to a nationality.
2. No one shall be arbitrarily deprived of his nationality nor denied the right to change his nationality.

ARTICLE 16

1. Men and women of full age, without any limitation due to race, nationality or religion, have the right to marry and to found a family. They are entitled to equal rights as to marriage, during marriage and at its dissolution.
2. Marriage shall be entered into only with the free and full consent of the intending spouses.
3. The family is the natural and fundamental group unit of society and is entitled to protection by society and the State.

ARTICLE 17

1. Everyone has the right to own property alone as well as in association with others.
2. No one shall be arbitrarily deprived of his property.

ARTICLE 18

Everyone has the right to freedom of thought, conscience and religion; this right includes freedom to change his religion or belief, and freedom, either alone or in community with others and in public or private, to manifest his religion or belief in teaching, practice, worship and observance.

ARTICLE 19

Everyone has the right to freedom of opinion and expression; this right includes freedom to hold opinions without interference and to seek, receive and impart information and ideas through any media and regardless of frontiers.

ARTICLE 20

1. Everyone has the right to freedom of peaceful assembly and association.
2. No one may be compelled to belong to an association.

ARTICLE 21

1. Everyone has the right to take part in the government of his country, directly or through freely chosen representatives.
2. Everyone has the right to equal access to public service in his country.
3. The will of the people shall be the basis of the authority of government; this will shall be expressed in periodic and genuine elections which shall be by universal and equal suffrage and shall be held by secret vote or by equivalent free voting procedures.

ARTICLE 22

Everyone, as a member of society, has the right to social security and is entitled to realization, through national effort and international co-operation and in accordance with the organization and resources of each State, of the economic, social and cultural rights indispensable for his dignity and the free development of his personality.

ARTICLE 23

1. Everyone has the right to work, to free choice of employment, to just and favourable conditions of work and to protection against unemployment.
2. Everyone, without any discrimination, has the right to equal pay for equal work.
3. Everyone who works has the right to just and favourable remuneration ensuring for himself and his family an existence worthy of human dignity, and supplemented, if necessary, by other means of social protection.
4. Everyone has the right to form and to join trade unions for the protection of his interests.

ARTICLE 24

Everyone has the right to rest and leisure, including reasonable limitation of working hours and periodic holidays with pay.

ARTICLE 25

1. Everyone has the right to a standard of living adequate for the health and well-being of himself and of his family, including food, clothing, housing and medical care and necessary social services, and the right to security in the event of unemployment, sickness, disability, widowhood, old age or other lack of livelihood in circumstances beyond his control.
2. Motherhood and childhood are entitled to special care and assistance. All children, whether born in or out of wedlock, shall enjoy the same social protection.

ARTICLE 26

1. Everyone has the right to education. Education shall be free, at least in the elementary and fundamental stages. Elementary education shall be compulsory. Technical and professional education shall be made generally available and higher education shall be equally accessible to all on the basis of merit.
2. Education shall be directed to the full development of the human personality and to the strengthening of respect for human rights and fundamental freedoms. It shall promote understanding, tolerance and friendship among all nations, racial or religious groups, and shall further the activities of the United Nations for the maintenance of peace.
3. Parents have a prior right to choose the kind of education that shall be given to their children.

ARTICLE 27

1. Everyone has the right freely to participate in the cultural life of the community, to enjoy the arts and to share in scientific advancement and its benefits.
2. Everyone has the right to the protection of the moral and material interests resulting from any scientific, literary or artistic production of which he is the author.

ARTICLE 28

Everyone is entitled to a social and international order in which the rights and freedoms set forth in this Declaration can be fully realized.

ARTICLE 29

1. Everyone has duties to the community in which alone the free and full development of his personality is possible.
2. In the exercise of his rights and freedoms, everyone shall be subject only to such limitations as are determined by law solely for the purpose of securing due recognition and respect for the rights and freedoms of others and of meeting the just requirements of morality, public order and the general welfare in a democratic society.
3. These rights and freedoms may in no case be exercised contrary to the purposes and principles of the United Nations.

ARTICLE 30

Nothing in this Declaration may be interpreted as implying for any State, group or person any right to engage in any activity or to perform any act aimed at the destruction of any of the rights and freedoms set forth herein.

NOTES

SECTION 3

1. Republished with permission from the National Association of Social Workers. See NASW's Undoing Racism initiative (https://www.socialworkers.org/Practice/Ethnicity-Race/Racial-Equity) for more information.

REFERENCES

AAUW. (2021). The simple truth about the gender pay gap. https://www.aauw.org/app/uploads/2021/09/AAUW_SimpleTruth_2021_-fall_update.pdf

Abramovitz, M. (1988). *Regulating the lives of women: Social welfare policy from colonial times to the present*. South End Press.

Ahmed, A. (2021, May 3). The father of environmental justice is not done yet. *The Nation*. https://www.thenation.com/article/politics/robert-bullard-isnt-done/

Almgren, G., Kemp, S., & Eisinger, A. (2000). The legacy of Hull House and the Children's Bureau in the American mortality transition. *Social Services Review*, 74(1), 1–27.

Alobuia, W. M., Dalva-Baird, N. P., Forrester, J. D., et al. (2020). Racial disparities in knowledge, attitudes and practices related to COVID-19 in the USA. *Journal of Public Health*, 42(3), 470–478. doi:10.1093/pubmed/fdaa069

Alston, P. (2018). *Report of the Special Rapporteur on Extreme Poverty and Human Rights on his mission to the United States of America, UN Human Rights Council*. https://digitallibrary.un.org/record/1629536?ln=en

American Psychiatric Association (APA). (2022). *Climate change and mental health connections*. https://www.psychiatry.org/patients-families/climate-change-and-mental-health-connections

Andorno, R. (2014). Human dignity and human rights. In H. A. M. J. ten Have & B. Gordijn (Eds.), *Handbook of global bioethics* (pp. 45–58). Springer.

Andrews, J., & Reisch, M. (1997). The legacy of McCarthyism on social group work: An historical analysis. *Journal of Sociology & Social Welfare*, 24(3), Article 13. https://scholarworks.wmich.edu/jssw/vol24/iss3/13

Androff, D. (2016). *Practicing rights: Human rights-based approaches to social work practice*. Routledge. https://doi.org/10.4324/9781315885483

Arnison, N. (2009). American exceptionalism and international human rights. *Journal of Lutheran Ethics*. https://www.elca.org/JLE/Articles/414

Arons, A. (2021). An unintended abolition: Family regulation during the COVID-19 crisis. *Columbia Journal of Race and Law*, 12(1). https://journals.library.columbia.edu/index.php/cjrl/article/view/9149

Asakura, K., & Maurer, K. (2018). Attending to social justice in clinical social work: Supervision as a pedagogical space. *Clinical Social Work Journal*, 46, 289–297. doi:10.1007/s10615-018-0667-4

Astor, M. (2022, May 4). Smoke and sandstorm seen from space. *New York Times*. https://www.nytimes.com/2022/05/04/climate/wildfire-smoke-dust-storm.

html?action=click&module=Well&pgtype=Homepage&section=Climate%20 and%20Environment

Bailey, Z., Feldman, J., & Bassett, M. (2021). How structural racism works: Racist policies as a root cause of U.S. racial health inequities. *New England Journal of Medicine, 384*, 768–773. doi:10.1056/NEJMms2025396

Banerjee, M. (2011). Social work scholars' representation of Rawls: A critique. *Journal of Social Work Education, 47*(2), 189–211.

Bannan, N. L. O. (2019). Human rights, economic justice and U.S. exceptionalism. *Pace International Law Review, 31*(2), 563–568.

Barker, R. L. (2013). *The Social Work Dictionary* (6th ed.). NASW Press.

Bauer, G. R., Churchill, S. M., Mahendran, M., Walwyn, C., Lizotte, D., & Villa-Rueda, A. A. (2021). Intersectionality in quantitative research: A systematic review of its emergence and applications of theory and methods. *SSM—Population Health, 14*, 100798. https://doi.org/10.1016/j.ssmph.2021.100798

Bayati, M., Noroozi, R., Ghanbari-Jahromi, M., et al. (2022). Inequality in the distribution of Covid-19 vaccine: A systematic review. *International Journal of Equity in Health, 21*(122). https://doi.org/10.1186/s12939-022-01729-x

Bazan, I. S., & Akgun, K. M. (2021). COVID-19 healthcare inequity: Lessons learned from annual influenza vaccination rates to mitigate COVID-19 vaccine disparities. *Yale Journal of Biological Medicine, 94*(3), 509–515. https://www.ncbi.nlm.nih.gov/pmc/articles/PMC8461587/

Betigeri, A. (2020). How Australia's Indigenous experts could help deal with devastating wildfires. *Time*. https://time.com/5764521/australia-bushfires-indigenous-fire-practices/

Beyleveld, D., & Brownsword, R. (1998). Human dignity, human rights, and human genetics. *The Modern Law Review, 61*, 661–680.

BlackPast. (2018). (1970) Huey P. Newton, "The women's liberation and gay liberation movements." https://www.blackpast.org/african-american-history/speeches-african-american-history/huey-p-newton-women-s-liberation-and-gay-liberation-movements/

Boetto, H. (2017). A transformative eco-social model: Challenging modernist assumptions in social work. *British Journal of Social Work, 47*(1), 48–67.

Bonilla-Silva, E. (1997). Rethinking racism: Toward a structural interpretation. *American Sociological Review, 62*(3), 465–480.

Bowleg, L. (2012). The problem with the phrase "women and minorities": Intersectionality—an important theoretical framework for public health. *American Journal of Public Health, 102*(7), 1267–1273. 10.2105/AJPH.2012.300750

Bowles, D., & Hopps, J. G. (2014). The profession's role in meeting its historical mission to serve vulnerable populations. *Advances in Social Work, 15*, 1–20.

Boyd, D. (2022). Human rights depend on a non-toxic environment. A/HRC/49/53, Special Rapporteur on human rights and the environment. https://www.ohchr.org/sites/default/files/2022-03/ToxicsSummary.pdf

Boyer, D. (2020, March 18). Trump spars with reporter over accusation that staffer called coronavirus "Kung flu." *Washington Times*. https://www.washingtontimes.com/news/2020/mar/18/trump-spars-reporter-over-accusation-staffer-calle/

Brantley, N. A., Nicolini, G., & Kirkhart, K. E. (2021). Unsettling human rights history in social work education: Seeing intersectionality. *Journal of Human Rights and Social Work, 6*(2), 98–107. https://doi.org/10.1007/s41134-020-00138-w

Breitman, R., & Lichtman, A. J. (2013). *FDR and the Jews*. Harvard University Press.

Brennan, T. (2022, January 19). Maine becomes the first US state to recognize the right to food in a constitutional amendment. Universal Rights Group. https://www.universal-rights.org/blog/maine-becomes-the-first-us-state-to-recognise-the-right-to-food-in-a-constitutional-amendment/

Brown, R. (2000). Social identity theory: Past achievements, current problems and future challenge. *European Journal of Social Psychology, 30*, 745–778.

Bullard, R. D., Johnson, G. S., & Torres, A. O. (2005). In R. D. Bullard, *The quest for environmental justice: Human rights and the politics of pollution* (pp. 279–297). Sierra Club Books.

Butler, L. J., Scammell, M. K., & Benson, E. B. (2016). The Flint, Michigan, water crisis: A case study in regulatory failure and environmental injustice. *Environmental Justice, 9*(4). doi:10.1089/env.2016.0014

Cappucci, M., & Samenow, J. (2022, May 7). "Potentially historic" wildfire event threatens New Mexico, Southwest. *Washington Post*. https://www.washingtonpost.com/weather/2022/05/07/wildfires-new-mexico-southwest-calfcanyon/

Carlton-LaNey, I., & Hodges, V. (2004). African American reformers' mission: Caring for our girls and women. *Affilia, 19*(3), 257–272.

Carpenter, K. D. (2000). The International Covenant on Civil and Political Rights: A toothless tiger. *North Carolina Journal of International Law, 26*(1). http://scholarship.law.unc.edu/ncilj/vol26/iss1/1

Carson, R. (2002). *Silent spring* (40th anniversary ed.). Houghton Mifflin Co.

Cato Institute. (2022). Economic freedom of the world. https://www.cato.org/economic-freedom-world/2022

Cave, D. (2020a, September 14). Australia's witnesses to fire's fury are desperate to avoid a sequel. *New York Times*. https://www.nytimes.com/2020/09/14/world/australia/bush-fires-preventive-burns.html

Cave, D. (2020b, September 19). Fire lessons from Australia's South Coast. *New York Times*. https://www.nytimes.com/2020/09/19/world/australia/fire-lessons-south-coast.html?referringSource=articleShare

Center for Economic and Social Justice. (n.d.). Defining economic justice and social justice. https://www.cesj.org/learn/definitions/defining-economic-justice-and-social-justice/

Centers for Disease Control and Prevention. (2021). Impact of racism on our nation's health.https://www.cdc.gov/minorityhealth/racism-disparities/impact-of-racism.html

Centers for Disease Control and Prevention. (2022). Disparities in COVID-19-associated hospitalizations, racial and ethnic health disparities. https://www.cdc.gov/coronavirus/2019-ncov/community/health-equity/racial-ethnic-disparities/disparities-hospitalization.html

Climate Psychiatry Alliance. (2022). *IPCC report urges climate action*. https://www.climatepsychiatry.org/featured-articles/2022/3/14/ipcc-report-urges-climate-action

Collins, P. H. (1990). *Black feminist thought: Knowledge, consciousness, and the politics of empowerment*. Taylor & Francis Group.

Collins, P. H., & Bilge, S. (2016). *Intersectionality*. Polity Press.

Combahee River Collective. (1977). Combahee River Collective statement. https://americanstudies.yale.edu/sites/default/files/files/Keyword%20Coalition_Readings.pdf

Combahee River Collective. (1983). A Black feminist statement. In C. Moraga & G. Anzaldua (Eds.), *This bridge called my back: Writings by radical women of color* (2nd ed., pp. 210–218). Kitchen Table: Women of Color Press. Original work published 1977.

ConstitutionFacts.com. (n.d.). U.S. Bill of Rights. Retrieved July 4, 2022.

Conway, M. M., Ahern, D. W., & Steuernagel, G.A. (2003). Women and public policy: A revolution in progress. In J. C. Gornick & M. K. Meyers (Eds.), *Families that work: Policies for reconciling parenthood and employment* (3rd ed., p. 28). Russell Sage Foundation.

Coughlin, B. J. (1965). *The church and state in social welfare*. Columbia University Press.

Council on Social Work Education. (2022). Educational Policy and Accreditation Standards (EPAS) for Baccalaureate and Master's Social Work Programs. https://www.cswe.org/getmedia/94471c42-13b8-493b-9041-b30f48533d64/2022-EPAS.pdf

Council on Social Work Education. (2015). Curricular guide for environmental justice, 2015 EPAS Curricular Guide Resource Series. Council on Social Work Education.

Crenshaw, K. (1989). Demarginalizing the intersection of race and sex: A Black feminist critique of antidiscrimination doctrine, feminist theory and antiracist politics. *University of Chicago Legal Forum, 1*(8). http://chicagounbound.uchicago.edu/uclf/vol1989/iss1/8

Crenshaw, K. (1991). Mapping the margins: Intersectionality, identity politics, and violence against women of color. *Stanford Law Review, 43,* 61.

Cunsolo, A., & Ellis, R. E. (2018). Ecological grief as a mental health response to climate change-related loss. *Nature Climate Change, 8*(April), 275–281. https://uwosh.edu/sirt/wp-content/uploads/sites/86/2020/04/Cunsolo-and-Ellis-2018.pdf

Cusick, D. (2020, January 21). Past racist "redlining" practices increased climate burden on minority neighborhoods. *Scientific American E&E News.* https://www.scientificamerican.com/article/past-racist-redlining-practices-increased-climate-burden-on-minority-neighborhoods/

D'Amato, A. (2010). *Human rights as part of customary international law: A plea for change of paradigms.* Northwestern University Faculty Working Papers, Paper 88. http://scholarlycommons.law.northwestern.edu/facultyworkingpapers/88

Daly, E., & May, J. R. (2019). Exploring environmental justice through the lens of human dignity. *Widener Law Review, 25,* 177–193.

Daniel, G. R., & Sterphone, J. (2019). Shame, anti-semitism, and Hitler's rise to power in Germany. *EC Psychology and Psychiatry, 8*(5), 334–345.

Deegan, M. J. (2010). Jane Addams on citizenship in a democracy. *Journal of Classical Sociology, 10,* 217–238.

den Hertog, P. (2020). *Why did Hitler hate the Jews? The origins of Adolf Hitler's anti-semitism and its outcome.* Frontline Books.

Denchak, M. (2018, November 8). *Flint water crisis: Everything you need to know.* https://www.nrdc.org/stories/flint-water-crisis-everything-you-need-to-know

Department of Economic and Social Affairs (DESA). (2009). *State of the world's Indigenous peoples.* ST/ESA/328. United Nations Division for Social Policy and Development, Secretariat of the Permanent Forum on Indigenous Issues. https://www.un.org/esa/socdev/unpfii/documents/SOWIP/en/SOWIP_web.pdf

Dicke, K. (2002). The founding function of human dignity in the Universal Declaration of Human Rights. In D. Kretzmer & E. Klein (Eds.), *The concept of human dignity in human rights discourse* (pp. 111–120). Kluwer Law International.

Dominelli, L. (2013). Environmental justice at the heart of social work practice: Greening the profession. *International Journal of Social Welfare, 22*, 431–439.

Dominelli, L., & Campling, J. (2002). Anti-oppressive practice in action. In J. Campling (Ed.), *Anti-oppressive social work theory and practice* (pp. 85–108). Palgrave. https://doi.org/10.1007/978-1-4039-1400-2_5

Donnelly, J. (1984). Cultural relativism and universal human rights. *Human Rights Quarterly, 6*(4), 400–419.

Dower, J. D. (1999). *Embracing defeat: Japan in the wake of World War II*. W. W. Norton.

drworksbook. (n.d.). Racism defined. https://www.dismantlingracism.org/racism-defi ned.html

Economic Policy Institute. (2020). Black workers face two of the most lethal preexisting conditions for coronavirus: Racism and economic inequality. https://www.epi.org/publication/black-workers-covid/

Élysée. (n.d.). *The Declaration of the Rights of Man and of the Citizen*. https://www.ely see.fr/en/french-presidency/the-declaration-of-the-rights-of-man-and-of-the-citizen

Environmental Protection Agency (EPA). (2021). *Carbon pollution from transportation*. https://www.epa.gov/transportation-air-pollution-and-climate-change/car bon-pollution-transportation

Environmental Protection Agency (EPA). (2022). *Environmental justice*. https://www. epa.gov/environmentaljustice

Environmental Transformation Movement of Flint (n.d.). https://www.etmflint.org/

Everytown for Gun Safety Support Fund (n.d.). Mass shootings in America. Everytown Research & Policy. https://everytownresearch.org/maps/mass-shootings-in-america/

Faiola, A. (2021, December 15). Amid drought, conflict and skyrocketing prices, a global food crisis could be nearing, expert warns. *Washington Post*. https://www.washingtonpost.com/world/2021/12/15/global-food-crisis-pandemic/

Findling, M., Blendon, R., Benson, J., & Koh, H. (2022, April 12). COVID-19 has driven racism and violence against Asian Americans: Perspectives from 12 national polls. *Health Affairs*. 10.1377/forefront.20220411.655787

Fisher, J. (1936). *Rank and file movement in social work 1931–1936*. New York School of Social Work.

Foday-Musa, T. (2010). Is UDHR a mere expression of western values? *The Patriotic Vanguard*. http://thepatrioticvanguard.com/is-udhr-a-mere-expression-of-west ern-values

Foner, E. (1999). *The story of American freedom*. W. W. Norton.

Freire, P. (1994). *Pedagogy of Hope*. New York: Continuum.

Friedlander, W. A. (1963). *Introduction to social welfare* (2nd ed.). Prentice-Hall, Inc.

FSIN and Global Network Against Food Crises. (2021). Global report on food crises 2021. https://www.wfp.org/publications/global-report-food-crises-2021

Galea, S., & Abdalla, S. M. (2020). COVID-19 pandemic, unemployment, and civil unrest: Underlying deep racial and socioeconomic divides. *Journal of the American Medical Association, 324*(3), 227–228. https://doi.org/10.1001/jama.2020.11132

Gary B. v. Snyder, 16-13292, U. S. Dist. Ct., East. Dist. Mich. Southern Div. 2018.

Gatenio Gabel, S. (2016). *A rights-based approach to social policy analysis*. Springer.

Gatenio Gabel, S., Mapp, S., Androff, D., & McPherson, J. (2022). Looking back to move us forward: Social workers as human rights professionals delivering justice. *Advances in Social Work, 22*(2), 416–435.

Gilio-Whitaker, D. (2019). *As long as grass grows: The Indigenous fight for environmental justice, from colonization to Standing Rock*. Beacon.

Gilliam, C. C., Sloan, L. M., & Schmitz, C. L. (In press). Climate change: Environmental justice, human rights, and peaceful practices. In L. Reimer, K. Standish, & K. Anderson (Eds.), *Finding hope: Human rights, justice, indigeneity, gender, and security*. University of Manitoba Press.

Gitterman, A., & Germain, C. (1976). Social work practice: A life model. *Social Service Review, 50*(4), 601–610. doi:10.1086/643430

Goldman, N., Pebley, A. R., Lee, K., Andrasfay, T., & Pratt, B. (2021). Racial and ethnic differentials in COVID-19-related job exposures by occupational standing in the U.S. *medRxiv: the preprint server for health sciences*. https://doi.org/10.1101/2020.11.13.20231431\

Gover, A. R., Harper, S. B., & Langton, L. (2020). Anti-Asian hate crime during the COVID-19 pandemic: Exploring the reproduction of inequality. *American Journal of Criminal Justice, 45*(4), 647–667. https://doi.org/10.1007/s12103-020-09545-1

Groulx, M. (2017). Other people's initiatives: Exploring mediation and appropriation of place as barriers to community-based climate change adaptation. *Local Environment, 22*(11), 1378–1393. https://doi.org/10.1080/13549839.2017.1348343

Gypen, L., Vanderfaeillie, J., De Maeyer, S., et al. (2017). Outcomes of children who grew up in foster care: Systematic review. *Children and Youth Services Review, 76*, 74–83.

Hacker, J. S., & Pierson, P. (2010). Winner-take-all politics: Public policy, political organization, and the precipitous rise of top incomes in the United States. *Politics & Society, 38*(2), 152–204. https://doi.org/10.1177/0032329210365042

Hancock, A. M. (2007). When multiplication doesn't equal quick addition: Examining intersectionality as a research paradigm. *Perspectives on Politics, 5*(1), 63–79. https://10.1017/S1537592707070065

Hanks, A., Solomon, D., & Weller, C. E. (2018). Systematic inequality: How America's structural racism helped create the Black-White wealth gap. Center for American Progress. https://www.americanprogress.org/wp-content/uploads/sites/2/2018/02/RacialWealthGap-report.pdf

Hannah-Attisha, M. (2019). *What the eyes don't see: A story of crisis, resistance, and hope in an American city*. One World.

Harvey, D. (2007). *A brief history of neoliberalism*. Oxford University Press.

Hayek, F. A. (1998). *Law, legislation and liberty*. Routledge. (Original work published 1973–79.)

Haynes, K. S., & Mickelson, J. S. (1992). Social work and the Reagan era: Challenges to the profession. *Journal of Sociology and Social Welfare, 19*(1), 169–183.

Haynes, K. S. (1998). The one-hundred-year debate: Social reform versus individual treatment, *Social Work, 43*(6), 501–509. https://doi.org/10.1093/sw/43.6.501

Healy, L. M. (2008). Exploring the history of social work as a human rights profession. *International Social Work, 51*(6), 735–748. https://doi.org/10.1177/0020872808095247.

Healy, L. M. (2008). Socioeconomic history of social work as a human rights profession. *International Social Work, 51*(6), 735–748. doi:10.1177/0020872808095247

Herf, J. (2005). The "Jewish War": Goebbels and the antisemitic campaigns of the Nazi propaganda ministry. *Holocaust and Genocide Studies, 19*(1), 51–80. https://doi.org/10.1093/hgs/dci003

Hershkoff, H., & Loffredo, S. (2011). State courts and constitutional socioeconomic rights: Exploring the underutilization thesis. *Penn State Law Review, 115*(4), 923–982.

Highsmith, A. R. (2009). Demolition means progress: Urban renewal, local politics, and state-sanctioned ghetto formation in Flint, Michigan. *Journal of Urban History, 35*(3), 348–368. https://doi.org/10.1177/0096144208330403

Hill, D. H. (2016). Avoiding obligation: Reservations to human rights treaties. *The Journal of Conflict Resolution, 60*(6), 1129–1158. https://www.10.1177/0022002714567947

Hoffman, J. S., Shandas, V., & Pendelton, N. (2020). The effects of historical housing policies on resident exposure to intra-urban heat: A study of 108 US urban areas. *Climate, 8*(1), 1–15. doi:10.3390/clii8010012

Hopkins, H. L. (1926). The place of social work in public health. Presentation at the National Conference of Social Work, 53rd Annual Session, Cleveland, Ohio. https://socialwelfare.library.vcu.edu/social-work/the-place-of-social-work-in-public-health/

Horowitz, J. M., Igielnik, R., & Kochhar, R. (2020). Most Americans say there is too much economic inequality in the U.S., but fewer than half call it a top priority. Pew Research Center. https://www.pewresearch.org/social-trends/2020/01/09/trends-in-income-and-wealth-inequality/

Houle, C. (2009). Inequality and democracy: Why inequality harms consolidation but does not affect democratization. *World Politics, 61*(4), 589–622. doi: 10.1353/wp.0.0031

Hume, D. (1740). *A treatise of human nature* (Book III, Part II). https://www.earlymoderntexts.com/assets/pdfs/hume1740book3.pdf

ICESCR. (2008). General Comment No. 15, The Right to Water.

ICESCR. (2008). General Comment No. 19, The Right to Social Security (art. 9), U.N. Doc. E/C.12/GC/19.

Ife, J. (2012). *Human rights and social work: Towards rights-based practice.* Cambridge University Press.

Intergovernmental Panel on Climate Change (IPCC). (2018). *Global warming of 1.5 C.* http://www.ipcc.ch/pdf/special- reports/sr15/sr15_ts.pdf

Intergovernmental Science-Policy Platform on Biodiversity and Ecosystem Services (IPBES). (2018). *Summary for policymakers of the assessment report on land degradation and restoration of the intergovernmental science-policy platform on biodiversity and ecosystem services.* https://www.ipbes.net/event/ipbes-6-plenary

International Association of Schools of Social Work. (2018). *Global social work statement of ethical principles.* https://www.iassw-aiets.org/wp-content/uploads/2018/04/Global-Social-Work-Statement-of-Ethical-Principles-IASSW-27-April-2018-1.pdf

International Federation of Social Workers & International Association of Schools of Social Work. (2018). *Global social work statement of ethical principles.* https://www.ifsw.org/global-social-work-statement-of-ethical-principles/

International Labour Organization. (n.d.). History of the ILO. https://www.ilo.org/
global/about-the-ilo/history/lang--en/index.htm

Ivanovich, C. (2018, January 3). A look back at 2017: The year in weather disasters
and the connection to climate change. Environmental Defense Fund. http://
blogs.edf.org/climate411/2018/01/03/a-look-back-at-2017-the-year-in-weat
her-disasters-and-the-connection-to-climate-change/?_ga+2.202446545.133
7490733.15423783-442978275.1542423783

Jackson, M., & Holzman, B. (2020). A century of educational inequality in the United
States. *Proceedings of the National Academy of Sciences, 117*(32), 19108–19115.
doi:10.1073/pnas.1907258117

Jacobs, M. D. (2013). Remembering the "Forgotten Child": The American Indian
child welfare crisis of the 1960s and 1970s. *American Indian Quarterly, 37*(1),
136–159.

John Jay Research Advisory Group on Preventing and Reducing Community
Violence. (2020). *Reducing violence without police: A review of research evidence.*
Research & Evaluation Center, John Jay College of Criminal Justice, CUNY.

Johns Hopkins Center for Gun Violence Solutions. (2022). A year in review: 2020 gun
deaths in the U.S. https://publichealth.jhu.edu/gun-violence-solutions.

Johnson, A. G. (2006). *Privilege, power, and difference* (2nd ed.) McGraw Hill.

Johnson, M. G., & Symonides, J. (1998). *The Universal Declaration of Human Rights: A
history of its creation and implementation 1948–1998.* UNESCO. http://unesdoc.
unesco.org/images/0011/001144/114488E.pdf

Kahn, P. W. (2000). Speaking law to power: Popular sovereignty, human rights, and
the new international order. *Yale Law School* Faculty Scholarship Series. http://
digitalcommons.law.yale.edu/fss_papers/329

Kaiser, M. L., Himmelheber, S., Miller, S., & Hayward, R.A. (2015). Cultivators of
change: Food justice in social work education. *Social Work Education, 34*(5),
544–557. doi:10.1080/02615479.2015.1063599

Kandaswamy, P. (2007). Beyond colorblindness and multiculturalism: Rethinking
anti-racist pedagogy in the university classroom. *Radical Teacher, 80*(80), 6–11.

Kaplan, S. (2021, December 14). Climate change has destabilized Earth's poles,
putting the rest of the planet in peril. *Washington Post.* https://www.washing
tonpost.com/climate-environment/2021/12/14/climate-change-arctic-antarc
tic-poles/

Kaplan, S., & Dennis, B. (2021, December 17). 2021 had wave of extreme weather
disasters: Scientists say worse lies ahead. *Washington Post.* https://www.was
hingtonpost.com/climate-environment/2021/12/17/climate-change-extreme-
weather-future/

Katznelson, I. (2013). *Fear itself: The New Deal and the origins of our time.* Liveright
Publishing Corporation.

Kennedy, M. (2016, April 20). *Lead-laced water in Flint: A step-by-step look at the
makings of a crisis.* https://www.npr.org/sections/thetwo-way/2016/04/20/
465545378/lead-laced-water-in-flint-a-step-by-step-look-at-the-makings-of-a-
crisis

King Jr., M. L. (1963, August 28). *I have a dream* [Speech audio recording]. American
Rhetoric. https://www.americanrhetoric.com/speeches/mlkihaveadream.htm

King Jr., M. L. (1967). America's chief moral dilemma. National Conference for New
Politics. https://www.rimaregas.com/2015/08/08/martin-luther-king-jr-spe
ech-the-three-evils-of-society-civilrights-on-blog42/

Korff, J. (2022). *Mental health and Aboriginal people*. https://www.creativespirits.info/aboriginalculture/health/mental-health-and-aboriginal-people

Landers, A. L., & Danes, S. M. (2016). Forgotten children: A critical review of the reunification of American Indian children in the child welfare system. *Children and Youth Services Review, 71*(December), 137–147.

Landrigan, P. J., Fuller, R., Acosta, N. J. Jr., et al. (2018). The Lancet Commission on pollution and health. *Lancet, 391*(10119), 462–512. doi:10.1016/S0140-6736(17)32345-0

Leopold, A. (2020). *Sand country almanac: And sketches here and there*. Oxford University Press.

Lanford, D., & Quadagno, J. (2021). Identifying the undeserving poor: The effect of racial, ethnic, and anti-immigrant sentiment on state Medicaid eligibility. *The Sociological Quarterly, 63*(1), 1–20. doi:10.1080/00380253.2020.1797596

Lauren, P. G. (2013). *The evolution of international human rights: Visions seen*. University of Pennsylvania Press.

Leighninger, L. (2004) Social work and McCarthyism in the early 1950s. *Journal of Progressive Human Services, 15*(1), 61–67. doi:10.1300/J059v15n01_04

Leonard, P. (2001). The future of critical social work in uncertain conditions. *Critical Social Work, 2*(1). https://ojs.uwindsor.ca/index.php/csw/article/download/5617/4590?inline=1

Lewis, B. (2012). Human rights and environmental wrongs: Achieving environmental justice through human rights law. *International Journal for Crime, Justice and Social Democracy, 1*(1), 65–73. https://doi.org/10.5204/ijcjsd.v1i1.69

Lewis, N. M., Friedrichs, M., Wagstaff, S., et al. (2020). Disparities in COVID-19 incidence, hospitalizations, and testing, by area-level deprivation—Utah, March 3—July 9, 2020. *MMWR Morbidity and Mortality Weekly Report, 69*, 1369–1373. http://dx.doi.org/10.15585/mmwr.mm6938a4

Lindenmeyer, K. (1997). *A right to childhood: The U.S. Children's Bureau and child welfare, 1912–1946*. University of Illinois Press.

Lindsey, R., & Dahlman, L. (2021). *Climate change: Global temperature*. https://www.climate.gov/news-features/understanding-climate/climate-change-global-temperature

Liu, J., Clark, L. P., Bechle, M. J., et al. (2021, December 1). Disparities in air pollution exposure in the United States by race/ethnicity and income, 1990–2010. *Environmental Health Perspectives, 129*(12). https://doi.org/10.1289/EHP8584

Lubove, R. (1963). *The Progressives and the slums tenement house reform in New York City, 1890–1917*. University of Pittsburgh Press.

Luken, A., Nair, R., & Fix, R. L. (2021). On racial disparities in child abuse reports: Exploratory mapping the 2018 NCANDS. *Child Maltreatment, 26*(3), 267–281. https://doi.org/10.1177/10775595211001926

Maathai, W. (2003). *The Greenbelt movement: Sharing the approach and the experience*. Lantern Books.

Maathai, W. (2006). *Unbowed: A memoir*. Knopf.

Mantler, G. (2013). *Power to the poor: Black–Brown coalition and the fight for economic justice, 1960–1974*. University of North Carolina Press.

Mapp, S., McPherson, J., Androff, D., & Gatenio Gabel, S. (2019). Social work is a human rights profession. *Social Work, 64*(3), 259–269. https://doi.org/10.1093/sw/swz023

Marks, S. P. (2016). *Human rights: A brief introduction*, Working paper. Harvard School of Public Health. https://www.coursehero.com/file/94205348/Human-Rights-A-brief-intro-2016pdf/

Marsh, J. C. (2005). Social justice: Social work's organizing value. *Social Work, 50*(4), 293–294. doi:10.1093/sw/50.4.293

Marshall, T. H., & Lipset, S. (1964). *Class, citizenship, and social development.*

Martinez, D., & Irfan, A. (2021). Colonialism, the climate crisis, and the need to center Indigenous voices. *Environmental Health News.* https://www.ehn.org/indigenous-people-and-climate-change-2655479728.html

Massimo, R. (2018, May 18). Resurrection City: An overlooked protest of the 1960s turns 50. WTOP News. https://wtop.com/local/2018/05/resurrection-city/

Mattson, D. J., & Clark, S. (2011). Human dignity in concept and practice. *Policy Science, 44,* 303–319.

McGurty, E. M. (1997). From NIMBY to civil rights: The origins of the environmental justice movement. *Environmental History, 2*(3), 301–323. https://doi.org/10.2307/3985352

McLean, K. G. (2012). *Land use, climate change, adaptation and Indigenous peoples.* United Nations University. https://unu.edu/publications/articles/land-use-climate-change-adaptation-and-indigenous-peoples.html

Merton, L., & Dater, A. (2008). *Taking root: The vision of Wangari Maathai* [DVD]. Marlboro Productions. https://m.youtube.com/watch?v=BQU7JoxkGvo

Millet, G. A., Jones, A. T., Benkeser, D., et al. (2020). Assessing differential impacts of COVID-19 on Black communities. *Annals of Epidemiology, 47,* 37–44. https://doi.org/10.1016/j.annepidem.2020.05.003

Morgaine, K. (2014). Conceptualizing social justice in social work: Are social workers too bogged down in the trees? *Journal of Social Justice, 4,* 1–18.

Mullaly, B. (2009). *Challenging oppression and confronting privilege: A critical social work approach.* Oxford University Press.

Naidu, S., Rodrik, D., & Zucman, G. (2020). Economics after neoliberalism: Introducing the EfIP Project, AEA Papers and Proceedings. *110,* 366–371. doi:10.1257/pandp.20201000

National Association of Social Workers. (2021). *NASW Code of Ethics.* https://www.socialworkers.org/About/Ethics/Code-of-Ethics/Code-of-Ethics-English

National Public Radio (NPR). (2021, September 7). *Climate change is the greatest threat to public health, top medical journals warn.* https://www.npr.org/2021/09/07/1034670549/climate-change-is-the-greatest-threat-to-public-health-top-medical-journals-warn

Nesmith, A., Schmitz, C., Machado-Escudero, Y., et al. (2021). *The intersection of environmental justice, climate change, community, and the ecology of life.* Springer International.

Newdom, F. (1994). Beyond hard times. *Journal of Progressive Human Services, 4*(2), 65–77.

Nicotera, A. (2019). Social justice and social work, a fierce urgency: Recommendations for social work social justice pedagogy. *Journal of Social Work Education, 55*(3), 460–475. doi:10.1080/10437797.2019.1600443

Nozick, R. (1974). *Anarchy, state, and utopia.* Basic Books.

Obergefell v. Hodges, No. 14-556, U.S. 2015.

Office of the High Commissioner of Human Rights. (n.d.). *Economic, social and cultural rights.* https://www.ohchr.org/en/human-rights/economic-social-cultural-rights

Office of the High Commissioner of Human Rights (OHCHR). (n.d.). *What are human rights?* https://www.ohchr.org/en/what-are-human-rights

Office of the United Nations High Commissioner for Human Rights. (n.d. a). https://www.ohchr.org/EN/HRBodies/HRC/Pages/Home.aspx

Office of the United Nations High Commissioner for Human Rights. (n.d. b). https://www.ohchr.org/en/what-are-human-rights

Ostry, J. D., Loungani, P., & Berg, A. (2018). *Confronting Inequality: How Societies Can Choose Inclusive Growth*. Columbia University Press. https://doi.org/10.7312/ostr17468-005

Oxford Languages (n.d.). Dignity. https://www.google.com/search?q=definition+of+dignity%5D&rlz=1C5CHFA_enUS953US955&ei=M-RvZO6kKa6uiLMPsImO wAg&ved=0ahUKEwiuitaexZH_AhUuF2IAHbCEA4gQ4dUDCBA&uact=5&oq=definition+of+dignity%5D&gs_lcp=Cgxnd3Mtd2l6LXNlcnAQAzIPCAAQigUQ sQMQQxBGEPkBMgUIABCABDIFCAAQgAQyBQgAEIAEMgUIABCABDIFCA AQgAQyBQgAEIAEMgUIABCABDIFCAAQgAQyBQgAEIAEMiUIABCKBRCxA xBDEEYQ-QEQlwUQjAUQ3QQQRhD0AxD1AxD2AxgBOgoIABBHENYEE LADOiUIABCKBRCxAxBDEEYQ-QEQlwUQjAUQ3QQQRhD0AxD1AxD2Axg BSgQIQRgAUJ0HWNcKYIQLaAFwAXgAgAFIiAFIkgEBMZgBAKABAcABAcg BCNoBBggBEAEYEw&sclient=gws-wiz-serp

Porter, B. (2015). *Rethinking progressive realization: How should it be implemented in Canada?* Background paper for a presentation to the Continuing Committee of Officials on Human Rights. http://www.socialrights.ca/documents/publicati ons/Porter%20Progressive%20Implementation.pdf

Porter, J. R. (n.d.). The world's food supply is made insecure by climate change. https://www.un.org/en/academic-impact/worlds-food-supply-made-insecure-climate-change

Powers, M., Schmitz, C., & Moritz, M. B. (2019). Preparing social workers for ecosocial work practice and community building. *Journal of Community Practice*, 27(3-4). doi:org/10.1080/10705422.2019.1657217

Powers, R. G. (1998). *Not without honor: The history of American anticommunism*. Yale University Press.

Prüss-Ustün, A., Wolf, J., Corvalán, C., et al. (2018). Preventing disease through healthy environments: A global assessment of the burden of disease from environmental risks. World Health Organization. https://www.who.int/publi cations/i/item/9789241565196

Rawls, J. (1999). *A theory of justice* (rev. ed.). Oxford University Press.

Rawls, J. (2001). *Justice as fairness: A restatement*. Belknap.

Reardon, S. F., & Bischoff, K. (2011). Income inequality and income segregation. *American Journal of Sociology*, 116(4), 1092–1153. https://doi.org/10.1086/657114

Regilme Jr., S. S. F. (2019). The global politics of human rights: From human rights to human dignity? *International Political Science Review*, 40(2), 279–290.

Reisch, M., & Andrews, J. L. (2002). *The road not taken: A history of radical social work in the United States*. Routledge.

Reisch, M., & Garvin, C. D. (2016). *Social work and social justice*. Oxford University Press.

Rengger, N. (2011). The world turned upside down? Human rights and international relations after 25 years. *International Affairs*, 87(5), 1159–1178. https://doi.org/10.1111/j.1468-2346.2011.01026.x

Richmond, M. (1922). *What is social case work? An introductory description*. Russell Sage Foundation.

Robinson, G. (2001). *By order of the President: FDR and the internment of Japanese Americans*. Harvard University Press.

Rogers, K. (2020, March 10). Politicians' use of "Wuhan virus" starts a debate health experts wanted to avoid. *New York Times*. https://www.nytimes.com/2020/03/10/us/politics/wuhan-virus.html

Roosevelt, F.D. (1944). The economic bill of rights. U.S. history.com https://www.ushistory.org/documents/economic_bill_of_rights.htm

Sable, M., Schild, D., & Hipp, J. A. (2012). Public health and social work. In S. Gehlert & T. Browne (Eds.), *Handbook of health social work* (2nd ed., pp. 64–99). Wiley.

Sanchez-Paramo, C., Hill, R., Narayan, A., & Yonzan, N. (2021). COVID-19 leaves a legacy of rising poverty and widening inequality. *World Bank Blogs*. https://blogs.worldbank.org/developmenttalk/covid-19-leaves-legacy-rising-poverty-and-widening-inequality

Schiele, J. H., & Jackson, M. S. (2020). The Atlanta School of Social Work and the professionalization of "race work." *Phylon: The Clark Atlanta University Review of Race and Culture*, *57*(2), 21–40.

Sege, R., & Stephens, A. (2021). Child physical abuse did not increase during the pandemic. *JAMA Pediatrics*, *176*(4), 338–340. doi:10.1001/jamapediatrics.2021.5476

Seligman, H., Laraia, B., & Kushel, M. (2010). Food insecurity is associated with chronic disease among low-income NHANES participants. *Journal of Nutrition*, *140*(2), 304–310.

Sensen, O. (2011). *Kant on human dignity*. De Gruyter.

Singh, G. (1996). Promoting anti-racist and Black perspectives in social work education. *Social Work Education*, *15*(2), 35–56.

Sloan, L. M., & Schmitz, C. L. (2019). Environmental degradation: Communities forging a path forward. *Journal of Transdisciplinary Peace Praxis*, *1*(1), 13–38. http://jtpp.uk

Sloan, L. M., Joyner, M. C., Stakeman, C. J., & Schmitz, C. L. (2018). *Critical multiculturalism and intersectionality in a complex world* (2nd ed.). Oxford University Press.

Soohoo, C., & Goldberg, J. (2010). The full realization of our rights: The right to health in state constitutions. *Case Western Reserve Law Review*, *60*(4), 997–1072. http://scholarlycommons.law.case.edu/caselrev/vol60/iss4/5

Specht, H. (1991). Should training for private practice be a central component of social work education? No! *Journal of Social Work Education*, *279*(2), 102–107.

Specht, H., & Courtney, M. E. (1994). *Unfaithful angels: How social work has abandoned its mission*. Free Press.

Stanford University. (n.d.). Poor People's Campaign. The Martin Luther King, Jr. Research and Education Institute, Stanford University. https://kinginstitute.stanford.edu/encyclopedia/poor-peoples-campaign

Steen, J. (2006). The roots of human rights advocacy and call to action. *Social Work*, *51*(2), 101–105. doi:10.1093/sw/51.2.101

Steinhauer, J. (2012, December 4). Dole Appears, but G.O.P. Rejects a Disabilities Treaty. The New York Times. https://www.nytimes.com/2012/12/05/us/despite-doles-wish-gop-rejects-disabilities-treaty.html

Stiglitz, J. (2011, May). Of the 1%, by the 1%, for the 1%. *Vanity Fair*, p. 126.

Stone, C., Trisi, D., Sherman, A., & Beltrán, J. (2020). A guide to statistics on historical trends in income inequality. Center on Budget and Policy Priorities. https://www.cbpp.org/research/poverty-and-inequality/a-guide-to-statistics-on-historical-trends-in-income-inequality

Strides in Development. (2010). *Wangari Maathai & the Green Belt Movement*. https://youtu.be/BQU7JOxkGvo

Suh, E. M. (2000). Self, the hyphen between culture and subjective well-being. In E. Diener & E. M. Suh (Eds.), *Culture and subjective well-being* (pp. 63–86). The MIT Press.

Sutto, M. (2019). Human rights evolution, a brief history. *The CoESPU Magazine, 3*, 18. doi:10.32048/Coespumagazine3.19.3

Swedo, E., Idaikkadar, N., Leemis, R., et al. (2020). Trends in U.S. emergency department visits related to suspected or confirmed child abuse and neglect among children and adolescents aged <18 years before and during the COVID-19 pandemic. *MMWR Morbidity & Mortality Weekly Report, 69*, 1841–1847. doi:10.15585/mmwr.mm6949a1

Tajfel, H., & Turner, J. C. (1979). An integrative theory of intergroup conflict. In W. G. Austin & S. Worchel (Eds.), *The social psychology of intergroup relations* (pp. 33–47). Brooks/Cole.

Tajfel, H., & Turner, J. C. (1986). The social identity theory of intergroup behaviour. In S. Worchel & W. G. Austin (Eds.), *Psychology of intergroup relations* (pp. 7–24). Nelson.

Tallamy, D. W. (2020). *Nature's best hope: A new approach to conservation that starts in your yard*. Timber Press.

The Green Belt Movement. (2018). *Wangari Maathai: Biography*. http://www.greenbeltmovement.org/wangari-maathai/biography

The Royal Society. (2022). *Reversing biodiversity loss: Why is biodiversity so important?* https://royalsociety.org/topics-policy/projects/biodiversity/why-is-biodiversity-important/

Thiebeault, D., & Spencer, M.S. (2019). The Indian Adoption Project and the profession of social work. *Social Service Review, 93*(4). https://doi.org/10.1086/706771

Thompson, N. (1997). *Anti-discriminatory practice* (2nd ed.). Macmillan.

Trattner, W. (2007). *From poor law to welfare state, 6th Edition: A History of Social Welfare in America*. Free Press.

Turns, A. (2019). *Eco-grief: Why climate change anxiety is keeping us awake at night*. https://welldoing.org/article/eco-grief-why-climate-change-anxiety-keeping-us-awake-night

U.S. Department of Agriculture, Economic Research Service. (2022). Food security status of U.S. households in 2020. https://www.ers.usda.gov/topics/food-nutrition-assistance/food-security-in-the-u-s/key-statistics-graphics/

UN Committee on Economic, Social and Cultural Rights. (2000). *General Comment No. 14: The Right to the Highest Attainable Standard of Health (Art. 12 of the Covenant)*, 11 August 2000, E/C.12/2000/4, available at: https://www.refworld.org/docid/4538838d0.html

UN Environment. (2019). *Environmental rule of law: First global report*. United Nations Environment Programme, Nairobi.

UN General Assembly, *International Convention on the Elimination of All Forms of Racial Discrimination*, 21 December 1965, United Nations, Treaty Series, vol. 660, p. 195, available at: https://www.refworld.org/docid/3ae6b3940.html

UN General Assembly. (1966a). International Covenant on Civil and Political Rights. https://www.refworld.org/docid/3ae6b3aa0.html

UN General Assembly. (1966b). International Covenant on Economic, Social, and Cultural Rights. https://www.ohchr.org/en/instruments-mechanisms/inst ruments/international-covenant-economic-social-and-cultural-rights

UN General Assembly. (2010). UNGA A/RES/64/292, p. 2. https://digitallibrary. un.org/record/687002?ln=en

UN General Assembly. (2021). The human right to a clean, healthy and sustainable environment, Resolution 48/13. https://digitallibrary.un.org/record/3945 636?ln=en

UN Human Rights Committee (HRC), *CCPR General Comment No. 18: Non-discrimination*, 10 November 1989, available at: https://www.refworld.org/ docid/453883fa8.html

Underwood, J. (2018, January 20). Education as an American right? *Phi Delta Kappan*, *99*(5), 76–77. https://www.kappanonline.org/underwood-education-ameri can-right/

United Nations Framework Convention on Climate Change (UNFCCC). (2021). *Glasgow climate pact*—https://digitallibrary.un.org/record/3945636?ln=en. *Advance unedited version.* https://unfccc.int/sites/default/files/resource/cop26_ auv_2f_cover_decision.pdf

United Nations General Assembly (1966). International Covenant on Economic, Social and Cultural Rights, Treaty Series 999: Preamble.

United Nations General Assembly. (1948). Universal Declaration of Human Rights.http://www.un.org/en/universal-declaration-human-rights/

United Nations Human Rights Council (UNHRC). (2012). Human rights and the environment, Resolution 19/10. https://www.right-docs.org/doc/ a-hrc-res-19-10/

United Nations Human Rights Council (UNHRC). (2021). The human right to a clean, healthy and sustainable environment, A/HRC/48/L.23/Rev.1. https://digitallibrary.un.org/record/3945636?ln=en

United Nations News. (2021, October 21). *Madagascar: Severe drought could spur world's first climate change famine.* https://news.un.org/en/story/2021/10/1103 712

United Nations Treaty Collection. (n.d.). Chapter IV : Human Rights. https://treaties. un.org/pages/Treaties.aspx?id=4&subid=A&clang=_en

United Nations. (1945). *Charter of the United Nations.* United Nations, Office of Public Information. https://www.un.org/en/about-us/un-charter

United Nations. (1948). *Universal Declaration of Human Rights.* http://www.un.org/ Overview/rights.html

United Nations. (n.d.). *History of the declaration.* https://www.un.org/en/about-us/ udhr/history-of-the-declaration

van Heugten, K. (2014). *Human service organizations in the disaster context.* New York: Palgrave.

Vernick, D. (2020). *3 billion animals harmed by Australia's wildfires.* World Wildlife Fund. https://www.worldwildlife.org/stories/3-billion-animals-harmed-by-australia-s-fires

Wight, V., Kauhal, N., Waldfogel, J., & Garfinkel, I. (2014). Understanding the link between poverty and food insecurity among children: Does the definition of poverty matter? *Journal of Children and Poverty, 20*(1), 1–20.

World Health Organization (WHO). (1999). *The mental health of indigenous peoples: An international overview.* https://apps.who.int/iris/bitstream/handle/10665/65596/WHO_MNH_NAM_99.1.pdf?sequence=1

World Health Organization (WHO). (2021a). *Climate change and health.* https://www.who.int/news-room/fact-sheets/detail/climate-change-and-health

World Health Organization (WHO). (2021b). *COP26 special report on climate change and health: The health argument for climate action.* https://www.who.int/publications/i/item/9789240036727

Young, I. M. (1988). Five faces of oppression. *Philosophical Forum, 29*(4), 270–290.

Young, I. M. (1990). Five faces of oppression. In I. M. Young (Ed.), *Justice and the politics of difference* (pp. 39–65). Princeton University Press.

Zapf, M. K. (2009). *Social work and the environment: Understanding people and place.* Canadian Scholars' Press.

Ziegler, J. (2005). Statement by Jean Ziegler Special Rapporteur on the Right to Food on the Occasion of World Food Day, United Nations Office of the High Commissioner on Human Rights. https://www.ohchr.org/en/statements/2009/10/statement-jean-ziegler-special-rapporteur-right-food-occasion-world-food-day

Ziemele, I., & Liede, L. (2013). Reservations to human rights treaties: From draft guideline 3.1.12 to guideline 3.1.5.6. *European Journal of International Law, 24*(4), 1135–1152. doi:10.1093/ejil/cht068

INDEX

For the benefit of digital users, indexed terms that span two pages (e.g., 52–53) may, on occasion, appear on only one of those pages.

Tables and figures are indicated by t and f following the page number.

racial/ethnic minority hospitalization
rates, 108–9
racial/ethnic minority transmission
rates, 108
racial/ethnic minority unemployment
rates, 108
racial/ethnic minority vaccination
rates, 107f, 109
social justice and, 106–12
UDHR and, 110
CRC. *See* United Nations (UN) Convention
on the Rights of the Child
Crenshaw, Kimberlé, 75, 76, 77. *See also*
intersectionality
CRPD. *See* Convention on the Rights of
Persons with Disabilities
CSWE. *See* Council on Social Work
Education
CSWE EPAS. *See* Council on Social Work
Education Educational Policy and
Accreditation Standards
cultural imperialism, 64–65
cultural level oppression, 65, 66f
cultural marginalization, 64
customary law, 22

Declaration of Independence (U.S.), 81
Deer, Ada, 30–31, 31f
Determination of Right and Unity
for Menominee Shareholders
(DRUMS), 30
dignity (human dignity). *See also* respect
benefits of, 12
definitions, 11
finding common ground
(example), 11–12
historical background, 11
international law and, 13
Kant on, 11
philosophers/scholars view of, 13
relation to human rights, 11, 13
discrimination
age-related, 114–15
defined, 66–67
economic justice and, 123–24
gender-related, 112–14
human rights instruments' stance
against, 43, 46t, 49, 104, 105
othering of Asian immigrants, 121
UDHR stance against, 104

distributive justice, 87, 89, 144
diversity, 59–61
celebration of, 4
defined, 60–61
privilege and, 61–63
sameness vs., 59
social constructs and, 60–61
valuation of, 1
Dole, Bob, 47
drug testing, 62
DRUMS. *See* Determination of Right and
Unity for Menominee Shareholders
(DRUMS)
Due Process Clause (U.S.
Constitution), 52
Duke, Charles, 13–14

ecological perspective, of social
work, 162–63
Economic Bill or Rights (U.S.), 130–31
economic inequalities
causes of, 133–34
growth of, 131–35
low/middle income households, 132f
upper vs. low/middle income
families, 133f
wealth gap, 133f
economic justice, 123–36
Black vs. White households, wealth
comparison, 124f
categorization of, 90f
definition, 91, 125
discrimination against
minorities, 123–24
examples of unjustice (U.S.), 123
future directions, 135–36
gains made in, 81
intersectionality and, 123
links with environmental justice, 139
Occupy Wall Street movement, 134–35
economic rights
adequate standard of living, 125
Cato Institute on, 127
CEDAW's references to, 126–27
CRC's references to, 126–27
CRPD's references to, 126–27
education, 125
family assistance/protection, 125
health, 125
ICESCR references to, 126

macro-approach (to social work), xi, 23, 173

Malik, Charles, 13–14

Mao Zedong, 83

marginalization
  of Jews, by Hitler, 68–70
  as oppression, 63–64
  political, 64
  positionality and, 72
  powerlessness and, 72
  social/cultural, 64
  steps leading to, 59
  strategy for avoiding, 40–41

McCarthy, Joseph, 97–98

McCarthyism, 97–98

McKeever, Linda, 139

Menominee Restoration Act (1972), 30

mental health
  Asian American data, 121
  environmental connections with, 148–49, 151, 162
  ICESCR/Right to Health, 104
  impact of police violence on, 122
  right to care for, 52, 74f, 140–41
  treatment-related worker bias, 96

#MeToo movement, 135

micro-approach to social work, ix, 173

microsystems, mezzosystems, macrosystems, 163f, 163, 171

Moore, Gwen, 62–63

Morton, Samuel, 115–16

National Association for the Advancement of Colored People (NAACP), 23–24, 27–28, 139–40

National Association of Social Workers (NASW)
  apology for past practices, 95–96
  assistance to the FBI, 98
  Code of Ethics, 2–4, 93–94, 95, 101–2
  description, 3
  fight for justice by, 93–96
  Joyner's leadership of, 96
  roles of, 2–4, 93–94
  social justice, defined, 91

National Child Labor Committee, 27–28

National Organization for Women (NOW), 75–76

National Puerto Rican Forum, 29

Native Americans (American Indians)

activism against Indian Relocation Acts, 28

American Indian Movement (AIM), 30

child welfare workers/children (social work example), 98–99

creation of DRUMS, 30

Deer's advocacy for, 30

impact of environmental devastation, 138–39

Indian Child Welfare Act, 99

Morton's denigration of, 116

NASW's apology for mistreatment of, 95

Nazis/Nazi Germany, 68–70

needs-based approach (medical model), 159–61, 160f

non-binary people, 74f, 113

Northeast Community Action Group (Texas), 139

Nozick, Robert, "entitlement theory" of justice, 86–87

Nuremberg Race Laws, 70

Obergefell v. Hodges (2015), 52

Occupy Wall Street movement, 134–35

oppression, 63–70. See also oppression, types of
  Addams' stance against, 23–24
  civil rights and, 35
  comparison with privilege, 63
  contributions to, 72
  defined, 63
  diversity, privilege, and, 7, 60–61
  positionality and, 72
  prejudice and, 66
  social identity and, 72
  societal symptoms leading to, xv, 59
  structural oppression, 65
  U.S. history and, 18
  wheel of (figure), 73f
  wheels of (figure), 73f, 74f

oppression, types of
  cultural imperialism, 64–65
  cultural level, 65, 66f
  discrimination, 66–67
  exploitation, 63
  marginalization, 63–64
  personal level, 65, 66f
  powerlessness, 65, 72
  stereotypes, 66

structural, 65, 66f
violence, 65
othering
of Asian immigrants to the U.S., 121
defined, 67

pansexual persons, 73f, 113
Pantoja, Antonia, 28–29, 29f
Peng Chung Chang, 13–14
personal level oppression, 65, 66f
Personal Responsibility and Work
    Opportunity Reconciliation Act
    (1966), 62
person-in-environment (PIE)
    perspective, 161–64
    description, 161–62
    ecological perspective, 162–63
    historical background, 162
    life model theory, 162–63
    limitations of, 164
    microsystems, mezzosystems,
        macrosystems, 163f, 163, 171
    physical environment connection, 162
    systems theories explanations, 162
phrenology, 115–16
pioneers of social work, 23–31
    Addams, Jane, 23–24, 24f
    Barrett, Janie Porter, 25f, 25–26
    Deer, Ada, 30–31, 31f
    Pantoja, Antonia, 28–29, 29f
    Wald, Lillian, 26–28, 27f
policy approach (to social work), xi
political marginalization, 64
Poor People's Campaign, 128–29
positionality, 72–75, 73f
post-structuralist theory, 76–77
power
    depiction of, in the U.S., 73f
    history of, in China, 83
    history of, in France, 83
    wheels of (figure), 73f, 74f
Preamble, United Nations (UN)
    Charter, 13
Pregnancy Discrimination Act (1978), 82
prejudice
    defined, 66
    against Puerto Ricans, 28
    racism and, 115
    social identity theory and, 71–72
    social work focus on, 67

privilege, 61–63
    cisgender men/women and, 61–62, 74f
    comparison with oppression, 63
    contributions to, 72
    defined, 61
    depiction of, in the U.S., 72, 73f
    diversity and, 61–63
    drug testing and, 62–63
    France/American Revolution and, 18
    social identity and, 72
    social work pioneers and, 23
    societal positionality and, xii, 7, 62
    wheel of (figure), 73f
procedural justice, 89, 127
"The 1619 Project" (New York Times), 119
Puerto Rican Research and Resource
    Center, 29
Puerto Ricans, Pantoja's advocacy
    for, 28–29

queer theory, 76–77

racism (race/ethnicity/color). See also
    ethnicism/ethnic cleansing
    child welfare system, NYC (case
        study), 168–70
    COVID-19 death rate data, 107–8
    COVID-19 hospitalization rates, 108–9
    COVID-19 transmission rates, 108
    COVID-19 unemployment rates, 108
    COVID-19 vaccination rates, 107f, 109
    Crenshaw, intersectionality, and, 77
    environmental justice and, 138–39, 140
    food insecurity and, 166–67
    historical examples of
        discrimination, 115–16
    in NYC, vs. Puerto Ricans, 28
    oppression and, 63
    and policing/justice, in the U.S., 121–22
    positionality and, 73f
    Rwanda genocide, 116
    social justice and, 84–85, 115–16
Rawls, John, theory of justice, 86
Reed v. Reed, 52
Regilme, S. S. F., Jr., 14
respect. See also dignity (human dignity)
    benefits of, 12
    finding common ground (example), 11–72
restorative justice, 89
retributive justice, 89–108

Virginia Industrial School for Wayward
Colored Girls, 26
Virginia State Federation of Colored
Women's Clubs, 26

Wald, Lillian, 26–28, 27*f*, 94
War on Poverty (U.S.) (Johnson), 128
Wells-Barnett, Ida B., 75
Wilkerson, Isabel, 119–20
women/women's rights, 5
Addams' advocacy for, 23–24

Barrett's advocacy for, 25–26
changing workplace role of, 81–82
historical background, 75–76
Muslim women, face veil issues, 83
oppression/violence, and, 65
salary-related gender
inequality, 113
societal expectations of, 61
workers' rights treaties, 19

Young, I. M., 72